Can Markets Solve Problems?

Part of the Goldsmiths Press PERC series

Goldsmiths' Political Economy Research Centre (PERC) seeks to refresh political economy, in the original sense of the term, as a pluralist and critical approach to the study of capitalism. In doing so it challenges the sense of economics as a discipline, separate from the other social sciences, aiming instead to combine economic knowledge with various other disciplinary approaches. This is a response to recent critiques of orthodox economics as immune to interdisciplinarity and cut off from historical and political events.

At the same time, the authority of economic experts and the relationship between academic research and the public (including, but not only, public policy-makers) are constant concerns running through PERC's work.

For more information please visit www.gold.ac.uk/perc/.

Can Markets Solve Problems?

An Empirical Inquiry into Neoliberalism in Action

Daniel Neyland, Véra Ehrenstein, Sveta Milyaeva

Goldsmiths
Press

© 2019 Goldsmiths Press
Published in 2019 by Goldsmiths Press
Goldsmiths, University of London, New Cross
London SE14 6NW

Printed and bound in Great Britain by Clays Ltd, Elcograf S.p.A
Distribution by the MIT Press
Cambridge, Massachusetts, and London, England

A CIP record for this book is available from the British Library

ISBN 978-1-912685-15-8 (hbk)
ISBN 978-1-912685-21-9 (ebk)

www.gold.ac.uk/goldsmiths-press

Contents

Acknowledgements

Many thanks to all of those who have contributed to the MISTS (Market-Based Initiatives as Solutions to Techno-Scientific Problems) project and helped to produce this book. We are grateful to the European Research Council (ERC), who funded this project (grant agreement number 313173) and to our research participants for taking time to guide us through the intricacies of market-based interventions. We would like to give special thanks to those who took part in MISTS events: Laura Bear, Will Davies, Noortje Marres, Fabian Muniesa, Marc Boeckler, Sheila Jasanoff, Christian Frankel, José Ossandón, Trine Pallesen, Vincent Lépinay, Brice Laurent, Liliana Doganova, Joe Deville, Tom Osborne, Andrew Barry, Koray Çalışkan, Franck Cochoy, Lucia Siu, Tanja Schneider, Xaq Frohlich, Taylor Spears, Javier Lezaun, Mike Upton, Céline Cholez and Pascale Trompette. And those who contributed to sessions we organised at conferences and special issues that we published: Gay Hawkins, Liz McFall, Catherine Grandclément, Alan Nadaï and Zsuzsanna Vargha. We would also like to thank Goldsmiths for providing a stimulating intellectual environment where our ideas could develop, with particular thanks to Marsha Rosengarten, Martin Savransky, Alex Wilkie, Vikki Bell, Les Back, Jennifer Gabrys, Evelyn Ruppert, Francisca Grommé, Michael Guggenheim, Laurie Waller, David Moats, Nele Jensen and Jess Perriam. Finally we would like to thank organisers of events where we were fortunate enough to present our work, as well as editors of special issues and collective volumes to which we have contributed and colleagues with whom we have discussed various ideas present in this book: Damian O'Doherty,

Ann Kelly, Linsey McGoey, David Reubi, Steve Woolgar, Monika Krause, Claes-Fredrik Helgesson, Philip Roscoe, Hans Kjellberg, Kean Birch, Dean Pierides, David Stark, Ève Chiapello, Anita Engels, Kate Nash and Vik Loveday.

Daniel would also like to thank Sarah, George and Thomas for their unending support and cups of tea.

Sveta thanks Nestor and Yegor for their continuous patience and support.

Véra would like to thank Guillaume for his support and eagerness to discuss what markets are for.

1

Introduction

Opening

Market-based interventions designed to solve public problems have become a pervasive feature of collective life over the past 30 years in various fields, from education and social care, to climate change, the digital economy and health. Actions that might once have come under the remit of the state, now involve a variety of what would traditionally have been termed public and private sector actors trying to figure out who and what is responsible for what problem along with what might constitute a viable solution. The creation of these associations between problem and solution has been given greater focus by the formulation of specific market-oriented policies. For example, in researching the field of US data start-up firms, we find regulators seeking a commercial solution to the problem of privacy as a matter of consumer rights under the aegis of the Federal Trade Commission. In efforts to address climate change we find European manufacturing industry, tied into carbon trading through the European Union Emissions Trading System. As we enquired into the health problems of countries described as 'low-income', we encountered a new global partnership enforcing an Advance Market Commitment to organise the supply of a new vaccine. And in academic research itself we witness growing demands that such work should stimulate economic growth, with universities obliged to demonstrate ever-greater impact through such policies as the UK's Research Excellence Framework. What these share in common is that various market modes of engagement have been called upon to participate in political programmes of action to introduce efficiency and effectiveness into new configurations of intervention.

We are by no means the first to engage with these market-based interventions. Hence, at the same time as these interventions are proposed, introduced, carried out and reshaped, numerous critiques have suggested that such interventions come with their own social and economic costs, reducing their efficiency and effectiveness, creating exclusions, divisions and inequitable distributions of benefits, alongside unexpected and unanticipated consequences. As a result, the very nature of market-based solutions has been called into question, with apparent solutions to public problems becoming problems that then require a solution. One upshot of these questions is that we find ourselves compelled to explore the precise nature of what constitutes a public problem.[1]

What seems clear is that much of the discussion of these market-based interventions up to now has been in terms of neoliberalism and its relative (in)coherence (for example, Mirowski, 2013; Harvey, 2005), the discontent it inspires (Ericson, Barry and Doyle, 2000; Shamir, 2008; Strange, 1996)

---

[1] In order to accommodate this exploration, we adopt an emergent definition of public problem. In Chapter 8 we will consider the definition of public problem that emerges across our chapters.

or its role in recent government austerity drives (Blyth, 2013). Rather than repeat these critiques, we instead look to get close to the action, drawing out the means through which market-based interventions are composed, enacted and given effect. This opens up opportunities, we suggest, for questioning in detail what a market can come to mean, for whom, when, involving what sets of people, relations, resources, policies and devices. In place of a single global frame such as neoliberalism through which these interventions might be made to make sense, we can instead start to trace out market contours around such notions as competition, investment and return, property, trade and exchange. This helps to cast light on a series of means of intervention – what we will term market sensibilities – through which new critiques can take shape. In the following, we will emphasise the advantages of attuning analysis towards the relations, devices and practices involved in giving shape to these sensibilities. We will suggest that this approach offers a different basis for critique, one that gets close to the specificities of each intervention, their distinct politics and problematic consequences.

Our approach will draw on the upsurge of interest in markets over the past decade from Science and Technology Studies (STS) scholars. Taking inspiration from Callon's (1998) call for an up-close engagement with the laws of markets, have come studies of financial innovation (Lepinay, 2011; MacKenzie, 2008), pricing practices (Muniesa, 2007), trading algorithms (MacKenzie and Pardo-Guerra, 2014), and the exchange of globalised goods (Çalışkan, 2010). Through these works, markets as heterogeneous agencements (Çalışkan and Callon, 2010), the performativity of economics (MacKenzie, Muniesa and Siu, 2007), and the economic as provocation (Muniesa, 2014), among many other approaches, have come to provide a means through which up-close studies of markets can raise new questions, address contemporary concerns of markets and continue to provide a rich seam of challenging ideas. We will now endeavour to retune these analyses towards market-based interventions into public problems.

In order to get close to the action and start to explore some distinct ways that market-based interventions take shape, we begin with three examples of markets introduced into areas once dominated by the state. We will use these examples as heuristic devices to explore some different analytic approaches available for engaging with markets. Subsequently, we will introduce our methodological principles and the market sensibilities that will shape the rest of this book.

How to Get a Grip: Three Examples of Market-Based Intervention

Let's start with the Hooghly shipyards of contemporary India. Bear (2013) tells us that here outsourcing and audit have become dominant rationales for the assemblage of men, machines and materials. A non-unionised workforce use decrepit and obsolete equipment to produce ships at a low cost for international trade. Bear identifies a form of neoliberal outsourcing at the centre of work arrangements, with a decreasing focus on centralised control and an increasing managerial focus on holding together various intermediary organisations through assessment mechanisms. What was once the state is now a series of ever-more temporary and precarious work arrangements loosely bound by audit rationales. The emerging effect of this neoliberalism is a ramshackle shadowland of informal labour, made invisible to public oversight by its absence from debates about foreign direct investment, local manufacturing growth or even from discussion within parent companies. Land is owned by the Kolkata Port

Trust, a state institution, and rent extracted through short-term leasing arrangements to companies who then offer short-term employment to workers. Much of the land is also illegally sub-let to other temporary organisations, leading to even briefer short-termism. Standards, certification and audit ensure that the product – the ships – are certified, but the work practices are not and land ownership with its rentier regimes seems overlooked.

Now let's switch attention to post-war Iraq. Best (2007) describes attempts by the Bush administration to "liberate" Iraq through free market economics. Privatisation of state-owned industries and integration into international financial markets sit at the heart of regime change. A neoliberal free market democracy, held in place through the establishment of a national Trade Bank under the guidance of international financial institutions, is noted as key to putting in place risk-free trade for US and UK companies. Best suggests these moves are part of an ever-changing international movement involving organisations such as the International Monetary Fund and the World Bank. For the latter, priorities have moved from providing technical expertise for countries seeking further engagement in international trade, to insisting upon the institution of economic development that fits with Washington Consensus principles of free markets, to a modified focus on free markets coupled with measures to ensure stability. In line with these measures, structural adjustment policies have been replaced with poverty alleviation initiatives. However, Best suggests, difficulties sit centrally with moves to promote economic stability through, for example, forms of transparency designed to provide markets with ongoing and reliable information on the state of a country's economy. Transparency becomes a disciplinary mechanism enacted through standardisation. Such insistence on standardisation then effectively produces multiple and ongoing exceptions as various nations do not fit a narrow set of standards. Either exception then becomes the rule or further standardisation for all exceptions is insisted upon. The overall effect, Best suggests, is to promote a sense that both the optimistic (enhanced development and poverty alleviation for poorer states) and pessimistic accounts (greater controls and insistence on narrowly imposed standardisation) of financial institutions such as the IMF and World Bank are correct.

And let's move again, but this time to the US in the 1970s. Here Nik-Khah (2014) explains how neoliberal ideas aimed to shape the management of science, in particular pharmaceutical policies. Chicago School economists sought to effect a medical neoliberalism through which market-friendly regulation of drug licensure could emerge. By establishing the Center for the Study of Drug Development (CSDD) and building relations between academic researchers and the pharmaceutical industry, influence could be exerted on pharmaceutical policy, and calls made for a deregulation of the field and a greater emphasis on market-led governance. This continued a line of sceptical assessments of government control of economic life that emerged through the Chicago School. The combined efforts of the CSDD and the American Enterprise Institute involved producing numerous apparently independent, but supportive reports challenging contemporary positions on pharmaceutical regulation and calling for more market-led regulation. This created an echo chamber through which apparently distinct sources of support could appear to accumulate for a single argumentative position, but it was enabled by various joint memberships and shared activities across the two institutions. Nik-Khah suggests this echo chamber strategy became a standard feature of neoliberal advocacy for free market policies. It was joined by a series of similar activities in relation to other industries which Nik-Khah traces back to the Mont Pelerin Society (MPS), and the work of the Austrian economist Friedrich Hayek. Their aim was to build institutions that could introduce a permanent critique of the state. And the critique had a strong free market component, but also an array of political and philosophical principles. In particular, the MPS promoted the epistemic superiority of markets – that they could process more information, more effectively, than individuals, policy-making committees or the state.

In three brief examples, we have moved between locations, times and scales – from India to Iraq to the US, from the past to a shabby-looking present and from individual shipyard workers to global institutions. One entity that seems to link these examples is neoliberalism. And a quick perusal of some of the major recent texts on neoliberalism certainly seems to provide a grounds for making a neoliberal sense of these examples. We could draw on Harvey's (2005) work to show how neoliberalism as an idea proposes "liberating individual entrepreneurial freedoms and skills within an institutional framework characterised by strong private property rights, free markets and free trade" (2). And "if markets do not exist (in areas such as land, water, education, healthcare, social security or environmental pollution) then they must be created, by state action if necessary" (2). In all three examples we find efforts to introduce and hold steady market principles, with Hooghly shipyards subject to new forms of competition, Iraq opened to international trade and pharmaceutical companies calling for greater market freedoms. But, as Harvey (2005), Brown (2015), Mirowski (2013), Birch (2017) and Peck (2010) each suggest, we should not overlook the continual contradiction at the heart of this movement, to introduce markets through state administrative means. In this way neoliberalisation (rather than neoliberalism) is best thought of as "an open-ended and contradictory process of politically assisted market rule" (Peck, 2010: xii). In place of a simplistic reduction of the state, its roles replaced by the private sector, comes a continual process of change. And Brown (2015) suggests that through this ongoing change, neoliberalisation can be seen as: "a peculiar form of reason that configures all aspects of existence in economic terms, [that] is quietly undoing basic elements of democracy" (17). In subsequent chapters we will see how public and private sectors are assembled, and the continual moves made back and forth between demands for greater market efficiency and the building of significant bureaucratic infrastructure to support market-based interventions.

At the same time as neoliberalisation seems to provide a compelling backdrop against which the three examples can be made to make sense, attaching all the different forms of action to a single political programme might risk overlooking the specific and distinct detail of each example. Rather than utilise neoliberalism as a basis for organising analysis, an alternative would be to focus in on a different shared concern: the market. Sociology, and in particular economic sociology, has had much to say on this topic. Swedberg (2005) suggests that drawing on Coase, we might be led to treat the market as a social institution that facilitates exchange. This builds on a long sociological history that we can trace back through Durkheim (1902), for example, who suggested that entering into market exchanges establishes many other obligations, forming a kind of precarious and accidental order. Simmel (1955) develops this point further in positing that market competition may create bonds (for example, between seller and buyer) at the same time as it alienates (for example, different sellers offering similar products). According to Granovetter (1973) bonds in the form of networks of strong and weak ties can provide a dramatic corrective to mainstream economics, showing that economic actions are primarily social. In contrast to mainstream economics, here the social is not treated as the last 5% of the action or the variance that needs to be mopped up.[2]

For our study, these ideas provide one historical trajectory for making sense of the three opening market examples. We can build from Hirschman's (1982) suggestion that market relations are seen as a means to incorporate civilised principles. "At mid-eighteenth century it became the conventional wisdom ... that commerce was a civilizing agent of considerable power and range" (Hirschman, 1982: 1464), with prominent figures such as Montesquieu declaring: "it is almost a general rule that wherever manners are gentle [*moeurs douces*] there is commerce; and wherever there is commerce, manners are gentle" (1750: 8, 1464). These eighteenth-century figures, according to Hirschman, "proceeded to discover in 'interest' a principle that could replace 'love' and 'charity' as the basis for a well-ordered society" (1982: 1467). Having an interest – an economic stake – was thus a means to bind individuals to orderly society. Gibson-Graham (2003) suggests that we can see new lines emerging in this civilising role of markets in the promotion of such matters as ethical trade. Also pertinent for our purposes is Fourcade and Healy's (2007) suggestion that transformations in social welfare since the 1990s push a similar line of argument. "Welfare support, the argument went, encourages laziness and illegitimacy and prevents any meaningful form of social recognition. By contrast, incorporation into the market encourages dignity, opportunity, responsibility

---

[2] Although this approach has been criticised by, for example, Fligstein and Mara-Drita (1996) for being too sparse and failing to take into account politics or social preconditions.

and social solidarity" (293). In this way, the market as a civilising set of relations might solve public problems.

Returning to the opening examples, we can see that the
financial restructuring of post-war Iraq might be understood
as a reintegration of the nation into what are pushed forward
as the civilising protocols of global financial flows. Calls for
the deregulation of the US pharmaceutical industry might be
similarly recast as a piece of advocacy work for the market to
take on a civilising (de)regulatory role through its ability to
process more information than a regulator ever could. The
Hooghly shipyards of the Kolkata Port Authority might then
be characterised as a series of ever-weaker, more temporary
ties, an ineffectual building of relations with workers, leading
to an uncivilised exploitation of the labour force. And we could
draw on the work of scholars like Gane (2014a, 2014b, 2016)
to carefully elaborate the interconnections between economic
sociology's notion of the market and the preceding focus on
neoliberalism and its contradictions.

Yet strong and weak ties, and civilising markets, seem to
swap one kind of generality – in the form of a neoliberal political programme of action – with another kind of conceptual generality. The latter still seems to risk losing much of the specificity
of the examples in an unhelpful search for a form of universal-
ism through which each can become part of the same explanation. And these are not the only general means of explanation
available – we could also bring in work inspired by Foucault's
notion of governmentality, on New Public Management and the
audit society (Foucault, 1977; Power, 1997; Osborne and Rose,
1999; Rose, 1996; Rose and Miller, 1992; Miller, 1992) as a way to
account for the opening three examples. These general explanations will each have a place in the following chapters. But treating Hooghly shipyards, the US pharmaceutical industry and the
invasion of Iraq as part of the same phenomenon risks losing

their distinctiveness. While short-term, hazardous and insecure working conditions and the auditing of ships' build quality seem prominent as a means to engage with the Hooghly shipyards, the scale and scope of international financial institutions and their demands for standardisation seem more pertinent to Best's analysis of financial restructuring. Although it might be tempting to draw out audit, transparency, standards and accountability as shared themes, even here the examples tell distinct and important stories, omitting the shipyard workers from audit (Bear) or imposing standards from afar (Best).

Focusing on this theme of audit alone would require cutting out much else (international trade, the decline of unions, the policies pursued by elected representatives and so on). But even a broader thematic rendering of the examples around time, rent, exchange, competition, standards, pricing, institutions and scale, while undoubtedly providing a compelling series of narratives, would only achieve so much. A neatly classified and compartmentalised analysis of individual themes might emerge. What we need is a theoretical and methodological means to move between, on the one hand, these broad and general points that facilitate critique and commentary on the state of the world – for example, the ongoing efforts to neoliberalise, to assemble public and private actors in new associations, to use markets to solve problems – and on the other a specific attention to the particular details of each intervention. This is where we suggest an STS approach can prove helpful.

Science and Technology Studies: Generals, Particulars and Markets

In recent years STS research has in some part turned attention towards matters of markets (rather than just the market) and the work of economists and economics. Callon's (1998) work has had a profound influence in proposing a treatment of markets as accomplished, heterogeneous assemblages of people, things, relations, resources and devices. Drawing on a history of Actor-Network Theory (ANT) these entities are not assembled in a straightforward manner, simply drawn together from pre-existing states. Instead, the act of assembly is central to establishing the nature of the entities and the roles they will take up. As Holm (2007) suggests, this form of market assembly work involves the production of devices and framings that disentangle entities from their social, cultural and technical obligations, "setting them free to realize – put into reality – the market model" (234). Disentangling and re-entangling becomes a continual process through which the nature of market things are successively set. The insistent demand here is for up-close empirical research through which assembly work can be made to make sense or given flesh.

STS scholars suggest up-close studies are important for engaging with the details of market work because assembly is not a neutral practice. Studies of market assembly work suggest that disentangling and re-entangling sets in place and affirms various demarcations between, for example, value (through valuation), and provides a framing of the entities internal and external to a market assemblage. Developing the latter point, Callon argues that: "framing constitutes powerful mechanisms of exclusion, for to frame means to select, to sever links" (2007: 140). In this sense, market assembly work can generate clear demarcations between the included and excluded. Callon uses the term *orphans* to describe those entities that occupy positions as particular kinds of externalities or overflows. Orphans are the non-disentangled, non-modelled, unframed entities on the outside of market assemblages. Orphans can be enraged by their externality to the market assemblage or "choose to engage in a strategy of construction of the worlds in which they want to live" (Callon, 2007: 141). Entangling and disentangling, inclusion and exclusion are thus not benevolent activities. Instead they help establish a kind of market politics as Callon suggests: "Political and moral reflection is at the heart of markets and not pushed out to their fringes" (2016: 18).

For the opening examples, this suggests a number of potential avenues of exploration. Hooghly shipyard workers might become the market orphans, subject to market relations, but excluded from having a voice. Short-termism might be opened to treatment as the basis for a particular kind of assembly work, one that is focused on price within time rather than sustainable practice or value. Post-"liberation" Iraq might then be understood as a focal point for a global reframing, established along the insistent lines of standardisation fed from international financial institutions. Successive disentangling and re-entangling might then be said to provide a continually renewed characteristic for the emerging nation, emerging into a stable and regular form of exploitative international trade. And calls for the market liberation of pharmaceutical firms in the US in the mid-twentieth century might be similarly understood as the successive plaiting of entities into assemblies that shift from an awkward and cumbersome heterogeneity to a more or less smooth and coherent, dangerous form of deregulatory advocacy.

All this seems interesting, yet assembly work alone is insufficient for describing the array of activities that might take centre-stage in any particular market-based intervention. Already we are in danger of losing specificity and losing focus on what particularly matters in this book which is the problem-centred nature of these interventions. STS market work has proposed a number of distinct ways to draw on market assembly work and broaden out its analytic utility. Here we can briefly consider four starting points.

First, the nature of market entities have been opened to a kind of fundamental scrutiny, deflating their otherwise grandiose status in order to open up avenues of analytical enquiry (MacKenzie, 2008). Through such enquiries, questions are pursued of, for example, what counts as a market actor or entity. In particular, the exchange of goods between a producer and a consumer has been put centre-stage by Callon, Meadel and Rabehariosa (2002), building on Chamberlin's (1946) work to discuss the continual (re)qualification of products. This perspective has then drawn STS scholars' attention toward marketing. In Cochoy's (2009) work, the suggestion is made that the shopping trolley (or cart) can be conceived as a market actor, provocatively broadening the set of entities conventionally considered to play an active role in markets. This draws on ANT's history of provocation around the nature of entities. The flattened ontology of ANT is important here not for suggesting that there is no difference between market entities. Instead, the focus is on questioning the ways in which distinctions are accomplished through market assembly work. A flat ontology is thus a methodological prerequisite for attuning analysis toward a deep scepticism that refuses to accept the easy prior existence of distinctions and instead seeks to explore the means through which such distinctions are made. Through the adoption of a flat ontology it becomes possible to examine how the nature of precarity emerges in Hooghly shipyards, how standardisation attains its status in Iraq or how deregulation of the pharmaceutical industry attains a recognisable form.

Second has been a focus on markets and calculative collective devices. Such devices according to Callon and Muniesa (2005) enable entities to be disentangled from their previous connections and re-associated in new economic relations. Primarily these take the form of competitive relations. The notion of competition anticipated by Callon (2016) is one of continual innovative pressure. However, this is not a pressure designed to alleviate competition, but becomes an essential driver of competition, with organisations striving to singularise their offer as increasingly attuned to the unique needs of the buyer to achieve at least temporarily a kind of "bilateral monopoly" (2016: 10). In this approach, calculative activity sits centrally: rather than drawing together parties into a single space for the neutral application of choice, markets can bring together parties into the same space with differential calculative agency (Callon and Muniesa, 2005; Cochoy, 2010). In place of a smooth execution of choice, Callon (1998) suggests, drawing on the work of Weber, that "agents enter into competition with one another to secure points of monopoly and domination" (43) with the result that "the very nature of competition is to rarefy competition" (44). The market assembly is then opened to treatment as a form of agencement: an assembly through which rights, abilities and obligations to act are distributed. Hence, while market exchanges could be said to draw competitors into a single spatial or temporal frame, calculative devices might participate in the differential distribution of the ability to act.

Third, markets have been treated by STS scholars as performed by economics (see for example, MacKenzie et al., 2007; MacKenzie, 2008), drawing on the work of Austin (1962). MacKenzie suggests a distinction can be made between utterances that do something and those that report on an already existing state of affairs (2008: 16). The most frequently quoted example from Austin (1962), is the utterance "I declare this meeting open". Such an utterance is said to describe and bring into being the state that it describes. For Cochoy (1998):

a performative science is a science that simultaneously describes and constructs its subject matter. In this respect, the "performation" of the economy by marketing directly refers to the double aspect of marketing action: conceptualizing and enacting the economy at the same time. (218)

From this we could understand that marketing brings the world it describes into being at the moment that the world as configured is taken up. In relation to financial markets, MacKenzie looks at the ways in which the work of economists brings markets into being through three levels of performativity: "generic" performativity (in which an aspect of economics as an academic discipline is broadly used by participants in economic processes), "effective" performativity (which involves a specific use of economics in effecting an economic process) and drawing on the work of Barnes, there is "Barnesian" performativity (in which the use of economics "makes economic processes more like their depiction by economists"; MacKenzie, 2008: 17). We can see these approaches to performativity as moving from weakly formulated to more thorough forms of performativity.

Fourth, capitalisation has become a recent focus within STS. Birch, for example, suggests we need to understand how things "are turned into assets (i.e., resources that generate recurring earnings) and then capitalized (i.e., discounting future earnings in the present)" (2017: 463). Such matters as discounted cash flows then enable a potential investor to judge the present value of a future income stream (Muniesa et al., 2017). Consequently, financial risks, exposure and levels of liquidity provide grounds for market actors to do capitalisation (Doganova and Muniesa, 2015; Muniesa et al., 2017).

Now we are equipped with these analytic tools, the three initial examples might look somewhat different. The forecasts of Chicago School economists of the future of pharmaceutical regulation could be explored to make sense of how they are given performative effect. The calculative asymmetries of participants in building market relations in post-war Iraq could be investigated. The work done to capitalise on, at the same time as keep silent, the working relations of the Hooghly shipyards might be drawn centre-stage. This suggests an interesting and compelling programme of work. But how can we move from here with all its messiness and distinctiveness, back to neoliberalism; to what do these examples form part? We need to find a way to move between what Lee (1999) terms the general and the particular.

Market assembly work, performativity, an in-principle flat ontology, calculations and capitalisation have formed the emerging generals of STS market work. Prices, formulas, devices, experiments have been among their particulars. In retuning these STS approaches to market-based interventions into public problems, we suggest an analytically useful means to shift between the general and the particular is provided by orienting our analyses around market sensibilities. We propose that sensibilities are not rules or instructions, they are not singular, but nor are they illimitable. Instead, sensibilities are ways of helping to organise thought and action that share sufficient similarity in their application to be comparable while also being sufficiently distinct to be contrastable. A sensibility shares some characteristics with what Wittgenstein (1953) has called family resemblances, but here we want to use sensibility as a term to capture the kinds of similar courses of action that are navigated through market-based interventions.

Our suggestion will be that market sensibilities then take the form of economically derived principles that gain a specific shape within each market-based intervention, and are subject to change and reform over time, shift between interventions, but retain sufficient coherence to be analysed together. Already in the opening three examples we can see that trade, competition, pricing and selling are prominent market sensibilities that provide something like common reference points, shared ways of thinking about and devising intervention, but that also take very specific shape in each example. Hence competition is given a standardised shape in Best's work by international global financial institutions in post-war Iraq through a specified need to provide the conditions under which finance can flow and only be subject to ordinary market risks. Iraq is thus opened to competition. In Nik-Khah's account, calls are made for the US pharmaceutical industry to be similarly opened up for competition, but here the focus is on scientific reporting, neoliberal echo chambers, and the conscription of academic research. In Bear's study of the Hooghly shipyards, competition seems rife, but also corrosive. Workers compete and small organisations compete, enabling global firms to build reliable ships, but only on the back of financially exploitative labour conditions. Meanwhile, the state operates a rentier regime made invisible by its externality to this competition. In each case, we might say that competition is a sensibility recognisable to most participants in the action, even though it takes various forms and gives effect to a variety of consequences and critiques. From these particulars, we might then be given the chance to move toward engaging with the general; elaborating a stance from which we can say something about the nature and form of competition. In the following section we will set out the sensibilities that will give shape to the rest of this book, following a brief word on methods.

A Brief Word On Methodological Principles

Our challenge in completing this research into market-based interventions has been to find a way to empirically move between general and particular, all the while navigating the complex contours of specific interventions. These operate, sometimes, across broad geographical regions or even span the world (without encompassing it), employ particular devices, engaging individuals, industries, activists, politicians, and more-than-human things, all the while changing with some frequency. Our method has been broadly ethnographic, taking inspiration from some of our own favourite work by Strathern (1991), Law (2004), Latour and Woolgar (1979), and MacKenzie (2008). Along with up-close studies of interventions underway, we have collected documents, taken pictures, sought out histories and stories, speculative futures and carried out 147 semistructured interviews. We have sought to travel the world and, to some extent, brought it back to this book.

That the worlds we have seen do not straightforwardly fit into this book has been an obvious and slightly painful experience for us in compiling this text. Our five years of up-close fieldwork with market-based interventions has produced numerous encounters that cannot all be reported here. The sensibilities we will introduce in the next section, have to some extent helped us to organise our editing of events. But our methodological principles have also been important.

These methodological principles were pursued (and occasionally challenged, edited and redirected) through a series of acts of fieldwork. We pursued efforts to translate the chemical composition of the atmosphere around us into a tradeable commodity through up-close analysis of the European Union Emissions Trading System (EU ETS), moving across Europe to interview 24 participants including policy-makers, economists and activists. We engaged with the materials of heavy industry, stopping for a while in Brussels to collect our (and others') thoughts. We travelled in and between Europe and the United States in considering the future of privacy as a problem for which policy-makers sought a suitable market, interviewing 38 stakeholders in the emerging data economy. We encountered the basis for distributing vaccines to low-income countries through an Advance Market Commitment (AMC) when moving between the offices of a global partnership in

Geneva and health administrations in Africa, carrying out 31 interviews along the way. We engaged with activities that have sought to transform UK higher education into a marketplace for research through the Research Excellence Framework and for drawing students to universities through a series of student loans policies. Here a total of 44 interviews were conducted with policy-makers, academics and managers. Finally, we researched the ongoing and uncertain effects of a Social Impact Bond for children at risk of going into care on the east coast of England, through ten interviews with central figures involved in the Bond.

Our methodological principles for organising our field-work have been as follows. As previously mentioned, we have drawn inspiration from ANT to pursue an in-principle flat ontology among the entities and events we have encountered. In this way, we have not assumed that there are no distinctions between entities and concerns, but neither have we sought to straightforwardly adopt the brutish presence of entities and concerns as they have been initially presented to us (for example in popular media accounts). Plehwe's (2009) critique has been instructive here. By emphasising the important distinctions between, for example, neoliberalism and neoconservatism in the US, Plehwe's work seems to suggest that we need to take a step back from even the most obvious and apparent features of our research to give them scrutiny. Neoliberalism, Plehwe's work suggests to us, is not a straightforward or single thing and its translation into a political programme of action requires careful scrutiny. Translation establishes in varied ways the nature of the intervention. Instead of simply taking on entities and relations as they appear to first present themselves, we have tried to explore the basis through which the nature of entities are established within market-based interventions, while holding onto the methodological principle that the nature of any entity might be subject to change. In our accounts, we have thus tended to eschew the overly rigid categories of the public and private sectors, for example. Rather, we have tried to use qualifying terms attuned to the actions undertaken by the entities and their spokespersons involved in the interventions we have studied.

Investigating the nature of entities has been inseparable for us from the pursuit of market assembly work. It is in the assembly, endurance and occasional (or quite frequent) changes in market-based interventions into public problems that we have been able to witness how entities and relations are given shape, transformed and called upon to give effect to particular kinds of outcomes. At times the search for assembly work has been a reasonably straightforward starting point for research – investigating, for example, a specific policy such as the UK Research Excellence Framework (REF) that has a clear starting point in 1986 through the Research Selectivity Exercise and then the Research Assessment Exercise. At other times, the search for market assembly work has been an ongoing challenge, for example in US and EU policy-makers' search for a privacy market. On these occasions, the pursuit of assembly work has often been as illuminating as the detailed study of the assembly work itself.

Within such market assembly work, we have paid particular attention to the types of devices, relations and practices that characterised forms of association within market-based interventions. Devices, relations and practices, we suggest, are the means by which market-based interventions accomplish any kind of outcome. Here we have drawn inspiration from Mitchell's (2002) critique of Polanyi. In contrast to Polanyi's argument that the economy emerged through the separation of economic ties from other social relations, creating a self-regulating economy unable to regulate itself, Mitchell argues:

The economy came into being not by disembedding market relations from a larger social ground that previously contained them, but by embedding certain twentieth-century practices of calculation, description, and enumeration in new forms of intellectual, calculating, regulatory and governmental practice. (2002: 118)

In our approach, it was through these forms of calculation, governmental intervention, and ways of enumerating, among many other activities, that the assembly work, its devices, relations and practices through which market sensibilities are enacted, could be made witnessable. The EU ETS, for example, could only be made to make sense through a significant number of metrological devices. And yet we would also add that devices, relations and practices only ever establish a hesitant, provisional, always-likely-to-change nature of the order of things.

Our acts of fieldwork and the methodological principles through which they took shape, will be selectively represented in the following chapters by considering the market sensibilities they extol. We provide a brief introduction to these sensibilities here.

Six Sensibilities of Market-Based Interventions

Our suggestion is that the following six sensibilities provide a basis for navigating between the general and particular of market-based interventions. The sensibilities will be used to give detailed insight into specific moments of fieldwork while also providing a basis for drawing together this fine-grained detail in order to pose questions of what it means to utilise markets to try and solve public problems. As will become clear in the chapters, these market sensibilities appear in different ways in different interventions and depend upon the assembly of distinct devices, relations and practices. We have chosen to focus on what participants articulate as the central market sensibility in each intervention in order to explore one sensibility in depth in each chapter (from Chapters 2 to 7), while in Chapters 8 and 9 we will also offer an analysis across these sensibilities and interventions.

Our first market sensibility is *trade and exchange*. We have found this to be an incredibly pervasive orientation for organising market-based interventions. We find elements of trade and exchange in interventions into the environment, education, health and digital data. In Chapter 2 we will focus on the European Union Emissions Trading System (EU ETS) to explore some of the central tenets of trading and exchange attuned to address a particularly challenging environmental problem – climate change. As we will see, emissions trading, or cap and trade, is an economics-based form of climate policy, currently implemented in various places around the globe, from the European Union to California and China. On paper, it consists of setting a quantitative limit on CO_2 emissions (the cap), which reduces over time, and issuing a corresponding amount of tradable allowances, each representing one ton of CO_2. Regulated installations must then make sure they have enough allowances to cover their level of emissions or they will have to pay a fine.

An economic rationale is at the heart of these arrangements that seek to utilise trade and exchange to solve one of the world's most significant and complex challenges – climate change caused by greenhouse gas emissions. Making emission allowances scarce should mean that they acquire a price that will then turn CO_2 emissions into a cost for industrial installations. At the same time, introducing a marketplace in which allowances can become tradable should mean that the cap on the release of CO_2 is achieved at the lowest cost for all the installations incorporated in the scheme. This is because installations with a low cost of reduction would be expected to reduce their emissions cheaply and swiftly, creating a surplus of allowances to sell. Those installations with higher costs of reduction would then buy the surplus allowances. As all allowances add up to the total cap on emissions, the intervention is expected to make a positive impact on climate change. Trade and exchange should then provide a market-based rationale through which a complex problem can be solved by delegating responsibility onto the decision-making practices of polluters, who can now choose between investing in, for example, new technologies to emit less, buying more allowances, or a mixed strategy of the two.

Yet, in practice as we will see, this economic simplicity quickly disappears. In the chapter we will suggest that although emissions trading systems have been designed to introduce effectiveness and efficiency into the resolution of public problems, they often rely on time-consuming bureaucratic practices, passionate negotiations (which involve, among others, politicians, European civil servants, industrial lobbyists and environmental activists), and suffer from both ongoing fragility and the legacy of past decisions. In place of the counter-expectation that trade and exchange will provide a ruthless means to underscore a new way to render the environment open to economic intervention comes what we will term a form of negotiated technocracy. Various technical devices, measures and metrics form a technocratic focus shaped through ongoing political negotiations that give effect to a series of limitations on, and caveats to, the mode of trade and exchange to be put into practice.

In Chapter 3, we will explore an alternative market sensibility to trade and exchange that has been equally central to interventions into public problems, namely *competition*.

Although the term *competition* might appear to be fundamental to market-based interventions, we will suggest that taking the nature of competition for granted risks missing the delicate work of composition through which this term takes an interventionist form. When engaging in the resolution of public problems, we suggest, competition is not simply left to take shape (which is an assumption made in the EU ETS), but rather emerges through a variety of forms of infrastructural effort and institutional responses. Our empirical focus in this chapter is higher education and the particular practices that, together with specific policies, enact competition. The specific intervention that we focus on is the UK higher education REF. In theory the REF provides an infrastructure for pooling together and allocating finite public resources to fund academic research in a system that measures but also steers universities into a form of competition that assumes that the best performers win the most government funding. Such distribution of funds is oriented toward national competitiveness, with impact now designating a new field of competition through which universities must demonstrate their ability to contribute to the UK economy.

The UK has the longest-standing structure for drawing universities into this kind of competition over scarce public resources and thus stands as an exemplar of market-based intervention into public problems. Through our research with REF panellists, impact assessors and REF managers, it becomes apparent that behind the public face of the REF, a specific scoring system, algorithms for automated normalisation, formulas for reconciliation and an absence of external transparency bring the nature of competition into being in distinct ways. Analysing the transformation of the distribution of funding for academia through a market-based intervention thus brings to the fore complex and sometimes unanticipated features of competition. Whereas the preceding chapter on trading and exchange emphasised the bureaucratic requirements for holding in place a convoluted form of negotiated technocracy that changed through set phases, here we will look at the importance of specific moment-to-moment practices through which competition is given form, still within a significant bureaucratic infrastructure. Employing the flat ontology of ANT as a starting point, we investigate how the nature of competition emerges through practices of representation, accountability and consensus.

Following our suggestions in Chapters 2 and 3 that competition, and trading and exchange form key sensibilities for orienting market-based interventions into public problems, in Chapter 4 we will turn attention to *property and ownership* as a sensibility for intervention. Property has been a key matter for mainstream economics (for example, as establishing the very basis for buying and selling goods) and for sociologists (for example, in holding in place social inequalities). In market-based interventions into public problems, we will suggest that the form accorded to property and ownership is consequential not just for the nature of the intervention but for the way we think about the entities intervened upon. Here we will move from the UK, across Europe and to the US to investigate interventions in public problems prompted by the digital data market.

Discussions regarding the inequities of the online data market are numerous across the US, Europe and elsewhere. Concerns include who owns data, how it could and should (or should not) be capitalised, who is in control of data, and what happens to such matters as privacy when data can be freely scraped and then monetised (through, for example, behavioural advertising). Although the concerns are abundant, what will count as an effective intervention is less clear.

In this chapter we engage with a significant policy intervention in the field, the EU General Data Protection Regulation (GDPR). We will explore how and with what effect, reforming notions of property and ownership became central to intervening in the data market through the GDPR and how rewriting the nature of privacy as a form of control through property ownership involved distinct relations in the US in contrast to Europe. Whereas Chapters 2 and 3 both investigated significant bureaucratic infrastructures (REF and EU ETS), in this chapter we will contrast the regulatory apparatus of the EU GDPR with the less bureaucratic efforts of US regulators from the Federal Trade Commission to oversee market participants' provision of new means to intervene in privacy. Property and ownership will thus open up avenues for exploring interventions with greater or lesser degrees of regulatory infrastructure.

Continuing this theme of market-based interventions characterised by smaller and more distributed regulatory apparatus, we switch our attention to the sensibility of *investment and return*. In Chapter 5 we will use the development of Social Impact Bonds as a basis for examining this market sensibility. We will focus in on a particular Bond in the UK: Essex County Council's Social Impact Bond for children at risk of going into care. The aim here is for the local authority to save money by bringing in private investors to cover the upfront costs of intervention. For this to work as an investment–return relationship, a financial-contractual structure is required that provides sufficient security to investors (perhaps unused to working on public problems). Much of this security depends on timing: how much money will be put in, when, with returns triggered by what means and paid at what amount and at what time? What is bought and sold is not just a financial return, but a better imagined future for the children and an opportunity for the investors to promote their own positive role in the world.

Looking at the Bond up-close enables us to analyse the practices, devices and relations through which a future-oriented temporal structure was composed and its certainty and stability more or less retained to ensure that money invested led to a return for investors. Approaching analysis in this way also opened up the chance to enquire into the way outcomes were accomplished. For example, we can note here that these investments were provident in the sense of ensuring arrangements for future needs; they fixed in place a set of relations that almost guaranteed a return while also enabling investors to promote the social benefits of that return. However, we will also suggest that providence was inequitably distributed; an intervention that proved provident for the investors turned out to be less so for the local political authority looking to cut its costs. In comparing the Social Impact Bond with other interventions, we will suggest that unlike the trading and exchange model of the EU ETS, for example, wherein the intervention could be partially renegotiated through phases, the tightly structured contractual relationships of the Social Impact Bond fixed these inequitable outcomes in place.

In exploring the broad organising principles of market-based interventions (competition, trading and exchange, investment and return, property and ownership), we can also look at some of the specific economic devices through which non-coercive forms of action are introduced. In Chapter 6 we investigate how the *incentive* has become an important sensibility for the practical design of market-based interventions. Here we will go to Geneva and explore the Advance Market Commitment (AMC) for pneumococcal vaccines in countries described as 'low-income'. The AMC is directed toward making vaccination possible on a large-scale in poor regions of the world such as sub-Saharan Africa in order to reduce the burden of pneumococcal diseases (pneumonia and meningitis), particularly among children. It pools public and philanthropic donor resources together to create something akin to a market proxy; an amount of available funding that can stand as more or less equivalent to a population of disease sufferers financially equipped to set a level of demand and incentivise pharmaceutical firms to invest in scaling up their production capacity for pneumococcal vaccines. In contrast to several of our preceding market sensibilities, incentives appear to open up the opportunity for regulators to govern industry at arm's-length: in theory an incentive is set and it is up to industry to achieve the rewards that the incentive offers.

In practice, the provision of incentives also seems to demand its own bureaucratic life. For example, forms of quantification prove crucial to establishing the viability of the intervention. These include the projection of the global impact of vaccination based on clinical trials and epidemiological studies to raise donor funds, calculating vaccine prices and formalising payment conditions to incentivise the pharmaceutical industry to produce large amounts and supply their vaccines, and forecasting the demand represented by low-income countries' birth cohort. Although it retains its title "Advance Market Commitment", the intervention is as much about evidence and carefully prepared and nurtured relationships as it is about arm's-length regulation through an incentive. The price to be paid for vaccines must be justified, demand must be stimulated, manufacturing listened to, and time inconsistencies overcome through legal obligations. Holding in place incentives is not then reducible to a matter of abstract economic theorising, but provides a basis for navigating and managing relations required for an intervention to happen. For the Advance Market Commitment, notions of competition and trading and exchange are almost entirely absent, while investment and return is more metaphorical than in the case of the Social Impact Bond (with a "return", for example understood in terms of health rather than finance). Instead, we will suggest, the incentive plays a part among an array of calculative and relationship-building operations that are central to enabling or preventing the intervention from achieving its aims and addressing the public problem it was meant to solve.

Although economic matters such as incentives, along with competition, exchange, investment and ownership have held a prominent position in recent years as ways to think about, orient and organise market-based interventions into public problems, the notion of selling has tended to be associated with a particular form of intervention, namely privatisation and the sell-off of public institutions. This has begun to change as we will explore in Chapter 7 with a distinct sensibility emerging around *selling* (and the associated activities of price setting and valuation) as a way of organising intervention. The economic crash of 2008 onwards has been key, we suggest, to giving increasing attention to new ways of cutting government costs and enhancing the efficiency and effectiveness of policy interventions. Here the transformation of what were once costs into assets through the mobilisation of new accounting terms and devices has played a central part in reordering the nature of public costs and debts. Once transformed into assets, we suggest that public debts can now be sold in new ways.

In this chapter we will focus on the UK system for higher education student loans to make sense of the means through which a liability can be converted into a cash-generating asset that can then be sold. However, in place of any counter assumption that such sales are part of a smooth and consistent political programme of action, what we find are sales that: opportunistically make the most of a series of uncoordinated activities that were not initially directed toward selling;

making a sale requires a range of new calculative devices, forms of practice and new relations; and that what should count as a reasonable price remains somewhat mysterious until a sale is achieved (meaning that any figure achieved through the sale then needs to be retrospectively narrated as a good return). We will suggest that the sale of student loans has been the most recent act in an ongoing drama that gained momentum in the 1990s with increasing recognition of the difficulties in maintaining UK public financing of university teaching (particularly with rapid growth in the number of students). This uncertainty regarding the sustainability of funding was combined with a switch in government accounting techniques from cash to accruals accounting. This meant that student loans would be reclassified from an outright cost of government (a liability), to an asset – a source of future income streams. Yet controversy continues to plague the loan system, with income-contingent repayments, variations in interest rate, government bail-outs of the system, attempts to sell the loan book and political support for alternatives such as a graduate tax, all vying for attention. Selling tranches of the loan book does not sell off these problems, but it does broaden the number of responsible actors involved.

Alongside the important features of market-based interventions and the sensibilities that our research can draw to readers' attention, we also note two prominent troubles that will stalk the following chapters. The first trouble is that each of these interventions proposes not only to utilise what we have termed *market sensibilities* as a basis for intervening in a public problem, but that these sensibilities will also provide an important form of regulatory governance. That is, competition, for example, will not only be important, for instance, in drawing together various potential providers to compete to provide a solution through a Social Impact Bond for children at risk, apparently ensuring the economic efficiency of the intervention. The quality of the intervention itself will also be regulated along competitive principles, with the competition designed to ensure that the "best" interventions are the ones selected. In this sense, competition operates as a sensibility for arranging *and governing* the intervention. This raises significant questions, we suggest, for the future role of what has traditionally been conceived of as the state. The second trouble is that each of these interventions continually brings into being specific relations of problem and solution. These interventions do not straightforwardly solve problems and further solutions are frequently required to solve the problems caused by initial solutions. This seems to generate ongoing and unresolved relations of problem and solution as an enduring characteristic of market-based interventions. Not only then is the future of the state at stake, but so is the very notion that interventions are able to succeed in resolving problems. In place of resolution comes a series of recursive loops between problems and solutions. These two forms of trouble will be picked up on in our final chapters, as we look across our distinct interventions and sensibilities and move from particular to general. In Chapter 8 we investigate in-depth the problematic relations of problem and solution that these market sensibilities provoke. In Chapter 9 the book concludes with an analysis of the future of the state and the very idea of progress incorporated into market-based interventions.

References

Austin, C. (1962) *How To Do Things with Words*. Oxford: Clarendon Press.

Bear, L. (2013) The antinomies of audit: Opacity, instability and charisma in the economic governance of a Hooghly shipyard. *Economy and Society* 42(3): 375-97.

Best, J. (2007) Why the economy is often the exception to politics as usual. *Theory, Culture and Society* 24(4): 87–109.

Birch, K. (2017) Response (to review of *We Have Never Been Neoliberal*). *Antipode*. Available at: https://antipodefoundation.org/2015/04/07/critical-dialogue-birch-christophers/ (last accessed 3 April 2019).

Blyth, M. (2013) *Austerity: The History of a Dangerous Idea*. Oxford: Oxford University Press.

Brown, W. (2015) *Undoing the Demos: Neoliberalism's Stealth Revolution*. Brooklyn, NY: Zone Books.

Çalışkan, K. (2010) *Market Threads: How Cotton Farmers and Traders Create a Global Commodity*. Oxford: Princeton University Press.

Çalışkan, K. and Callon, M. (2010) Economization part 2: A research programme for the study of markets. *Economy and Society* 39(1): 1–32.

Callon, M. (1998) *The Laws of the Markets*. Oxford: Blackwell.

Callon, M. (2007) An essay on the growing contribution of economic markets to the proliferation of the social. *Theory, Culture, Society* 24: 139–63.

Callon, M. (2016) Revisiting marketization: From interface-markets to market agencements. *Consumption Markets and Culture* 19(1): 17–37.

Callon, M., Meadel, C. and Rabehariosa, V. (2002) The economy of qualities. *Economy and Society* 31(2): 194–217.

Callon, M. and Muniesa, F. (2005) Economic markets as calculative collective devices. *Organization Studies* 26: 1229–50.

Chamberlin, E. (1946) *The Theory of Monopolistic Competition: A Re-orientation of the Theory of Value*. Cambridge, MA: Harvard University Press

Cochoy, F. (1998) Another discipline for the market economy: Marketing as a performative knowledge and know-how for capitalism. In M. Callon (ed.), *The Laws of the Market*. Oxford: Blackwell, pp. 194–221.

Cochoy, F. (2009) Driving a shopping cart from STS to business, and the other way round: On the introduction of shopping carts in American grocery stores (1936–1959). *Organization* 16: 31–55.

Cochoy, F. (2010) Reconnecting marketing to "market-things". In L. Araujo, J. Finch and H. Kjellberg (eds.), *Reconnecting Marketing to Markets*. Oxford: Oxford University Press, pp. 29–49.

Doganova, L. and Muniesa, F. (2015) Capitalization devices: Business models and the renewal of markets. In M. Knornberger, L. Justesen, A. Madsen and J. Mouritsen (eds.), *Making Things Valuable*. Oxford: Oxford University Press, pp. 109–25.

Durkheim, E. (1902) *De la division du travail social [The Division of Labour in Society]*. New York: Free Press.

Ericson, R., Barry, D. and Doyle, A. (2000) The moral hazards of neoliberalism: Lessons from the private insurance industry. *Economy and Society* 29(4): 532–58.

Fligstein, N. and Mara-Drita, I. (1996) How to make a market: Reflections on the attempt to create a single market in the European Union. *American Journal of Sociology* 102(1): 1–33

Foucault, M. (1977) *Discipline and Punish*. London: Allen Lane.

Fourcade, M. and Healy, K. (2007) Moral views of market society. *Annual Review of Sociology* 33: 285–311.

Gane, N. (2014a) The governmentalities of neoliberalism: panopticism, post-panopticism and beyond. *The Sociological Review* 60: 611–34.

Gane, N. (2014b) The emergence of neoliberalism: Thinking through and beyond Michel Foucault's lectures on biopolitics. *Theory Culture and Society* 31(4): 3–27.

Gane, N. (2016) In and out of neoliberalism: Reconsidering the sociology of Raymond Aron. *Journal of Classical Sociology* 16(3): 261–79.

Gibson-Graham, J. K. (2003) Enabling ethical economies: Cooperativism and class. *Critical Sociology* 29(2): 123–61.

Granovetter, M. (1973) The strength of weak ties. *American Journal of Sociology* 78(6): 1360–80.

Harvey, D. (2005) *A Brief History of Neoliberalism*. Oxford: Oxford University Press.

Hirschman, A. (1982) Rival interpretations of market society: Civilizing, destructive or feeble? *Journal of Economic Literature* 20: 1463–84.

Holm, P. (2007) Which way is up on Callon? In D. MacKenzie, F. Muniesa and L. Siu (eds.), *Do Economists Make Markets? On the Performativity of Economics*. Oxford: Princeton University Press, pp. 225–43.

Latour, B. and Woolgar, S. (1979) *Laboratory Life*. London: Sage.

Law, J. (2004) *After Method: Mess in Social Science Research*. Oxford: Routledge.

Lee, N. (1999) The challenge of childhood: Distributions of childhood's ambiguity in adult institutions. *Childhood* 6(4): 455–74.

Lepinay, V. (2011) *Codes of Finance: Engineering Derivatives in a Global Bank*. Oxford: Princeton University Press.

MacKenzie, D. (2008) *An Engine, Not a Camera: How Financial Models Shape Markets*. London: MIT Press.

MacKenzie, D., Muniesa, F. and Siu, L. (eds.) (2007) *Do Economists Make Markets? On the Performativity of Economics*. Oxford: Princeton University Press

MacKenzie, D. and Pardo-Guerra, J. (2014) Insurgent capitalism: Island, bricolage and the re-making of finance. *Economy and Society* 43(2): 153–82.

Miller, P. (1992) Accounting and objectivity: The invention of calculable selves and calculable spaces. *Annals of Scholarship* 9(1/2): 61–86.

Mirowski, P. (2013) *Never Let a Serious Crisis Go To Waste*. London: Verso.

Mitchell, T. (2002) *Rule of Experts*. London: University of California Press.

Montesquieu, C. (1750) *De l'espirit de lois [The Spirit of Laws]*. Available at: https://archive.org/details/spiritoflaws01montuoft/page/n9 (last accessed 3 April 2019).

Muniesa, F. (2007). Market technologies and the pragmatics of prices. *Economy and Society* 36(3): 377–95.

Muniesa, F. (2014) *The Provoked Economy: Economic Reality and the Performative Turn.* London: Routledge.

Muniesa, F., Doganova, L., Ortiz, H., Pina-Stranger, Á., Paterson, F., Bourgoin, A., Ehrenstein, V., Juven, P.-A., Pontille, D., Saraç-Lesavre, B. and Yon, G. (2017) *Capitalization: A Cultural Guide.* Paris: Presses de Mines.

Nik-Khah, E. (2014) Neoliberal pharmaceutical science and the Chicago School of Economics. *Social Studies of Science* 44(4): 489–517.

Osborne, T. and Rose, N. (1999) Governing cities: Notes on the spatialisation of virtue. *Environment and Planning D: Society and Space* 17: 737–60.

Peck, J. (2010) *Constructions of Neoliberal Reason.* Oxford: Oxford University Press.

Plehwe, D. (2009) Introduction. In P. Mirowski and D. Plehwe (eds.), *The Road from Mont Pèlerin: The Making of the Neoliberal Thought Collective.* Cambridge, MA: Harvard University Press, pp. 1–42

Power, M. (1997) *The Audit Society.* Oxford: Oxford University Press.

Rose, N. (1996) *Inventing Our Selves.* New York: Cambridge University Press.

Rose, N. and Miller, P. (1992) Political power beyond the state: Problematics of government. *British Journal of Sociology* 43(2): 173–205

Shamir, R. (2008) The age of responsibilization: On market-embedded morality. *Economy and Society* 37(1): 1–19

Simmel, G. (1955) *Conflict and the Web of Group Affiliations.* New York: Free Press.

Strange, S. (1996) *The Retreat of the State.* Cambridge: Cambridge University Press.

Strathern, M. (1991) *Partial Connections.* Lanham MD: Rowman & Littlefield.

Swedberg, R. (2005) Towards an economic sociology of capitalism. *L'Annee Sociologique* 55(2): 419–50.

Swedberg, R. (2008) The centrality of materiality: Economic theorizing from Xenophon to home economics and beyond. In T. Pinch and R. Swedberg (eds.), *Living in a Material World*. London: MIT Press, pp. 57–87.

Wittgenstein, L. (1953) *Philosophical Investigations*. Oxford: Blackwell.

2

Trade and Exchange

Opening

We begin our empirical exploration of market-based interventions into public problems with a first market sensibility: trade and exchange. From everyday shopping in supermarkets (Cochoy, 2007), through the long-distance transport of commodities that make global trade (Çalışkan, 2010), to the conditional exchanges performed in a nanosecond by financial algorithms (MacKenzie, 2017), transfers of goods or contracts in return for monetary compensation or promise of payment appear central to the activities of markets. Here, we propose to examine how the market sensibility of trade and exchange is mobilised to engage with a significant public problem – climate change. Our focus will be on the European Union Emissions Trading System (EU ETS). Opening up the challenges of translating an issue as potentially amorphous as climate change into something that might be addressed through a market-based intervention will provide a basis for posing questions that will be initiated here and picked up again in subsequent chapters. We will use the EU ETS to ask what practices, relations and devices it takes to design and hold in place a market-based intervention, how market-like that intervention remains over time, what problems emerge and what consequences follow. By getting close to the action, we will investigate how this market-based intervention participates in the production of specific effects.

Emission trading has become a central component of Europe's climate policy, and has gained traction across the world, from California to China. The idea of relying on trade and exchange to address pollution originated within economics in the late 1960s (MacKenzie, 2009a; Lane, 2012), and emission trading or cap and trade systems appear to be economically oriented all the way through. When attuned to the problem of climate change, these interventions are designed to limit greenhouse gas emissions (in particular CO_2) released from the burning of fossil fuels and other industrial activities by stimulating industries to respond through a form of trade. The aim is to regulate the quantity of carbon emitted within a jurisdiction through the setting of an emission cap and the distribution of emission allowances (an allowance is often equivalent to one tonne of CO_2) that can be sold and bought by polluting installations and companies. Once a cap is set, a corresponding amount of tradable allowances is issued and distributed to the regulated entities. The existence of a limit is supposed to make allowances a scarce resource, turn the emission of CO_2 into a costly action and create an incentive for industries to reduce their pollution (for more on incentives, see Chapter 6). The purpose is to force producers to internalise an externality by making them take their emissions into account, including in their financial accounts, and transform their productive activities and technologies accordingly.

The economic rationale does not end here. Given the possibility of exchange through the purchase and sale of allowances, the cap is assumed to be met at the lowest possible aggregated cost. For economists, this assumption works as follows: a regulated entity that can reduce its emission of CO_2 at a low cost will do so and keep or sell the allowances it might have in excess, while a regulated entity facing high costs for reducing emissions will instead tend to buy the cheaper allowances. Through the possibility of trade and exchange, the distribution of the emission reduction effort is such that it takes place where it costs the least and thus efficiency is achieved. As this all happens within the limit of the cap, and in the case of the EU ETS the cap decreases over time, pollution will also decline. The price of allowances is set by exhausting all opportunities of trade and exchange and expresses this optimal state. Both for the regulator and the regulated entities, a cap and trade system amounts to a creative discovery process given that reduction costs and associated technological changes are not known in advance of the intervention.

Emission trading appears to set in place a very clear market sensibility derived from some equally clear economic expectations: capping allowances can place a cost on pollution; this can reset at least partially the business priorities of polluters and lead to an internalisation of externalities; trade and exchange will establish for polluters the viability of investing either in more environmentally friendly production processes or in the purchase of more allowances. If these assumptions were straightforwardly given effect they would move effortlessly from general (a logic justified through economics and a notion like efficiency) to particular (an operational climate policy for Europe), and there would be no need to get close to the action. And yet the notion that a carbon market is created, through which the complex problem of climate change is tackled via the creation of a finite quantity of tradeable allowances, seems somewhat simplistic. The market needs to be designed (Çalışkan and Callon, 2010) and held in place. We will suggest, through an up-close analysis of the EU ETS, that this intervention is as much dependent on the European legislative process and what one of our interviewees called "the

Brussels ecosystem" as it is on the economic expectations we have outlined here. We will see that the minimal, neat and simple economic logic of the market-based intervention begins to disappear once the EU ETS is operationalised and gives way to a convoluted set of rules, regularly modified through tedious technical negotiations. Indeed, as these rules are put into operation and their consequences scrutinised, the market's rules raise new issues in need of further adjustment. Passage from the general to the particular and back again requires careful scrutiny. The chapter will focus on two issues that have pervaded the EU ETS in order to explore the means through which the intervention is designed and held in place, but also begins to sink into a morass of detailed policy negotiations: the problem of the surplus and the question of carbon leakage. The chapter begins with an opening foray into what we will describe as a negotiated technocracy.

The EU ETS: A Negotiated Technocracy

To move from economic expectations on cap and trade to a set of regulatory practices routinely enforced by member states across the European Union has taken huge effort. A key aspect of this move from general theory to particular intervention has been legislative activity in Brussels. The genesis of the legal existence of the EU ETS and its early design choices have been extensively documented and analysed (Wettestad, 2005; Ellerman and Buchner, 2007; Voss 2007; Skjærseth and Wettestad, 2009, 2010; MacKenzie, 2009a; Ellerman, Convery and de Perthuis, 2010; Ellerman, Marcantonini and Zaklan, 2014, Voß and Simons, 2014). Emission trading took shape as an idea in the United States in the 1990s to regulate SO_2 emissions (a pollutant emitted by power plants responsible for acid rain and local health problems). The trade and exchange principle was then first adapted to the problem of CO_2 emissions within the United Nations negotiation process on climate change and the development of the Kyoto Protocol.[1]

These antecedents in US environmental regulations, international climate negotiations and academic papers were insufficient to introduce Europe-wide legislation. The European Commission is also said to have played a major role in bringing in the idea of market-based environmental policy and developing the EU ETS, with a few civil servants acting as "policy entrepreneurs" (Wettestad, 2005; Braun, 2009). In EU politics, the Commission is in charge of preparing legislative proposals and overseeing the implementation of endorsed legislation. Decisions are made jointly by the European Parliament, which is currently composed of 751 politicians elected across Europe, and the Council, which represents the voice of member states through their ministers (here those in charge of environmental issues). The Commission was enthusiastic about emission trading because it suited the decision-making procedures of the European Union. While fiscal measures like a unique carbon tax would have needed to be unanimously accepted within the Council – and a European carbon tax had been envisioned in the 1990s – a cap and trade system could be more easily agreed on as it would qualify as an environmental policy that only required a majority vote. The Directive creating the EU ETS passed in 2003 after three years of negotiation, with

---

[1] The Kyoto Protocol is a treaty negotiated in 1997, though which the so-called developed nations of the time complied with emission reduction objectives (compared to emission levels in 1990) for the period 2008–12. The treaty also established market-based interventions to facilitate compliance, including a cap and trade system.

regulated industries showing relative support for the quantity and market-based mechanism.

The EU ETS is a significant regulatory feat. It extends over 31 nation-states[2] and regulates more than 12,000 installations owning a fuel combustion unit of a certain size and whose total emissions represent around 45% of the total carbon dioxide released into the atmosphere within the European Union. Maintaining this market-based intervention is thus a remarkable task. Each year, a number of allowances (digital entities held in electronic registers) is created up to the corresponding Europe-wide cap. Some of these allowances are sold on auction platforms while the rest are handed out for free according to harmonised allocation rules applied by member states. The governments of these member states are then also in charge of translating and enforcing the legislation. Every installation must calculate its annual level of emissions according to guidelines, which have been increasingly standardised across Europe. Installations must report the results to a national administrative authority and surrender an equivalent quantity of allowances whose electronic existence will then be cancelled. In cases of non-compliance, financial sanctions are imposed through a penalty of €100 per tonne of CO_2. The whole process involves independent audit, administrative control and the maintenance of registers. An online interface provides the general public with information such as the annual emission levels and surrendered allowances for all installations. These range from New Cross Hospital in the south of London to a Polish coal-burning power plant close to the German border, from a cement plant in the middle of Spain to a blast furnace along the Mediterranean in France.

---

[2] The 31 participants are the EU's 28 member states plus Iceland, Lichtenstein and Norway.

The emergence of the EU ETS has inspired a range of academic analyses. This has focused on the "performativity" of economic theory given that cap and trade stems from the work of economists (MacKenzie, 2009a), the "innovation journey" of this new type of climate policy (Voß, 2007; Voß and Simons, 2014), discussions around the legal and accounting existence of allowances as a new asset class (Lovell, 2014) and the development of a financial sector, market intermediaries and derivatives (Knox-Hayes 2009). The neoliberal dimension of cap and trade systems, which supposedly delegate regulation to the market, is also discussed (Lohmann, 2005, 2010, 2011; Mirowski, 2013). However, unlike education (see Chapter 3) or health where an existing state sector might become in some sense marketised, turning climate change, or rather pollution from industrial activities, into an issue amenable to market-based intervention has required a variety of measures enforced by national, state-related authorities upon private companies that were already market agents. Through this enforcement, carbon emissions have been specifically targeted as a public problem, rendered measurable and distributed into tradable allowances equivalent to tonnes of CO_2. But this is a peculiar kind of enforcement: industrial installations have been identified and made responsible for the problem, yet the *trading* activity through which allowances are bought and sold is not regulated as such (Knoll, 2015). Companies treat allowances as they decide; some might set up an in-house financial desk while others rely on brokers; some might buy surplus while others keep only what they need. But decisions on how many allowances are available for trade (the cap) and who, at first, owns them (allowance allocation) are subject to continual debate and public scrutiny.

The complexity of the system will become apparent in this chapter. But complexity is also partly what inspires critique. Complexity might be a smokescreen. For example, making emission trading the cornerstone of climate action is said to divert attention from "initiating a new historical pathway that leads away from the dependence on fossil fuels" (Lohmann, 2010: 80). Designing and maintaining a cap and trade system is mainly about establishing an emission limit and agreeing on the allocation of a corresponding amount of allowances. The intervention is meant to initiate a decentralised process whereby industrial sectors and companies explore and invent their own technological responses, but whether and how this happens is not the main focus of the EU ETS. As a result, in Brussels, the EU ETS is considered at a distance in an aggregate form, through an "endless algebra" (Lohmann, 2011). Much effort is dedicated to set its number-based rules, percentage targets, quantitative criteria and threshold values, rather than to discuss what kinds of production processes and consumption patterns could lead to a durable decrease in emissions. Such a rule-by-numbers intervention might thus appear disconnected from the profound matters that should be at stake with climate change – the dependency on fossil fuels as an energy source and the large-scale transformation of organic matter for industrial purposes.

It would, however, be reductive to dismiss the EU ETS altogether. Instead we need to get close to the detail in order to understand how the market-based intervention is given effect. The intervention has made CO_2 a problem recognised by European politicians and industries. Its design and redesign provide a focal point for a particular problematisation of global warming (see Callon, 2009), a number-oriented collective problematisation that happens in various meetings and paperwork. This problematisation is traceable in the comments on the legislative process elicited during our interviews with industrial representatives (company executives, in particular from the cement sector, and lobbyists), staff members of the European Commission, parliamentary assistants, national civil servants, academic economists and environmental activists, who have all become experts in the technicality of the EU ETS.

To better characterise the EU ETS, the market-based intervention can then be described by the oxymoron a *negotiated technocracy*, a technocratic intervention whose calculative technicality is subjected to intense political negotiations. Such ongoing technocratic negotiations were foreseen in the genesis of the EU ETS. From the start, the system was structured in sequential phases (Mackenzie, 2009a), which means that its rules are regularly reopened for negotiation. When the EU ETS was launched in 2005, it was for a first pilot phase, then followed by a second phase from 2008 to 2012. From 2013, a third phase with new rules started that would last until 2020, and in December 2017, the rules of a fourth phase (2021–30) were agreed on. Getting close to the negotiated technocracy will enable us to make sense of the ways in which the EU ETS is involved in producing particular kinds of consequence. We can even suggest that, within the Brussels ecosystem, given the centrality of the legislative process and ceaseless negotiations, the kind of exchange that matters most in relation to the EU ETS might not be the trading of allowances. Instead the exchange of arguments to agree on the number-based rules that give existence to the trading of allowances sits centrally. In order to explore this negotiated technocracy in action, we now turn our attention to two main issues subject to intense negotiation: first, the surplus and, second, carbon leakage.

The Surplus Problem

Time and Negotiated Technocracy

A central feature of the market's design – its emission cap – and the provenance of the numbers used for this purpose must be unpacked if one wants to understand a current major topic for negotiation in the EU ETS – the surplus of allowances. As we will see, the surplus is in many ways the pinnacle of negotiated technocracy. It relates to the cap (the emission limit) in the cap and trade system; that is, the total quantity of tradable regulatory units (emission allowances) that can be exchanged among market agents.

Since 2013, the market has operated with a unique Europe-wide emissions limit. This has been a central change. In phase 2, each member state had set its own cap, a constant value for five years (2008–12), and was in charge of distributing the corresponding amount of allowances to installations located in its territory. Caps and allocation plans were national matters then, finalised around 2006–07 through tense interactions between national administrations and the European Commission who tried to ensure constraining limits and comparability across countries (MacKenzie, 2009a).

[In phase 2, from 2008 to 2012] it was expected that national caps [he draws a flat line] would more or less match emissions levels. But emissions tremendously dropped because of the economic crisis and because it was a time when lots of funding went to renewable energies and so electricity producers started using renewables, which emit less CO_2. Europe has globally emitted less CO_2 due to the recession and renewables. Emissions did like this [he draws a decreasing curve], which means that all this area [between the curve and the line] corresponds to allowances that have not been used. People can surrender them at any time, they have the allowances in their accounts, it's their ownership and there is no rule to cancel them. (Interview, civil servant, French ministry of environment)

The phenomenon described above is usually referred to as the surplus. It becomes tangible when on paper through diagrams and numbers, the market is conceived as the aggregation of all installations reporting their emissions and all member states handing out allowances. The accumulation of unused allowances results from the difference between emission caps and actual emission levels and from the possibility for regulated entities to bank allowances. The latter's lifespan, if not surrendered for compliance, is theoretically indefinite. In an emission trading system, the cap ought to be a constraint and force emission reductions upon the regulated activities. But in Europe since 2009, the amount of tradable allowances created every year has exceeded what is released into the atmosphere across all installations. According to all interviewees with whom we discussed the problem, from industrial representatives and environmental activists to civil servants (see above), the surplus has resulted from a significant and enduring decline in industrial activities and their demand for energy together with a move toward cleaner sources of energy. This double effect was attributed to policy incentives established at the initiative of European decision-makers to encourage the development of renewable energies (like feed-in tariffs) and the 2008 economic recession.[3]

The financial crisis in Europe provides a clear example of the difficulties of setting a cap and issuing allowances. As the following economist suggests, surplus might actually be a more general feature of cap and trade systems.

------

[3] This situation was exacerbated by the import of emission offsets (or emission reductions) from international market-based interventions, a UN policy established as part of the Kyoto Protocol (see MacKenzie, 2009b). These offsets added to the surplus of allowances before European decision-makers put an end to their fungibility with allowances.

It's actually very hard to fix a cap, very, very hard. First, because you need to set it several years in advance, and then in the meantime, you have many surprises, because you can't predict energy prices, you can't predict the economic situation. And if you set a constraining cap, you take the risk that the price increases and plants close and manufacturers say "it's the carbon market's fault". Even if they close their plants for other reasons, they'll say it. And so because politicians won't take the risk, they set a cap that is not ambitious enough.[4]
(Interview, economist 1)

For some economists, over-allocation is an inherent feature of cap and trade systems attributable to politicians' fear of generating economic and social troubles and because of an "upward bias" observed in the mid-term modelling used to inform such climate policy decisions (Grubb and Ferrario, 2006). There is too much optimism and "false confidence" in growth projections and the simulation of business-as-usual energy prices and emissions levels (Grubb and Ferrario, 2006). A numerical value that appears to be reasonably ambitious in baseline modelling, might not be so once, as a policy target, it is compared to the emissions of industrial activities whose life is full of contingencies, even in the absence of a major crisis. To address this intrinsic flaw, economists tend to advocate for what they call *production-based allocation*; that is, an annual update of the total amount of allowances to be put into the market according to the observed activity level of the regulated sectors. The rule is practised in the Californian cap and trade system, but has never been seriously considered in the legislative proposals of the European Commission. One reason seems to be the

---

[4] As will be clear in the next section, the argument that an overly rigorous EU ETS would badly hurt European industry has a great deal of traction in the Brussels ecosystem.

political importance of the cap; the EU climate effort is captured by one simple number and becomes easy to advertise
and justify (we noticed, for example, that European civil servants used the expression "the cap is the cap" when they wanted
to nuance some critiques of the EU ETS).

Given the timing of phases and decision-making required
in advance of each phase, the surplus problem was not resolved
as the EU ETS entered its third phase in 2013. In a move towards
a stronger integration of Europe's climate and energy policies
and in line with the single market objective, the heads of states
and governments of European countries agreed in 2009 to have
a unique Europe-wide cap and harmonised allocation rules
(see next section). A couple of times a year these politicians
convene as the European Council, a diplomatic gathering that
provides unanimously endorsed directions to be operationalised into legislative texts. In EU politics and policy-making,
what appears in the conclusions of the European Council is
endowed with a higher authority. According to our interviewees, it is very difficult, almost impossible, to renegotiate what
has been unanimously agreed on at the European Council
and the design of the EU ETS in the third phase was affected
by such a political constraint. Its unique emissions cap was
set in accordance with a broader target already announced
by the European Council in 2007 as part of the forthcoming
2020 Climate and Energy Package. This was a time of particularly intense industrial activity across Europe, before the economic recession. Two years later in Spring 2009, despite signs
of change within the economy, the heads of states approved
the Package's commitments in the form of a series of items of
legislation, including a revised EU ETS Directive for phase 3
(OJEU, 2009).

The Climate and Energy Package was structured around
what a staff member of the European Commission referred

to as "20-20-20 by 2020" (interview, DG Research): by 2020 Europe should reach a 20% improvement in energy efficiency, 20% of European energy should be renewable and a 20% cut in emissions compared to 1990 should be achieved. The latter target applied to all greenhouse gases (not just carbon dioxide) and emitting sectors (including transport, agriculture, etc.). The distribution of the emissions reduction effort between sectors covered by the intervention and the rest was established through modelling whose purpose was to find the most cost-efficient partition. The Europe-wide EU ETS cap was eventually set at the following value: a 21% reduction compared to the 2005 emission level as quantified during the first year of market compliance (European Commission, 2008). The quantity of allowances to be issued every year during phase 3, from 2013 to 2020, was then obtained by calculating a 1.74% annual decrease, between an aggregated level derived from the national caps of phase 2 and the 2020 objective. Numbers and timing, as we can already see, are central to the design of the market-based intervention.

The phases of the EU ETS, to quote a member of the European Commission, allow "a lot of learning by doing" (interview, DG CLIMA 1) such as the move from national caps to a single objective. There is, however, a temporal rigidity. The need to decide far in advance on the emissions limit seems to encourage politicians (particularly heads of state) to fix in place targets that are relatively easy to achieve, which means that when an event such as an economic crisis happens, measured emissions remain below the regulatory limit. At the same time, the European Commission justify this inertia by the fact that "at least two years are needed for any decision to be reached and it makes sense to decide at once for eight- to ten-year-long phases" (interview, DG Research). Although the economic theory of the EU ETS portends of an intervention driven

by a market-based dynamic, its implementation is characterised by this staccato negotiated technocracy that swings into
action in advance of each new phase, and then fixes parameters for many years to come. But it would be misleading to suggest there is no room for manoeuvre. As we will see in the next
section, adjustments of a sort are possible.

Convoluted Adjustments

The surplus, the accumulation of allowances that are not
needed, not traded nor used, just kept in electronic accounts,
is a problem that emerged in the course of implementation of
the EU ETS. It becomes a tangible phenomenon when in an
administrative office, on paper, through diagrams and numbers, the market is conceived as the aggregation of all installations reporting their emissions and all member states handing
out allowances. This is how the phenomenon was identified in
2010 when for the second successive year, reported emissions
showed a strong decline. As the EU ETS moved on to its third
phase a few years later, the continuous growth of the surplus
was for some time passively witnessed given the temporal
rigidity of the market's design.

The legislative bodies of the European Union did, however,
aim to take action eventually. Several measures to address
the surplus were introduced, but slowly, given that specific
decision-making procedures had to be followed. A first emer-
gency measure called "back-loading" was agreed at the end of
2011 (OJEU, 2011). It consisted in delaying the issuance of a
certain quantity of allowances (900 million tonnes of CO_2) that
were due to enter into circulation in 2014, 2015 and 2016. The
corresponding amount of allowances temporarily levied would
be made available in auctions in 2019, 2020. Meanwhile, a second measure, the creation of a Market Stability Reserve, took

shape, which would more profoundly change the rules of the EU ETS. Negotiations on the topic started in 2012 and ended in 2015, with the Reserve to be put into operation from 2019 onwards (OJEU, 2015). The design adjustment would work as follows. Each year, the European Commission publishes a figure indicating the value of the surplus. A certain proportion of the quantity of allowances supposed to be issued the following year according to the cap is then put in the Reserve. This amount is set at 12% (the withdrawal rate) of the surplus, which should gradually decrease. But if its volume falls below a given limit (400 million tonnes of CO_2), allowances are taken out of the Reserve and become available again for trading. The Reserve is expected to operate as a mechanism of surplus reduction by keeping allowances outside the electronic accounts of regulated companies. It conceives of the EU ETS as a matter of aggregated supply and demand and aims to make it "more resilient in relation to supply-demand imbalances" in the words of the policy decision (OJEU, 2015).

These two successive decisions to render the supply of allowances more flexible were not unproblematic. Even the back-loading measure, which the European Commission had considered to be "a tiny little adjustment", created an "outcry" within the European Parliament, according to a former Parliamentary assistant.

The argument that was put forward was "you are interfering with the market." Which is a stupid argument I think. [...] But this is a very frequent argument. It has to be taken seriously. This is a point I have put in a lot of speeches, like "We interfere in markets all the time. Let's not forget this." (Interview, former Parliamentary assistant)

The back-loading measure, and later the Market Stability Reserve, raised the question of whether and to what extent policy-makers should interfere with the possibility of trade after a set of rules had been established (see Knoll, 2015). Interference here concerned the timing of the quantity of allowances placed into circulation. For a market analyst we interviewed, the EU ETS is "an artificial market", wherein "policy-makers basically define the supply side of the market by creating the rules" (interview, Point Carbon team, Reuters). Yet, adjusting the rules through the back-loading measure turned out to be "a very politically emotional debate" (interview, Point Carbon team, Reuters). Members of the European Parliament were using their Twitter accounts to comment in real-time on the evolution of the legislative process. This quite volatile "exchange of views" had repercussions on the price of allowances because regulated companies and financial intermediaries reacted to every new argument as if it would translate into "the market infrastructure" and durably shape the possibility of exchange (interview, Point Carbon team, Reuters). Such is the basis of designing this peculiar market-based intervention; if the designers (in this case European politicians) take part in volatile exchanges of views on the future of the market, this can lead to volatile market exchanges of contracts (derivatives) about future allowances. Real-time tweets can shape real-time prices for emissions allowances.

Time is a central issue in the EU ETS in many different ways, whether it is the timing of the conclusions of the European Council, the phased approach of the intervention, the delay between setting a cap and enforcing it or the real-time tweets of politicians creating price changes. To be prevented from further accusations of meddling with the market, the Reserve is presented as an automatic mechanism, whose detailed rules once agreed would not change. This aims to create the kind of predictability demanded by regulated companies, while risking again further rigidity in the intervention among much industrial flux.

In getting close to the action, we can see that negotiated technocracy is crucial to designing the market, redesigning its rules through phases, giving voice to and settling controversies, while also attempting to appear to remain at arm's-length from market meddling. The focus for negotiation also continues to change. As the legislative process on the rules of the market for phase 4 was initiated in the summer of 2015, environmental organisations began advocating for a much more stringent emissions cap. They based their request on the Paris Agreement, a treaty meant to coordinate global climate efforts, which was endorsed by most nations of the world (including EU member states) in December 2015. But aligning the EU ETS on the ambitions inscribed in the international treaty implied renegotiating policy targets decided by the European Council in 2014. And again, despite press releases, events in Brussels and face-to-face meetings with European Parliamentarians, the temporal rigidity of EU politics defeated this demand.

The demand for tighter constraints in the EU ETS was not only an environmental crusade. The power sector also supported the idea. For the spokesperson of the European power association, the prices at which allowances had been traded in phase 3 did not "provide incentives" and "visibility" for investment in, for example, gas rather than coal plants (interview, Eurélectrics).[5] Indeed, another way of conceiving of the surplus problem is to say that the price of allowances is too low

---

[5] In this respect, the official position of the power sector is very different from other industries. That the power sector advocates for a tighter cap (and thus a stronger constraint on their emissions) can be explained in part by the existence of a range of low-carbon alternative technologies, in particular nuclear energy which appears environmentally friendly when the only matter of concern is carbon emissions.

because they are not scarce enough. In 2016–18, it fluctuated between €4 to €10 a tonne of CO_2, whereas in the mid-2000s, at least €30 were talked about.[6] The reason why the price has not gone down to zero despite an excess of around two billion allowances (the equivalent of two years of total emissions) has been explained to us as a matter of expectation. Allowances are kept on companies' accounts to hedge against potentially more stringent rules in the future. In economic theory, making allowances tradable is supposed to distribute the emissions reduction effort (to meet the cap) among installations in the most cost-effective way and the price of allowances captures this optimal state. Studying the implementation of the intervention sheds light on a different dynamic, with hedging and speculative behaviour generating little investment in each tonne of CO_2 in a situation of surplus.

The EU ETS transforms climate change into technical discussions about emission levels and various sorts of numerical values, from the withdrawal rate of the Market Stability Reserve to the price of allowances. The emergence of a surplus of unneeded and thus untraded allowances and the attempts to adjust the market's design to address this problem illustrate well the centrality of technical matters in cap and trade systems. These technicalities, on which the possibility of trade and exchange eventually relies, have been endlessly debated in discussions that tied together the aftermath of the economic recession, overlapping policy effects, and a cost-effectiveness rationale with political authority in the EU. The fixed temporal phases of the EU ETS and their rules combined with the emergence of problems such as the surplus effectively demonstrate the convoluted nature of negotiated technocracy. The EU ETS is at once both incredibly technically detailed in its metrology

---

[6] www.theice.com/products/197/EUA-Futures/data

and subject to the vagaries of sometimes hesitant, sometimes changing and sometimes vehement political negotiation. In the next section we will show how this operates in relation to another emergent issue: carbon leakage.

The Carbon Leakage Problem

Competitiveness Matters

Carbon leakage emerged as a notable issue in the EU ETS through the allocation of emission allowances. In a similar manner to the surplus, allocation and carbon leakage became a feature of the negotiated technocracy. As the surplus was subject to an array of negotiations and subject to staccato changes characteristic of the phasing of this market-based intervention, allocating allowances is also subject to its own specific technical procedures, negotiations, complaints, stubborn endurance and sudden, partial transformations. However, the existence of the surplus was never disputed as a phenomenon and could be accounted for through simple procedures. In contrast, carbon leakage is a much less tangible phenomenon, whose existence is contested. Precisely because of this, it is an important matter of concern for the Brussels ecosystem. Whereas the surplus enabled us to engage with investment and financial crisis, carbon leakage allows us to explore competitiveness, what counts as adequate evidence and forms of risk.

In the first and second phases of the EU ETS (2005–07 and 2008–12), when caps and allocation plans were national matters, most allowances were given out for free. The amount distributed every year per installation was calculated by member states based on past emission levels. The decision to make allowances freely available was meant to encourage regulated industries to accept the new environmental constraint, without compromising the trading of allowances and their expected incentivising effect (MacKenzie, 2009a). According to economists, an installation would not use all the allowances it received for free if it could reduce emissions at a lower cost and derive revenues by selling the excess allowances. Moreover, installations' past emissions would not necessarily match future emissions and these discrepancies would further generate the sale and purchase of allowances (Ellerman et al., 2010). But the implementation of free allocation was not unproblematic. Governments seemed to engage in a sort of competition to set very generous rules that, according to a staff member of the European Commission, "were distorting the market" (interview, DG CLIMA 2). Whereas European politics ought to create a level playing field for economic activities across the whole Union, some national allocation plans amounted to unfair subsidies rewarding domestic industries with many free allowances (see Chapter 3 for more on the practices of competition).

The new harmonised rules did not terminate free allocation but established two treatments: one for the power sector and the other for the rest of industry. Economic analysis suggested that in phase 1, power companies were able to increase electricity prices as a result of the EU ETS (MacKenzie, 2009a). The phenomenon attracted much attention and the power sector's potential windfall profits were condemned (Point Carbon, 2008).[7] It was eventually decided that from 2013 onwards,

_____

[7] Economists expected the phenomenon to happen and passing through cost was a desired outcome. In an ideally liberalised market, it meant that power suppliers who were able to reduce emissions by using renewable sources of energy could decrease the price of their electricity and be rewarded for it by gaining consumers attracted to cheaper prices.

power plants would no longer get anything for free (expect in some Eastern European countries heavily dependent on coal that were deemed to be in transition). Electricity companies would have to buy allowances on auction platforms or market exchanges.

Free distribution of allowances, amounting to around half the cap, continued for other industries supposedly unable to pass on costs to their consumers in the manner of the power sector. The new allocation rule was still based on installations' past emissions but was now weighted according to the exposure of the industrial activity to carbon leakage. Carbon leakage is first and foremost an economic concept to capture the intuition that an increase in emissions can occur outside a circumscribed jurisdiction as a result of climate policy enforced within this jurisdiction (Hourcade, Demailly, Neuhoff, and Sato, 2007; Dröge et al., 2009). This dynamic is usually expressed as a rate that partially counterbalances the climate objective (here the emissions cap). Leakage might take place through two means. The first is the price of fossil fuels: the latter would decrease within the regulated space because demand for polluting energy sources would decline as cleaner sources are sought and this price reduction might in turn increase the consumption of fossil fuels in unregulated spaces leading there to higher emission levels. The second means is called "the competitiveness channel": because of additional cost associated with emissions, domestic industries might lose market share to products manufactured outside the regulated space and lead to more imports sold at lower prices. As production would increase outside the regulated space, so would carbon emissions. In the longer-term, investments in new plants and equipment might even relocate to these unregulated jurisdictions in order to avoid the costs of equipping plants with cleaner, more expensive machinery or using cleaner, more expensive fuels.

Carbon leakage through the so-called competitiveness channel was not an issue for the power sector because the physical constraint of electricity networks prevented consumers from choosing non-European energy providers if faced with price increases due to European companies passing on costs.[8] The situation was different for industrial activities whose products were or could become globally traded (e.g., steel, glass, cement, etc.). Professional associations suggested these sectors would become uncompetitive and subject to carbon leakage in order to obtain generous levels of free allowances from member states in phases 1 and 2 when such jurisdictions were in charge of the EU ETS (Godard, 2005; interview, economist 2). By alleviating some of the cost of emitting carbon, a cost supposedly created by the constraints of the emissions cap and the limited amount of allowances, free allocation ought to protect against carbon leakage.

In phase 3, it was decided that the exposure to such risk should be more carefully assessed following a unique procedure enforced by the European Commission. The negotiated technocracy of the Brussels ecosystem produced two new criteria, "carbon intensity" and "trade intensity" as proxies to detect those industrial sectors threatened by foreign competitors and unable to retain consumers if they tried to pass on the cost of complying with the EU ETS into the prices of their products. An activity was judged to be at risk of carbon leakage through loss of competitiveness if its cost intensity (the additional cost incurred due to the EU ETS compared to the gross value added of the product) is above 30%, or if its trade intensity (total value

---

[8] Except in Baltic countries where the interconnection of the grid with non-EU space has endured from Soviet times (see Kama, 2014).

of imports from, and exports to, non-EU countries compared to the total EU market size) is above 30%, or if cost intensity is at least 5% and trade intensity at least 10%. Cost intensity would capture the financial burden exerted on industrial activities that consume significant amounts of energy (steel, cement, glass, aluminium, oil refining, etc.) by giving a price to carbon emissions through the cap and trade system. Trade intensity was in contrast a less precise indicator and a number of unanticipated businesses ended up on the so-called carbon leakage list.

Operationalising the criteria to establish an updatable carbon leakage list was a daunting task. Staff members of the European Commission recall a "heavy" process involving "a lot of data crunching". It required, first of all, the delineation of what an industrial sector is. This relied on "a certain level of disaggregation" in the Statistical Classification of Economic Activities in the European Union (NACE), a data infrastructure that allows anyone in an office in Brussels to "grasp the economic activity" (interview, former DG CLIMA). With the chosen level, NACE 4, 250 distinct sectors were established. For each of them, the values of the two indicators – cost intensity and trade intensity – were calculated thanks to Eurostat's databases. The operation was particularly complicated for the cost intensity criterion. For economists whose analysis had inspired the choice of the indicator, the latter was straightforward because it clearly represented cost increases due to climate policy that in their economic logic would inevitably lead to loss of competitiveness. However, moving from such theoretical considerations to actual numerical values proved difficult. Production costs involved confidential information and assigning an additional cost to the EU ETS demanded a counterfactual reasoning to set what would have happened without the market-based intervention. The European Commission had no mandate to use an indicator that would be easier to compute. Despite being poorly suited, the ratio and threshold values were inscribed in a legal text (the Directive) and fixed in place for several years, another manifestation of the system's rigidity.

In the negotiated technocracy of the EU ETS even the mere application of criteria already decided turned out to be open to debate. Industrial representatives could further argue for their inclusion on the carbon leakage list. An activity could be considered at a more disaggregated level in the statistical classification when the chosen category was not representative of its specific products. Manufacturers had then to provide the European Commission with additional cost and trade data matching the criteria. The possibility of ad hoc inclusions allowed, for example, the sub-sector "Frozen potatoes, prepared or preserved (including potatoes cooked or partly cooked in oil and then frozen; excluding by vinegar or acetic acid)" to be added to the list of activities deemed at risk of carbon leakage (OJEU, 2013). As a result, the list in use during the third phase of the EU ETS covered more than 95% of manufacturing industry's emissions.

From 2013 to 2020, except for those of the electricity sector, all other installations are given some allowances for free in order to transition from the generous regime of phase 2 to a future regime when most allowances would be auctioned. A harmonised allocation formula computed the amounts of allowances given to regulated installations. The formula contained a carbon leakage factor;[9] for the sectors on the list, its

---

[9] The allocation formula relies on historic emissions levels (data specific to a given installation are adjusted with a benchmark value representative of the best performances of the sector), multiplied by a carbon leakage factor, multiplied by a linear reduction factor (indexed on the annual decrease of the cap).

value was set at 1, while for the others it was set at 0.8% in 2013 and decreased annually to reach 0.3% in 2020. As we see, engaging with percentages does not stop with debates about the emissions cap. These technicalities pervade the technocratic negotiation of the EU ETS. The design of the intervention is made of numbers that are given effect through legislation and the apparatus of administrative and legal enforcement. Whether it is the cap or free allocation, these number-based rules are fiercely negotiated.

A Contested Elusive Risk

The major consequence of being classified as vulnerable to carbon leakage is the number of free allowances an installation will receive. As carbon leakage is a risk that may occur if the EU ETS is overly stringent in its demands, the aim of issuing free allowances is to prevent leakage ever taking place. The very specific nature of carbon leakage, a phenomenon whose actualisation is a potentiality, occupies a particular position in the negotiated technocracy; it is one of its most contentious issues. The elusiveness of carbon leakage has been for quite some time a matter of academic comment (Dröge et al., 2009) and industry response, particularly from lobbyists who have tended to put forward impressive leakage rates. The cement lobby, for example, suggested phase 3 rules would mean more than 80% of European cement production "will be at risk of offshoring" (BCG, 2008). Even after the financial crisis, the cement lobby has continuously put the emphasis on the risk of leakage.[10]

---

[10] See the opinion papers and press releases available online: https://cembureau.eu/

While there was initially nothing more than models and numeric forecasts to testify to the possibility of the phenomenon, with the policy being implemented, retrospective analysis became possible. Through the progressive constitution of an archive of emission levels per installation, Eurostat's routine measurement of the economy and allowance prices recorded on market exchanges, correlations could be tested in order to detect or not phenomena such as the relocation of production. Empirically grounded analyses of the elusive risk thus entered the negotiated technocracy. In 2013, to prepare for the revision of the EU ETS for phase 4, the European Commission tasked a consortium of consultants with investigating "whether there is factual evidence for the occurrence of carbon leakage over phases 1 and 2 of the EUETS" (Bolscher et al., 2013). The conclusion was, there was none. Econometric studies, for example, suggested that changes in production and emission levels of specific industrial activities correlated with changes in demand for the industrial products and not with changes in the allowance price. The absence of observed leakage was due, it seemed, to the absence of a risk instead of the effectiveness of the protective measure. Gradually, a consensus grew around the fact that carbon leakage might have been overstated.

A sign that, even within industry, people tended to agree with the widely shared diagnosis of the absence of carbon leakage, is the switch in phrasing to a new lobbying term "investment leakage".

Investment leakage is when companies decide to invest less and less in a new capacity or invest less in maintaining and upgrading existing capacity and rather spend that money somewhere else. Whereas, carbon leakage is really the final station where a company decides to completely move out of Europe. (Interview, communication, Business Europe)

Carbon leakage had entered but could also leave the negotiated technocracy. Investment leakage might fare better, but
only if it could prove its own existence. To provide evidence of
this even more elusive process, the business lobbyist quoted
above relied on a survey that asked 200 industrial representatives how they saw things developing in the future and whose
results were released at a public event in Brussels in Autumn
2016. The timing was chosen to exert pressure on the legislative
process around the new rules of the market.

As for the emissions cap from 2021 to 2030, the distribution of allowances was another element of the EU ETS to be
renegotiated. Noting the absence of evidence of the carbon
leakage phenomenon but also the demand from the European
Council to pursue free allocation as a protective measure
(European Council, 2014), the European Commission's proposal for phase 4 suggested only a few changes. Besides replacing cost intensity with an indicator easier to calculate (emission
intensity), the text called for the use of a combined criterion
to exclude from the carbon leakage list sectors that were only
trade intensive. This single criterion would then work within
a "tiered approach" (European Commission, 2015). Instead of
a binary outcome, at risk or not, different degrees of exposure
would translate into differentiated treatments regarding free
allowances. The tiered approach aimed to ensure that, overall,
fewer free allowances would be handed out and their distribution would better match the vulnerability of regulated sectors.

To make the case for any legislative suggestion, the
European Commission first write an "impact assessment", in
which different policy options are laid out and consequences
investigated, often through modelling. This document and
the discussions it organises then translate into a Proposal
later amended by European Parliamentarians and ministers.
According to a staff member of the Commission, the difference

between their own proposal and politicians' amendments might be "disproportional in terms of level of thought and analysis" (interview, DG CLIMA 3). This opinion indicates a slight frustration from those in charge of the technical thinking called for by the negotiated technocracy of the EU ETS. When suggested rules enter the arena of the Parliament, numbers are used much more lightly (one could say as a means of bargaining, a bit more of this, a bit less of that). And so during Parliament's vote in 2017, the carefully thought through, and maybe too sophisticated, change in the assessment of carbon leakage risk was rejected to stick to how it used to be dealt with in phase 3.

Many industrial lobbies had actively contested the tiered approach. The European ceramic association, for example, representing 1,200 regulated installations (but less than 1% of total emissions covered by the EU ETS), "organized its people so well" to send out 200 similar online replies that rejected tiering when the Commission opened "stakeholder consultation" on the revision of the Directive (interview, DG CLIMA 3; Cerame-Unie, n.d,). The mobilisation of industry was not restricted to public releases and official participation channels. Lobbyists also enrolled Parliamentarians. As a result, debate at the European Parliament was shaped at a distance by steel unions in Germany, which organised a series of demonstrations at the time of the vote claiming that an overly stringent EU ETS would bring an end to the steel industry and increase unemployment in Saarland, Germany and Europe (interview, CAN Europe). The attempt to respond to the problem of the elusive risk of carbon leakage stalled and was abandoned.

Carbon leakage protection was probably one of the revision's most polarised topics. For a former Parliamentary assistant, "there is no ideal approach" to address the elusive risk (interview, former Parliamentary assistant). The issue seems irreconcilable due to its very nature: carbon leakage is a potentiality that makes sense within an economic logic but has not been observed and might not be observable in the short term anyway. When the EU ETS rules were revised in 2009 to move to a more harmonised system, distributing free allowances was talked about as a transition and an exception, auctions being the norm. Political discussions in subsequent years indicate that the exception has become the norm for manufacturing industries.

Free allocation is not unrelated to the surplus previously discussed. It has a direct impact on who owns the surplus and who bears or not the cost of emitting CO_2. Despite a decline in production following the recession, cement and steel companies, for example, have continued to obtain massive quantities of free allowances based on pre-crisis emission levels (Sandbag, 2010). It follows that in addition to deriving revenues from the sale of some of their surplus to sectors short of allowances such as refineries (Ellerman et al., 2010), these industries have had no reason to address their carbon problem.[11] Without judging the justification of the carbon leakage protective measure, based on our research, it seems possible to suggest that the market-based intervention has had little purchase, so far, on investment decisions in energy-intensive

---

[11] EU ETS rules are also said to enable the continuation of pollution. If an installation operates below 50% of its production capacity, it will lose half its allowances. But if the installation maintains 51% of its activity, full supply is secured. To secure full allocation, many cement plants maintained their activity, and emissions, above the threshold regardless of local demand for the material and exported the product manufactured in excess (Neuhoff et al., 2014).

industries, and even less so on innovation. The equipment and processes able to manufacture a material like cement remain almost unchanged since the 1970s and still involve the release into the atmosphere of large concentrations of CO_2.[12] For the negotiated technocracy of the EU ETS what is elusive, then, is not only the possible-future-existence of carbon leakage, but also the yet-very-tangible material realities of productive activities responsible for climate change.

Conclusion

Trade and exchange might be considered at the core of markets (see the centrality of the bilateral transaction in Çalışkan and Callon, 2010). In this chapter we examined how this market sensibility is employed to address a major public problem, climate change. By getting close to the action of the European Union Emissions Trading System, in place of a dynamic market activity derived from a clear and straightforward economic logic, we have instead been witness to a form of negotiated technocracy setting and resetting the rules of the market. The chapter highlighted the time-consuming and convoluted work that, since the creation of the EU ETS in 2005, has gone into making such a market-based intervention politically and legally possible.

To explore the negotiated technocracy we focused our attention on the relatively small world of the "Brussels ecosystem" that engages with the design and redesign of the number-based rules of the carbon market. We suggested that the EU ETS

---

[12] Cement is obtained from burning limestone and clay, a process that emits CO_2 from fuel combustion and the chemical transformation itself.

is an intervention dominated by hotly disputed and negotiated technical matters. One may say that the centrality of these debates about numerical values, thresholds, rates and categories is a smokescreen that keeps representatives of the public (elected members of the Parliament, ministers and even environmental activists) busy tinkering with the technical details of a very lax form of regulation, while allowing private companies to continue business as usual and even to derive profits from regulatory loopholes. This chapter indeed showed that the EU ETS has experienced such issues over time. However, other consequences can also be seen. In particular, the contentious nature of this negotiated technocracy foregrounds the multivalent complexity of the problem of carbon emissions: the urgency to act against climate change that must accommodate the slow rhythm of political decision-making; the intense lobbying of industries concerned by reduced profits as well as job losses; and the practical challenges of enforcing metrological requirements in the face of changes in the European economy.

Emission trading or cap and trade systems are often discussed as instances of "commodification" (see Lohmann, 2005). This chapter adopted a slightly different perspective. It suggested that the EU ETS has created a new tradable object, emissions allowances, in order to act upon companies and their markets. Setting a limit on emissions across Europe and distributing a corresponding amount of allowances, the intervention sought to generate a cost for emitting CO_2, which ought to be integrated into firms' financial accounts, investment decisions and productive processes. The EU ETS is, then, not so much an example of a market sensibility entering a non-market domain (which is what the term *commodification* often refers to), than that of a market sensibility meant to intervene on various existing market dynamics. With the problem of the surplus and the question of carbon leakage, we witnessed the difficulties of this form of intervention. The surplus of allowances started accumulating in the system following the 2008 economic crisis, with declining demand for industrial products such as cement and steel in many European countries. The surplus resulted from the inability of the EU ETS to react in a timely fashion to the contingencies of other markets (finance, housing, construction, etc.). The second issue we examined, the disputed assessment of carbon leakage risks, further pointed out how hard it is for the EU ETS to exert a constraint on other market dynamics. To prevent the elusive possibility of a geographical relocation of production and emissions abroad due to an overly stringent intervention, companies competing against foreign manufacturers have been protected from emission costs through free allowances. One result of this is that little appears to have happened with regard to their environmental performance. The fear of endangering competitiveness led to an exemption for some of the most polluting industries from the need to reduce emissions. Although the focus in this chapter has been on trade and exchange, as we can see competition (or at least competitiveness) is not far away (see Chapter 3).

The general economic expectations that we noted at the start of this chapter do not then straightforwardly translate into the particular details of intervention. Instead, the details dominate and their specific technical form (as measures, devices) is subjected to ongoing negotiation. The trade and exchange of opinions made witnessable through our study of negotiated technocracy is at times more apparent than the trade and exchange of allowances envisaged in the original design of this market-based intervention. Is this merely a quirky outcome of convoluted EU politics and a focus on trade and exchange? In the next chapter we will switch attention to a UK-based intervention into higher education research, away from the negotiated technocracy of the EU and the sensibility of trade and exchange, to look into the contours of competition. Here we will suggest some similar forms of bureaucracy pervade the intervention, providing further detail on the difficulties of moving from general principles to particular interventions and back again. Rather than simply retelling the story of negotiated technocracy in a new setting, we will use the competitive focus of interventions into UK higher education research to introduce some distinct questions of practice and their consequence.

References

Bolscher, H., Graichen, V., Hay, G., Healy, S., Lenstra, J., Meindert, L., Regeczi, D. and Timmons-Smakman, F. (2013) *Carbon Leakage Evidence Project: Factsheets for Selected Sectors*. Rotterdam: Ecorys.

Boston Consulting Group (BCG) (2008) *Assessment of the Impact of the 2013–2020 ETS Proposal on the European Cement Industry. Final Report – Executive Summary*. Boston: BCG.

Braun, M. (2009) The evolution of emissions trading in the European Union: The role of policy networks, knowledge and policy entrepreneurs. *Accounting, Organizations and Society* 34(3–4): 469–87.

Çalışkan, K. (2010) *Market Threads: How Cotton Farmers and Traders Create a Global Commodity*. Oxford: Princeton University Press.

Çalışkan, K. and Callon, M. (2010) Economization, part 2: A research programme for the study of markets. *Economy and Society* 39(1): 1–32.

Callon, M. (2009) Civilizing markets: Carbon trading between in vitro and in vivo experiments. *Accounting, Organizations and Society* 34(3–4): 535–48.

Cerame-Unie (n.d.) Ceramic industry position on post 2020 EU ETS review. Available at: http://cerameunie.eu/topics/climate-energy/emissions-trading-scheme/ceramic-industry-position-on-post-2020-eu-ets-review/ (last accessed 3 April 2019).

Cochoy, F. (2007) A sociology of market-things: On tending the garden of choices in mass retailing. In M. Callon, Y. Millo and F. Muniesa (eds.), *Market Devices*. Oxford: Blackwell-Wiley, pp. 109–29.

Dröge O, van Asselt H., Brewer T., Grubb M., Ismer, R., Kameyama, Y., Mehling, M. and Wang, X. (2009) Tackling leakage in a world of unequal carbon prices. *Climate Strategies*. Available at: https://climatestrategies.org/wp-content/uploads/2010/05/cs-greens-group-final-160610.pdf (last accessed 3 April 2019).

Ellerman, A. D. and Buchner, B. K. (2007) The European Union emissions trading scheme: origins, allocation, and early results. *Review of Environmental Economics and Policy* 1(1): 66–87.

Ellerman, A. D., Convery, F. J. and de Perthuis, C. (2010). Pricing carbon: the European Union emissions trading scheme. Cambridge University Press.

Ellerman, A. D., Marcantonini, C. and Zaklan, A. (2014). *The EU ETS: Eight Years and Counting*. EUI Working Papers, RSCAS 2014/04, Robert Schuman Centre for Advanced Studies Climate Policy Research Unit.

European Commission (2008) Proposal for a Directive of the European Parliament and of the Council amending Directive 2003/87/EC so as to improve and extend the EU greenhouse gas emission allowance trading system, Impact Assessment, Brussels.

European Commission (2015) Commission Staff Working Document.

European Council (2014) Conclusions – 23/24 October 2014, Brussels.

Godard, O. (2005) Politique de l'effet de serre. Une évaluation du plan français de quotas de CO_2. Revue française d'économie 19(4): 147–86.

Grubb, M. and Ferrario, F. (2006) False confidences: Forecasting errors and emission caps in CO_2 trading systems. *Climate Policy* 6(4): 495–501.

Hourcade J.-C., Demailly D., Neuhoff, K. and Sato, M. (2007) Differentiation and dynamics of EU ETS industrial competitiveness impacts. *Climate Strategies Report*. Available at: https://climatestrategies.org/wp-content/uploads/2007/12/1-climatestrategies-competitiveness-final-report-140108.pdf (last accessed 3 April 2019).

Kama, K. (2014) On the borders of the market: EU emissions trading, energy security, and the technopolitics of "carbon leakage". Geoforum 51: 202–12.

Knoll, L. (2015) The hidden regulation of carbon markets. *Historical Social Research/Historische Sozialforschung*, 132–49.

Knox-Hayes, J. (2009) The developing carbon financial service industry: Expertise, adaptation and complementarity in London and New York. *Journal of Economic Geography* 9(6): 749–77.

Lane, R. (2012) The promiscuous history of market efficiency: The development of early emissions trading systems. *Environmental Politics* 21(4): 583–603.

Lohmann, L. (2005) Marketing and making carbon dumps: Commodification, calculation and counterfactuals in climate change mitigation. *Science as Culture* 14(3): 203–235.

Lohmann, L. (2010) Neoliberalism and the calculable world: The rise of carbon trading. In K. Birch, V. Mykhnenko and K. Trebeck (eds.), *The Rise and Fall of Neoliberalism: The Collapse of an Economic Order?* London: Zed Books, pp. 77–93.

Lohmann, L. (2011) The endless algebra of climate markets. *Capitalism Nature Socialism* 22(4): 93–116.

Lovell, H. (2014) Climate change, markets and standards: The case of financial accounting. *Economy and Society* 43(2): 260–84.

MacKenzie, D. (2009a) *Material Markets: How Economic Agents Are Constructed.* Oxford: Oxford University Press.

MacKenzie, D. (2009b). Making things the same: Gases, emission rights and the politics of carbon markets. *Accounting, Organizations and Society* 34(3–4): 440–55.

MacKenzie, D. (2017) A material political economy: Automated trading desk and price prediction in high-frequency trading. *Social Studies of Science* 47(2): 172–94.

Mirowski, P. (2013) *Never Let a Serious Crisis Go To Waste.* London: Verso.

Neuhoff, K., Vanderborght, B., Ancygier, A., Tugba Atasoy, A., Haussner, M., Ismer, R., Mack, B. and Schopp, A. (2014). *Carbon Control and Competitiveness Post 2020: The Cement Report*. Final Report, Climate Strategies.

Official Journal of the European Union (OJEU) (2009) Directive 2009/29/EC of the European Parliament and of the Council of 23 April 2009 amending Directive 2003/87/EC so as to improve and extend the greenhouse gas emission allowance trading scheme of the Community.

Official Journal of the European Union (OJEU) (2011) Commission Regulation (EU) No 1210/2011 of 23 November 2011 amending Regulation (EU) No. 1031/2010 in particular to determine the volume of greenhouse gas emission allowances to be auctioned prior to 2013.

Official Journal of the European Union (OJEU) (2013) Commission Decision of 18 December 2013 amending Decisions 2010/2/EU and 2011/278/EU as regards the sectors and subsectors which are deemed to be exposed to a significant risk of carbon leakage.

Official Journal of the European Union (OJEU) (2015) Decision (EU) 2015/1814 of the European Parliament and of the Council of 6 October 2015 concerning the establishment and operation of a market stability reserve for the Union greenhouse gas emission trading scheme and amending Directive 2003/87/EC.

Point Carbon (2008) EU ETS Phase II: The potential and scale of windfall profits in the power sector, a report for WWF. Available at: www.wwf.de/fileadmin/fm-wwf/Publikationen-PDF/Point_Carbon_WWF_Windfall_profits_Mar08_Final_01.pdf (last accessed 3 April 2019).

Sandbag (2010) *The Carbon Rich List: The Companies Profiting from the EU Emissions Trading Scheme*. London: Sandbag. Available at: https://sandbag.org.uk/wp-content/uploads/2016/11/carbon_fat_cats_march2010.pdf (last accessed 3 April 2019).

Skjærseth, J. B. and Wettestad, J. (2009) The origin, evolution and consequences of the EU emissions trading system. *Global Environmental Politics* 9(2): 101-22.

Skjærseth, J. B. and Wettestad, J. (2010) Fixing the EU emissions trading system? Understanding the post-2012 changes. *Global Environmental Politics* 10(4): 101–23.

Voß, J. P. (2007) Innovation processes in governance: The development of "emissions trading" as a new policy instrument. *Science and Public Policy* 34(5): 329–43.

Voß, J. P. and Simons, A. (2014) Instrument constituencies and the supply side of policy innovation: The social life of emissions trading. *Environmental Politics* 23(5): 735–54.

Wettestad, J. (2005) The making of the 2003 EU emissions trading directive: An ultra-quick process due to entrepreneurial proficiency? *Global Environmental Politics* 5(1): 1–23.

3

Competition

Opening

In Chapter 2 we noted that trade and exchange is a market sensibility that is given specific shape in the European Union Emissions Trading System (EU ETS) by a significant bureaucratic infrastructure. In place of free market competition, which seems a central preoccupation for scholars of neoliberalism, came a somewhat expensive administration, governed by a system of rules that are reconsidered in each phase of the EU ETS. Negotiated technocracy deputised for ruthless efficiency and effectiveness. What this situation points towards is the importance of the particular form given to the sensibility at the centre of a market-based intervention. We could not assume that trade and exchange took shape as anticipated or stayed the same throughout the phases of the EU ETS. What got to count as trade and exchange, along with how central trade and exchange was as an organising principle for intervention, shifted over time and required careful research. Within the EU ETS, these shifts were accomplished through the phasing of the intervention, which was shaped, for example, by such powerful bodies as industrial lobbies who looked to utilise features of the trade and exchange model to reduce the competitive pressures their industry faced. And as a result, trade and exchange, counter to any expectation that it might orient the EU ETS toward dynamic market-like relations, slipped into a morass of extensive metrological discussions. In this sense, the form given to the market sensibility of trade and exchange, over time seemed to lose some of its market-like character. In this chapter we will focus in more explicitly on competition in order to tease out its key features. In a similar manner to Chapter 2, we will note along the way the extensive and costly bureaucratic infrastructure required to hold in place this market sensibility. We will also see how holding the focus steady on competition depends on a specific set of practices.[1] We will suggest that the practices through which competition is enacted invoke questions of representation, accountability and consensus. These have become important, we will suggest, for ensuring that the inevitably inequitable outcomes of competition can also seem fair.

The chapter is focused on higher education and the introduction of competition between UK universities to try and secure as great a share as possible of the fixed resource of government research funding. Although multiple governments around the world have introduced distinct systems for competitively allocating scarce government research funding (Wilsdon et al., 2015), we will analyse the particular contours of the UK's Research Excellence Framework (REF). This is the world's longest-standing system for competitive allocation of government research funding, stretching back to 1986 through the Research Selection Exercise and then the Research Assessment Exercise, before the first REF was carried out in

---

[1] In this chapter we will treat practice as the array of activities through which a specific subject matter (here competition) is formed and transformed (Schatzki, 2001).

2014. This ties into recent writing on neoliberalism that identifies competition as part of "the elevation of market-based principles and techniques of evaluation to the level of state-endorsed norms", within which "'competition' means that individuals, organisations [in this chapter, universities], cities, regions and nations are to be tested in terms of their capacity to out-do each other" (Davies, 2017: xvi). In this way, competition becomes part of a political programme of action, a "disciplining and coercive force" (Peck, 2010: 216) that "becomes generalized as a social and political principle" (Brown, 2015: 65). Following from this, we might be tempted to treat the REF as an illustration of this political programme of action. And yet by focusing on the programme of action, the specific practices of the competition itself seem to be underplayed. Once again we need to be able to move from the general principles (in this case of competition) to the particular features of the market-based intervention and back again. We need to know something of the practices of competition that compose the REF, not just the REF's position within a programme of action. In place of a study of the REF's position in the world, we want to know more about the REF practices that compose (at least a part of) the world.

In taking on this task, the chapter begins with an introduction to the REF and to the forms of competition it anticipates and demands. We then turn attention to the specific practices of the REF through interviews with participants and managers of the evaluation system. In contrast to the suggestion (above) of scholars of neoliberalism that the appropriate focus for analysis should be on competition as part of a political programme of action, we will instead argue that in order to understand competition in the allocation of fixed resource to higher education institutions, we need to explore the form that REF competition takes and how this form emerges. In the conclusion we will begin to explore the ways in which our first two chapters have started to engage with what is at stake in market-based interventions; this focus will be developed in subsequent chapters.

Competition and the Research Excellence Framework

Competition as the basis for selectively allocating the fixed resource of government research funding has a long tradition in the UK and remains central to research assessment. Funding Councils that managed the 2014 process, suggested in their "Key Facts" of the REF that their form of research assessment ensured: "a dynamic and internationally competitive UK research sector that makes a major contribution to economic prosperity, national wellbeing and the expansion and dissemination of knowledge".[2] Competitive allocation of research funding is then central to ensuring that UK research continues as a higher education market leader (always and already presupposing the existence and unquestionable importance of such a market) by concentrating scarce resources (government research funding) among those most able or likely to utilise those resources to good (market) effect.

We can see that competition as envisaged in the REF has two features. Competitive allocation of resources and the competitiveness of the UK on the world scene. The two are inseparable in the way the intervention is envisaged by those that manage the REF. The UK's economic prosperity depends on

---

[2] Funding Councils REF 2014: Key facts. Available at: www.ref.ac.uk/2014/media/ref/content/pub/REF%20Brief%20Guide%202014.pdf

being competitive with other nations; this competitiveness is (at least partly) underpinned by research and innovation stemming from universities; universities must then compete on the basis of how much they have contributed to that competiveness (particularly in the form of impact as we shall see); and universities will be rewarded according to their position in the competition – with greater rewards allocated to those most able to demonstrate their contribution to UK competitiveness. Whereas in Chapter 2, the problem being engaged was pollution and industries raised concerns regarding limits placed on competitiveness by the EU ETS, here the problem is ensuring an efficient and effective means of distributing scarce government research funding that will then contribute to national competitiveness.

We can see how the REF anticipates a movement from competition between universities to international competitiveness in Lord Stern's (2016) review of the REF. This review strongly emphasises the role and importance of competition in research funding as a basis for ensuring research market leadership and the position of the UK in trading relations with other nations. "Past Research Assessment Exercises and the 2014 REF have contributed productively to driving competition and fostering research excellence" (7). Driving competition, according to Stern is vital, as: "We live in a world where intellectual enquiry is global and competition is increasing so that our outstanding [UK research] leadership requires constant investment: key competitors are increasing theirs ... We live in turbulent as well as competitive times" (35). Competition for scarce government research funding is here presented as a means to ensure the quality of research, the productivity of academics, the strength of UK universities, the vitality of the national economy and even as a means to guard against global turbulence.

The competitiveness of the UK is an anticipated outcome of the form given to the market sensibility of competition. Competition is enacted in specific ways through the REF structure and the allocation of research funding to UK universities. One way to investigate the form given to competition is to explore the rules of UK research assessment. The REF rules are designed to work as follows. Each university department in the UK is expected to submit a REF return, composed of the most suitable research active staff based on internal assessments carried out by university departments. In 2014 each academic selected to take part had to submit their four "best" research outputs, although books could be double-weighted and part-time and early career staff could submit fewer outputs. For 2021 these submission rules have changed from four outputs per academic to a departmental total based on staff numbers, with a minimum of one output per staff member to a maximum of five (until the required total departmental number of outputs has been fulfilled). All submitted articles and books are peer reviewed and scored on a four/five part scoring system (from 0 to 4, with 4 being highest) and the peer review should constitute the basis for scoring, not the medium of publication or any external metrics.[3] As a result, peer review provides one means to give form to the market sensibility of REF competition, how much funding and what kind of future an academic department ought to have.

Peer review takes place through four Main Panels (Panels A, B, C and D), each of which covers a broad academic area (medicine, health and life sciences; physical sciences, maths and engineering; social sciences; arts and humanities) and

---

[3] Although some experiments with metrics have now begun to emerge in the REF.

these are divided into 36 discipline specific sub-panels (such as sociology or clinical medicine). The chairs of each sub-panel make up the membership of the Main Panels, also under the stewardship of a further chair. Chairs allocate outputs (articles, books) to members of their sub-panel in line with their expertise to carry out peer review. On most sub-panels, two reviewers examine each output. Departments can also highlight staff circumstances that panels should take into account in considering an academic with fewer publications (including maternity leave, sickness and so on). Further direction can be given by departments on such matters as interdisciplinary work that might need the attention of assessors from other sub-panels. If there are identified gaps in the expertise of the members of the sub-panel (for example, initially sociology had no STS expert in 2014) then a further specialist can be nominated and appointed. Each assessor then enters a score for each article they review in the REF computer system. These scores are then combined to work out the average score for each department that has submitted to a sub-panel and an initial ranking is calculated. In this way, the kind of significant bureaucratic infrastructure that we witnessed in Chapter 2 that was necessary to give form to trade and exchange is also apparent here in competition; estimates of the cost of the 2014 REF are around £250 million with most of this cost falling to universities.[4] With the significant bureaucratic infrastructure and scale of the REF comes a significant workload. Some individual assessors on some sub-panels were given between 800 and 1,000 articles to peer review.

---

[4] See: http://webarchive.nationalarchives.gov.uk/2018032211 1235/; www.hefce.ac.uk/pubs/rereports/year/2015/refreview costs/

Yet, the annual distribution of up to £1.6 billion of quality-related (QR) research funding between English universities (with smaller amounts for Scotland, Wales and Northern Ireland) does not only depend on reviewing outputs. Along with outputs, departments also submitted to the 2014 REF impact cases and an environment statement. These were both new to REF 2014. The environment statement provided a narrative of research life in each department submitted, setting out how much research grant income had been received, and how many PhD students were in the department, the major research centres and their activities, and so on. Impact cases had to demonstrate the non-academic impact of the work of the department. These cases had to fit a four-page template and set out the impact achieved, evidence for that impact and a link to at least a 2-rated academic publication. Although for assessment of research outputs, items had to be published within a single assessment period (for the 2014 REF this was 2008 to 2013), impact case studies could draw on a 20-year history. The number of impact cases required by a department, depended on the number of staff submitted to the assessment (in 2014 this required two cases for up to 14.99 full-time equivalent staff, then one more for every ten extra staff). The impact cases were crucial for underpinning the anticipatory link between REF competition and national competitiveness. Impact was anticipated as a means for academia to step outside its own internal conversations and instead talk up its contribution to the UK.

Once the ranking for academic outputs is combined with the scores for research environment and impact cases, only then is a formula publicly released and used to transform rankings into amounts of funding distributed to each department. The rules of the REF, then, are useful for understanding some initial features of REF competition, its anticipation of competitiveness and how the REF is expected to bring about specific effects. But this tells us little of how such anticipation is given flesh: just how is peer review conducted, scores given, rankings made and impacts assessed? To address these questions we need to get close to the practices of the REF.

As a research task, this is by no means straightforward. Beyond anodyne minutes of sub-panel and Main Panel meetings that reveal nothing of any use for getting close to the details of assessment practices, the REF and its predecessor the Research Assessment Exercise are characterised by a curious absence of accountability and transparency (particularly in comparison with other publicly funded initiatives which depend on openness for their democratic legitimacy[5]). This goes beyond the traditional anonymity of peer review: REF sub-panel and Main Panel members must destroy all records, including notes relating to any assessments they have carried out, messages they have exchanged regarding assessments, concerns or questions they have raised or any accounts of disputes that were resolved. No one is allowed to record the means by which an assessment took place. Only the scores are held on record and made public in an aggregate form. As a publicly funded competition, the REF is more black hole than black box awaiting to be opened. However, with the support of the Higher Education Funding Council for England (HEFCE) and a commitment to complete anonymisation, we have carried out lengthy interviews with Main Panel and sub-panel members, specially invited academic assessors and impact assessors. This has produced a corpus of more than 1,000 pages of interview transcript. What we present in the following analysis is necessarily a brief rendition of REF practices that give form to competition and anticipate future forms of competitiveness.

---

[5] See Woolgar and Neyland (2013).

Getting Close to the Practices of Competition

Research assessment stalks the corridors of UK universities, with academics put under pressure to continually work in ways that will contribute to their REF submission. As quality-related (QR) research funding is distributed according to REF results, academic careers and the future of some departments can be at stake. This is not a bland competitive sensibility in name only that masks a little-changed area of the public sector; the REF and the competition it institutes has become of fundamental importance to UK academia. Like philosophers with their coffee cups (Latour, 2004), academics have been swift to write about UK research assessment, as it has taken place every five to six years since 1986 and appears close to hand. The vast literature on research assessment tends to fall into three categories. First, there are studies that draw on ideas of New Public Management and the audit society to make arguments similar to those expressed by neoliberal scholars in the introduction to this chapter: that these kinds of assessment are part of a broader programme of political action that shapes the activities of academic research (see, for example, Power, 1999; Sayer, 2014). A second literature is more focused on the work done by universities to prepare for research assessments, analysing in-depth the efforts required to produce, for example, REF submissions, REF-able departments or individual impact cases (see, for example, Watermeyer, 2012; Watermeyer and Hedgecoe, 2016; Chubb and Watermeyer, 2017). A third literature is more focused on outcomes, investigating the effects accomplished in relation to the numbers produced as a result of research assessment (for a broad summary, see de Rijcke, Wouters, Rushforth, Franssen, and Hammarfelt, 2016).

In this literature, important questions are raised regarding the ways research assessment measures become targets that problematically shape the trajectory of academic work (Strathern, 2002), how research assessment enables the marketisation of UK higher education (Brown, 2014) and to what extent research assessment is costly and unreliable (Sayer, 2014). Building on these efforts, our concerns are how competition is given a specific form through the practices of research assessment, what constitutes peer review and the precise ways in which scores are accomplished. To address these concerns we needed to get close to the assessment practices and devices that gave effect to the REF. This has required working through our transcripts from interviews with REF participants in a dedicated manner. In the following sections, we will first explore the practices that gave form to the market sensibility of competition. Here we will work our way through practices of representation, accountability and consensus. We will then assess the practices through which the REF anticipates UK competiveness.

Practices of Representation

Many of our interviewees, particularly the chairs of Main Panels and sub-panels, reflected on what they took to be important features of the composition of a panel. Composing a Main Panel or sub-panel's membership involved a careful practice of deciding who and what ought to be represented in discussing and assessing the work of a discipline. Who should take part and what kinds of sub-disciplines should be represented on a sub-panel assessing UK sociology or geography or physics, for example? This was a normative question (what should count as part of an academic field) alongside a practical concern (who might be good at assessing so many outputs).

So the first thing was to get the Main Panel right, which was to pick the chairs of the subpanels, the sorts of human beings who would be good at doing that and we had a list of different ones that were put forward by various organisations. So because the human qualities of these individuals was going to dictate their performance in this new world of interdisciplinarity, we couldn't have narrow thinking, and it would be unacceptable to have somebody trading their own particular biased interest in such a setting. So the key thing was to get those chairs sorted first, and that was great fun, picking the right qualities of the individuals. [...] Once we got them, then of course working with them to pick the people who would populate the subpanels. (Interviewee 32)[6]

We can already see here that one challenge for participants in the REF was to choose other academics who would also participate – participants with the appropriate "human qualities" (interdisciplinarity, no narrow thinking or biased interest) who would act as representatives of a field and carry out assessment. Furthermore, covering various aspects of a sub-discipline's work was also deemed important, as sub-panel members would be assigned the task of peer reviewing a huge number of outputs (books and articles) from within each area of a discipline's work. Interviewees suggested that not having adequate representation would mean a huge effort on the part of a sub-panel and its chair to try and work out how outputs could be peer reviewed if there was no relevant expert in a specific area. Competitive outcomes, then, depended on very specific practices of representation that could combine a normative concern for what ought to count and a practical concern for how to do the counting. Appointing sub-panel members even included appointing experts in the process of assessment, who had been assessors in previous evaluations.

---

[6] Interviewees are simply given numbers in this chapter in order to respect their request for anonymity.

However, composing a representative panel proved more difficult than simply assembling an array of experts. The Higher Education Funding Councils that ran the 2014 REF also demanded that sub-panels had appropriate geographical, gender and university representation (for example older and newer universities should be included). This led to Main Panel and sub-panel chairs considering potential participants from different types and sizes of academic departments, different age groups (although these were not early career academics) and different regions of the UK. Some sub-panel chairs looked in vain for representative participants:

> I, as Chair, had to [...] say to them, for example, "We need more women. We need people in these subject areas," and so on. [...] I think we ended up with about a third of women on the panel. It should have been more. (Interviewee 15)

We might read into these demands that a form of diversity was key to composing representation. Indeed this seemed to be the case for the Funding Councils. But diversity was not the only concern in building a sub-panel. Sub-panel chairs also suggested that drawing together and holding together sometimes more than 30 different academics from within a discipline, preventing internecine conflicts from developing, stopping certain universities or even sub-fields from dominating the scoring, was an ongoing challenge.

Competition as a market sensibility was given an initial form by practices of representation that introduced various possibilities of tension (regarding the appropriateness of the membership of a sub-panel) and conflict (between members of a sub-panel). Although it might be a commonplace assumption of neoliberal scholars that competition turns organisations against each other, interviewees also suggested to us that even those participating in the assessment system were likely to fractionalise, take advantage of the chair and sew things up in their own interests. Competition between universities in the UK, instituted by peer review tied to the selective allocation of research funding, could not be accomplished without these practices of representation (unless peer review was removed from the assessment). Competition was accomplished through these tensions. Yet representational practices and their challenges did not cease here. Sub-panel chairs also had to represent their sub-panel internally to the rest of the REF. Within the REF, sub-panel chairs had to go to their Main Panel and demonstrate that their scores had been composed appropriately – they represented the assessment practices of their sub-panel. And outside the REF, sub-panel chairs had to communicate to the relevant academic community (for example, sociologists) that the scores produced by their sub-panel (for example, sociology) were in some way defensible. The actions of the sub-panel must not be reported, but must be deemed legitimate by stakeholders (comprising, for example, the sociological community not on the sub-panel). This was mostly achieved through publicly presenting the representativeness of the sub-panel, as the list of members is one of the few pieces of information from the REF that is made public. The list is designed as a means to communicate to the relevant academic community that their interests – their subject, expertise, the assessment of their work, the eventual distribution of funding and even, sometimes, the future of their department – have been taken into account and will be well represented. Representativeness is a requirement for demonstrating that, although the outcomes of the REF might be inequitable, they will be fair.

Representation has thus become a delicate practice within research assessment, discussed in terms of adequate representation of "human qualities", an academic field, geography, gender, age and university type, taking on sub-panel members' views and responding, representing the discipline internally within the REF and externally to the academic community. In order for government research funding to be competitively allocated, these practices of representation seem to have become necessary. However, on occasions participants suggested that adequate representation proved elusive. Interviewees suggested that, even though they were members of a sub-panel, they did not feel their views were listened to, their scores got to count or their co-members adequately encompassed the discipline (either in expertise, age or gender). What we began to see is that in the REF, representation was both crucial for some participants and on occasions deemed inadequate as a basis for carrying out assessments of academic work. Interviewees suggested there was little representation from institutions previously ranked lower in research assessment league tables. Some participants had moved into senior management roles and were thought by other sub-panellists to be some distance from the cutting edge of a discipline. Other sub-panellists thought that those doing original, cutting-edge research would not join a sub-panel as they were either too busy or opposed to the apparent conservatism of the assessment system. And some sub-panellists felt intimidated by the consensus of their sub-panel – a consensus into which they felt they did not fit.

The overall effect, as the following interviewee suggests, could be quite dramatic. Practices of representation did not just compose a sub-panel, but could shape a discipline.

[W]hile one would never, ever say, "You're privileging certain things over other things," nevertheless there were decisions to be made. Of course, that's being done at the level of who you appoint as the assessors and all that sort of thing, which has an inevitable effect on how the whole process is regarded and how people think the discipline is being treated. [...] So, you are giving off – you're undoubtedly giving off – messages about how you view the discipline, in every decision that is taken, to be honest [Laughter]. (Interviewee 27)

To include (or not) a specific field by having a representative of that field on a sub-panel is to suggest that such a field is important (or not) to a discipline and should be important (or not) to universities with those departments. There is no REF mechanism for making these concerns raised by sub-panellists regarding representation publicly available. Nevertheless, we can note across our interviews a range of views on the importance of representation and its limitations – age, gender and university type were all deemed relevant categories of representation for these interviewees to discuss. The twin move of representation outwardly (to demonstrate that representation was adequate to the academic community being assessed who were not part of a sub-panel), and inwardly (ensuring that each sub-panel was adequately represented within the REF) both connected closely to assessment practices. The outward move was an attempt to ensure that the inequitable outcomes of assessment seemed fair: the scores had been produced by a representative group. And the inward move often involved reporting to Main Panels that the sub-panel interaction had been reasonable. Competition, then, was given a very particular form through these representative practices, a form that could shape the academic discipline being assessed. To be on a sub-panel or not was a kind of competition in its own right, but not one characterised in 2014 by conventional forms of accountability and transparency, whereby the basis for making decisions might be made available for external scrutiny. The REF competition, then, involved practices of representation that simultaneously provoked concerns and neatly contained these concerns.

When issues were aired by a range of interviewees, they each put human representatives at the centre of the matter of concern. However, as we will see in the next section, the entities that were produced by, moved through and eventually went out into the world as representatives that could say something (and be used to say something) about university departments, were not people but scores, and their production depended on specific practices of accountability.

Practices of Accountability

Alongside the composition of representative sub-panels, peer review of journal articles, books and impact cases has been a major preoccupation of the REF. Peer review was a key means through which competition could be given form as the outcomes of peer review fed into the league tables for competitively ranking UK universities. Peer review, according to our interviewees involved a specific type of accountability.

The precise form of competition that is accomplished through the peer review system of the REF might initially appear to stand outside the traditions of democratic political accountability. If a democratic process depends for its legitimacy on being transparent and open to question – or accountable – to the populace who will experience the consequences of the decisions being made, then REF assessments certainly appear to be outside this realm of accountability. In contrast to the transparency initiatives of organisations that make information available about their internal workings in order to demonstrate that they have taken seriously their responsibility for their environmental impact, for example, or their employees or supply chains (Gray, 1992; Wall, 1996; Neyland, 2007), the REF makes no such efforts. The insistence on destroying all material that contributes to the process of giving a score, leaving aggregate departmental scores alone to stand testament to the process that has produced them, appears to systematically eliminate the possibility for departments or individual academics to question or hold to account their scores.

However, a particular practice of account and accountability does pervade the REF system of peer review. A more ethnomethodological sense of accountability is at work.[7] In place of traditional political accountability with a public face, comes an enclosed moment-to-moment, situated accountability of sub-panel peer review scoring. It is through this scoring system that numeric representatives are produced that go on to talk on behalf of departments and their value (once they are translated into a league table position and an amount of funding). If practices of representation gave competition a specific form by deciding who and what would participate in research assessment, these internal practices of accountability produced numeric representatives that would help give effect to competition.

But how did this internal accountability work? Interviewees devoted some time to discussing the sheer number of outputs they had to review (from around 200 articles or books to over 1,000) and the length of time this took. In our interview transcripts, we can also discern various practices of reading that characterised peer review. Some sub-panellists spoke of the dedication required to carefully read through a huge number of articles or books and give scores. Others talked of developing a skill or technique for quickly compiling scores or of losing quality in their assessment practices if they took too long to produce a score for an individual piece of work. Interviewees spoke of taking outputs they had to assess on family holidays, some were given sabbatical leave, while others struggled to fit scoring into their already busy schedules. While

---

[7] See Garfinkel (1967); Sacks (1972); Suchman (1993).

one interviewee spoke of scoring 892 outputs in a week, others suggested it took them several months to score around 200. It is here that something akin to an ethnomethodological (Garfinkel, 1967) sense of accountability is at work. In order for sub-panel members to move from reading to the practices of giving a score (from 0 to 4) through peer review was a locally demonstrable, accountable matter. That is, in having more than one reviewer for each output on most sub-panels, the work of reading and reviewing became a situated practice through which, what made sense as a 4 (or 3 or 2 or 1), was an interactionally agreed, and demonstrably accountable, outcome of moment to moment practice.

I knew what was coming and the way we did it was every output was read by two people, with a third in case [...] So the ones which were the first assessing team had more responsibility than the second. The third quite often just arbitrating. [...] So the outputs, I think we had about three or four months to do that. So I was sort of setting aside Mondays and Fridays to work on REF. (Interviewee 26)

As we can see in this excerpt, an initial score acted as an interactional turn, a kind of putative account, through which demonstration could be offered of a reviewer's act of reading, level of relevant expertise, and ability to allocate an appropriate score. The scores provided by second reviewers could then complete this turn-taking sequence either by demonstratively attending to the same matters (reading, expertise, allocation of a score) and providing a similar or identical score, or provide the basis for further accounts and turns in holding to account if the scores were discrepant. On these occasions, interviewees talked about first assessors holding sway in the maintenance of their score (often situating their closer expertise in the topic as providing a moral warrant for the score), or agree a score somewhere between the two discrepant scores, or call in a third assessor to hold to account both assessments already made.

Competition required this accountability in order for the sub-panellists' initial scores to pass through this process of discussion. At the same time as scores were produced, the ability of these scores to act as numeric representatives and stand in for or talk on behalf of the quality of a piece of work became contentious (in a similar manner to the way that questions were raised regarding the extent to which a panel of academics could act as representative of a discipline). For example, the apparent accuracy of the numeric representatives was deemed spurious by several interviewees. As the following excerpt makes clear, to rank institutions by decimal points was considered problematic:

> how this all figures through to the way in which the GPAs [grade-point averages] work out when everybody tries to rank all the institutions, and there's 0.01 of a ... This is a kind of spurious accuracy, I think, in some of the ways in which this was done. (Interviewee 28)

Despite these concerns, the value of peer review, even if an impaired concept, was deemed essential by most interviewees for the future of research assessment because of the local accountability that peer review offered. That a putative score could be proposed and questioned, providing an antagonistic situation through which a numeric representative might emerge, was highly valued. The existence of the antagonistic situation, even if its details were not publicly revealed, could attest to the strength of each numeric representative produced – that they were outcomes that had already been subject to interrogation. In this way the numeric representatives were the outcome of an internally oriented, deliberative practice. The competitive outcomes of the REF depended on this internal, preparatory competitive practice: deciding who was the best-positioned to give a score and what score an output ought to receive. Even when concerns of spurious accuracy or precision were raised, these remained carefully contained within the REF, in a similar fashion to containing concerns over sub-panel representativeness. In the same way that releasing the names of sub-panellists was intended as a limited form of transparency designed to assure an academic community that their work had been subject to assessment by experts, here limiting the transparency of the scoring system was designed with the same intent. The academic community might be satisfied that their work was scored fairly through this antagonistic situation (rather than, for example, a purely metric system[8]), even if they would not be informed of the details of individual scores and scoring practices. Inequitable outcomes were an assured feature of the competitive allocation of research funding. But concerns regarding inequity and the absence of transparency for the most part might be assuaged by these limited releases of information (the names of sub-panellists, the existence of expert judgement) that promoted the fairness of inequitable outcomes.

As we will see in the next section, producing a numeric representative did not rely on peer review alone. The very means of internal accountability was always and already shaped by the practices of consensus and the need to settle scores.

Practices of Consensus

As we have noted, interviewees participated in scoring academic outputs through peer review, then agreed those scores

---

[8] Drawing on, say, journal rankings, impact factors or citations.

with other assessors and reconciled any differences between scores, generating an internally oriented form of accountability. Giving a score and making that score locally accountable was essential for the maintenance of the research assessment system in the UK, producing numeric representatives that would stand in for qualities (scoring academic work) and quantities (eventually an amount of funding). The antagonistic situations that accountability composed were noted as important for preventing the further questioning of scores – the numeric representatives had already been subject to interrogation – and the inequitable outcomes of the REF competition – that one university would get more than another. Yet building up a consensus on the most appropriate method for producing numeric representatives was not anticipated by the Funding Councils as a straightforward matter.

The Funding Councils insisted on a variety of calibration exercises in order to ensure consensus in scoring practices. First, sub-panel chairs were gathered together on the Main Panels to agree on criteria that would be used in their sub-panels. Sub-panel chairs were also given a small selection of outputs (journal articles and books) to score and results were compared across the members of each Main Panel (who were each chairs of a sub-panel) to establish an appropriate, calibrated average of what kinds of scores ought to be given in line with the criteria. Interviewees talked about the initial, wide scattering of marks that were produced by sub-panel chairs and the need for more direction to be provided in assessments. Much emphasis was placed by interviewees on the initial calibration exercise providing evidence of the need for more calibration. Despite these difficulties, many of the Main Panel and sub-panel chairs found calibration to be a useful exercise, "establishing appropriate community interaction" as one interviewee put it, around how work should be read and scores given. Calibration thus provided a basis for establishing an emerging normative consensus not on scores as such, but on the practices of how assessors could work together to accomplish their scoring activity. In this way, calibration among chairs aimed to create a pacified environment in which disagreements and divergences did not disappear, but instead distributions of scores were produced that could accommodate a degree of difference among scorers.

Second, each sub-panel chair then had to run a calibration exercise with their sub-panel assessors, building on the calibration they had just practiced in the four Main Panels. Assessors were given a shared, limited, range of outputs to assess and scores were compared. Again, this was designed to calibrate an appropriate average for the type of score that ought to be given to outputs and what ought to count as an appropriate scoring practice. This also provided sub-panel chairs with an initial indication of generous and less generous assessors that they could check on throughout the period of assessment – marking out what one interviewee called the "tough guys and the softies" who would be further scrutinised and calibrated, as deemed necessary by sub-panel chairs. Calibration also provided sub-panellists with some steer on how to score work with which they were unfamiliar. They would turn to the guidance offered on what ought to count as appropriate scoring practice to try and ensure that the method of scoring, even if not the score, was correct. Calibration became a means for assessors to draw closer their distributions of scores, their scoring practices and tolerance for work with which they were unfamiliar.

Third, assessors got on with the task of scoring their huge allocation of outputs. Assessors entered their scores on the Funding Councils' computer system, and could start to see their distribution curve of scores emerging (how many outputs they allocated to each scoring category from 0 to 4). As a result, the collective tuning of the scoring process could continue.

[Scoring] kept having to be re-explored. We were each sent our own individual distribution of scores regularly, as we uploaded our rankings. Then I could see where I was relative to other people, for example. I think calibration is something that was ongoing. There was a calibration exercise early on. [...] But there was [also] constant calibration. (Interviewee 10)

In this way, calibration involved not referencing an external standard or a historically established basis for correct scoring,[9] but instead relied on an internally oriented averaging process from which further decisions could be made. As sub-panel chairs had overviews of the distribution of these score curves among sub-panel members, and then Main Panel chairs had overviews of the distribution of scoring curves across whole sub-panels, they could carry out further interventions. They could choose to warn generous or less generous scorers of the relative position of their curves:

There was an individual in our panel who scored very low, right the way across the board. The other panel members were uncomfortable because they were consistently getting different marks to him. I had to deal with that. I had to say to him, "You don't appear to be in line, why is that? Is it that everybody else is wrong?" (Interviewee 20)

As this excerpt suggests, consensus could be accomplished along majoritarian lines: if most sub panellists were deemed to be scoring one way, then any other way could be marked out as discrepant and the discrepancy addressed. This means of accomplishing the outcomes of competition was also prevalent in other activities. For example, on some sub-panels

---

[9] See Mallard (1998) on external and historical bases for calibration.

as deadlines neared and scores needed to be agreed, chairs would settle differences between assessors in scores for the same output by averaging out the score, rather than discussing at length the subtle or nuanced differences between scores, scoring or the work being scored. On other occasions, first assessors' scores would be given more weight. If necessary, chairs could carry out an automated normalisation of the distribution curves of scores in order that discrepant curves were pushed closer to average curves as the following interviewee makes clear:

> [I]t turned out that our panel was marking everything lower than any other panel [...] Then at a certain point they just applied an algorithm and pulled up the entire middle of the field, which I gather is completely legal and acceptable. (Interviewee 4)

The competition required that scores were settled. A consensus of sorts was reached on the settlement of what scores ought to be and what scoring practices ought to be and what form reconciliation ought to take. But unlike a traditional democratic process of lengthy discussion and compromise, REF consensus comprised a human and non-human assemblage, an agreement settled between assessors, software and numeric representatives. In the same way that calibration was achieved through an internal orientation to an emerging average, so was normalisation.[10] As the following interviewee makes clear, it is not the scores that assessors attach to outputs that matter, but

------

[10] This is what Foucault (2004) suggested was the normalisation characteristic of moments of security (whereby the norm for normalisation emerges from within a set of observations) in place of a disciplinary normalisation (that requires the pre-existence of an external norm).

the distribution of scores in relation to the emerging norm that are important:

My individual ratings for papers, or whatever outputs, doesn't matter. It's irrelevant. What is relevant is, how accurate my overall assessment of the set of papers was. [...] I mean, how well it represents the quality of the outputs against the criteria identified. [...] The point is that individual rankings for papers does not matter. It's not what the methodology is about, it serves no purpose whatsoever. (Interviewee 7)

As a result of these processes of calibration and normalisation, the scores for outputs reached a kind of assembled consensus and assessments from 0 to 4 got to stand as numeric representatives of quality and quantity. The competition had settled scores. As Callon (1986: 211) argues in his study of scallops, the ability of a consensus to hold together depends on "the solidity of the equivalencies that have been put into place". In the REF, these equivalences (that a 4 is a 4 and not a 3, and that this 4 is a meaningful representative of quality and quantity) are dependent on a form of relativism. In contrast, many scoring systems rely on notions of objectivity developed on a referential basis. An item is given a score, not because of a localised, personal preference, but because of some matter it references in the world outside the scoring system (see, for example, global MBA rankings; Espeland and Sauder, 2007). To return to Callon (1986), we could say that in these scoring systems a referential consensus would depend on the alliances that have been built between a score and the world outside the scoring system. Achieving consensus in such a way would mean "the margins of manoeuvre of each entity will then be tightly delimited" (1986: 211). A referential REF might involve reviewing a journal article, giving it a score, then defending that score through reference to the article's number of citations or the impact factor of the journal within which it was published. The external existence of the reference beyond the scoring system could then be used to attest the strength, reliability, objectivity and so on of the score and the scoring system – building allies and limiting manoeuvrability through referential consensus. Aside from some limited experiments with citations, the REF eschews these referential forms of evidence. Instead, it depends for consensus on a type of relativism: each Main Panel and sub-panel produces a criteria to guide scoring; initial calibration on the Main Panels and sub-panels is oriented toward establishing a calibrated average scoring system in relation to the scores of the members of the Main Panels and sub-panels; generous and less generous assessors are marked out through their position in relation to other REF assessors; automated normalisation, where it is required, is accomplished in relation to the emerging distribution curves of scores of other sub-panellists.

What we can note here, then, is that peer review in the REF is not about objectivity in the sense of composing an object successively cut free from human hands. Peer review here is about expert judgement and is celebrated and defended by participants on that basis. REF scores are deliberately relativistic and such matters as calibration anticipates this relativism. Furthermore, the REF's modes of normalisation depend on relativism, as normalisation cannot work without shifting the distribution of scores relative to each other. A referential consensus would make this kind of manoeuvre difficult. What got to count as a score for an output in REF 2014 was thus settled through a relativist scoring system such that assessors did not know if a score they gave would be a score that an output received. A score was only a score relative to the other scores that assessors themselves provided, relative to the distribution curve of each other member of their sub-panel, relative to the cumulative curve of their sub-panel as a whole, relative to other sub-panels drawn together in each Main Panel.

Although we can say, then, that the form given to the market sensibility of competition depended on practices oriented towards settling scores that could only be achieved through a form of consensus, this was only part of the story. By getting close to the action we can also see that scores given by peer reviewers were only ever a putative pre-truth of the numeric representative that each score might become as a result of the consensus achieved between human reviewers, distribution curves, non-human algorithms and software systems. Furthermore, the final league table for each sub-panel – the final settling of scores – was only revealed at the end of the assessment process and without much time for comment from sub-panellists. The formula through which the Funding Councils would translate scores and league table positions into funding was also only revealed after the scoring process was complete. What got to count as an adequate assessment practice and form of consensus were only ever partially known to human participants. The stark certainty of the competitive outcome in the final league tables and their distribution of funds stands in contrast to practices of representation, accountability and consensus that seem to emerge through various decisions by sub-panel and Main Panel chairs, ever-changing distribution curves and software for normalisation.

From Competition to Competitiveness

In the preceding sections we have noted a variety of ways in which a specific form is given to the market sensibility of competition through practices of representation, accountability and consensus. This does not tell the whole story of the REF. The form given to competition is oriented toward a future that anticipates a contribution by universities to the UK's global competitiveness. Whereas the REF scoring system produces a rank order of competition among universities, competitiveness is more outwardly directed toward an understanding of the UK's position in relation to the rest of the world. However, the move from competition to competitiveness takes places among many of the same practices that we have already witnessed. In particular, competitiveness is anticipated through assessments of research impact.[11]

Impact case studies articulate a university department's role in shaping life beyond academia. They must be submitted to the REF along with academic outputs and an environment statement. The impact cases then travel through many of the same practices of assessment as journal articles and books. The case studies are scored on the same 0 to 4 scale, by academic members of sub-panels along with specially appointed industry assessors. The same questions arose for many of our interviewees with regards to who would be an appropriate (industry) *representative* for a discipline, how initial scores could result from local forms of *accountability* and through what means *consensus* around appropriate scoring practices could be accomplished.

The REF system for assessing impact case studies – much like the scoring system for academic outputs – has not been without its controversy. Among our research participants, views ranged from impact being "one of the most wonderful" aspects of the REF through to "it stinks". Alongside the practices of representation, accountability and consensus, assessing impact case studies seemed to promote a new set of concerns.

---

[11] For more on the specificities of impact in the social sciences, arts and humanities, see Watermeyer and Chubb (2018).

For some interviewees, impact had provided yet another way of distorting academic life, for example, with recruitment strategies now oriented toward finding candidates with potential future impact. Alternatively, impact had not been supported through adequate guidance to departments on what should constitute impact. Or cases were largely un-evidenced, as the following interviewee made clear:

[T]he emphasis put on impact is largely unevidenced and is simply a case document [...] It's completely unevidenced and highly problematic. (Interviewee 13)

In a similar manner to the scoring of academic outputs, these concerns regarding impact remained carefully restrained within the REF. Regardless of these concerns or perhaps as a direct result of their silent containment, the move from competition to competitiveness continued. Here individual academics and departments submitting to the REF in 2014 became aware of the need to fulfil new requirements to write and submit impact cases that portrayed their contribution to national competitiveness, as the following interviewee explains:

If the purpose of the REF is just to distribute QR, that's one thing. But it's not just to distribute QR. Actually, it's about other mechanisms, other policy-related goals. [...] It is about drawing attention of researchers to the primacy which policy attaches to certain classes of impact. It is about driving up the global position of the UK, with respect to its competitors, against certain key measures. (Interviewee 7)

As the interviewee suggests, the anticipatory move from competition to competitiveness was about "drawing attention" to the new impact requirements. It might be tempting to describe this as a form of incentive (see Chapter 6), but for the 2014 REF, writing most impact case studies involved reworking already complete research.[12] Producing cases involved a post-hoc rationalisation of research that had already been carried out that now required conscription to the cause of impact and had to be re-narrated to fit the confines of the impact template provided by the funding councils. It was not, at least in 2014, mostly about incentivising new work.

Two aspects of this move from competition to competitiveness stand out. First, despite letters being written to newspapers about the distorting effects of impact case studies by academics and despite concerns being raised by research participants, those involved in impact assessment often held back from public critique of impact. Second, instead of being noted as an incentive for changing research activity, for many of our research participants the move from competition to competitiveness offered a means to archive a specific set of academic cases. That is, impact case studies had the effect of establishing what one interviewee referred to as an "evidence base" of UK academia's impact beyond the academy. The critical silence and accumulation of evidence were connected by participants in our research as part of the same cause: that what was at stake in demonstrating impact was a need to defend already scarce government resources for research funding against possible budget cuts and the continued existence of the Funding

---

[12] This is likely to change in subsequent REFs as academics will have a greater lead time in producing impact cases, there is more time for department and university managers to build up expectations that current and future research work should have impact and research funders have placed a greater emphasis on the importance of impact as a feature of assessing funding bids.

Councils. To be able to produce an evidence base that could be used to talk up the (newly emergent or recently reworked) ability of academia to contribute to the UK's international competitiveness was crucial to safeguarding future funding. For some interviewees this even led to a downscaling of competition. In place of a ruthless competition against each other, UK universities understood the new emphasis on competitiveness as evidence of forthcoming change:

I think that we, certainly on the subpanels and probably academics generally, up to a point at least, suddenly twigged [...] that we, as subpanels, needed to help [the funding councils], but, of course, already by that stage there [...] were threats in the air and somehow that they had to sort of pull the rabbit out of the hat with the impact stuff. [...] Whereas in previous exercises it was all competitive between the institutions all the time, the bigger show here was to show that these subject areas matter, and that we have an international and disproportionate reputation for the work that we do, and that we push the boundaries in practice research and all those kinds of things. [...] almost became a kind of, "Let's see if we can save [the Funding Councils], or at least save QR and any future REFs, for fear of what worse may follow." (Interviewee 27)

Anticipating the movement from competition to competitiveness offered the prospect of changes in the practices that formed competition. UK academics took note of these changes as the harbinger of new and more direct concerns regarding the importance of contributing to competitiveness. Scholarly excellence would no longer retain its privileged position as the mainstay of the UK's research assessment competition: the new practice to develop was impact because it also helped the academic community as a whole to justify its need for public resources in times of cuts within the UK's public budget (see also Chapter 5).

Conclusion

We have noted in this chapter that the market sensibility of competition is given shape by a changing array of practices, involving representation, a locally oriented accountability, consensus and a move toward competitiveness. Unlike the literature on neoliberalism that situates competition within a general programme of political action, we have focused in on the particular practices demanded by, and required for, competition to take shape. Here antagonistic situations are generated, expertise and "human qualities" drawn together, scores and scorers calibrated and normalised, numeric representatives produced and competitiveness anticipated. The settled scores act as representatives that say something of quality (the scores denoting the varied worth of academic outputs), quantity (with formulas translating scores into amounts of money) and contributory competitiveness (that UK academia can and does feed into the nation's wealth). Efforts to demonstrate representativeness, meagre amounts of transparency and accountability, and the silent containment of critique each seem to be a requirement for maintaining the idea that the inequitable outcomes of competition are also fair. These practices have also shifted toward a defence by academics of research funding, Funding Councils and the current peculiarities of funding competition as a basis for maintaining the REF's inequitable fairness in the face of what else might come to take its place.

From this chapter we can see that competition does not just happen, it cannot just be effortlessly subsumed within a broader programme of political action from whence we will already know what it is, how it works and what consequences will follow. Instead, competition depends on forms of participation and representation that set demands for a thoroughgoing relativism. The peer review at the centre of this competition, its calibration and normalisation, can only happen when relativism is pursued and referential-ism eschewed. The integrity and dignity of the scoring system, the legitimacy of the competition, depends upon the containment of counter-voices; concerns over representation and questions regarding the adequacy of accuracy that the scoring system seems to inspire cannot be allowed to unsettle the scores. The absence of transparency means that it is only from detailed discussions with participants that this internal ordering can be made apparent. These features of competition can only be ascertained through close scrutiny, by moving from general (in this case the notions of competition and competitiveness, and the broad public goals of the REF) to particular (the practices through which the REF is accomplished).

Looking across Chapters 2 and 3, we have focused on two sets of practices that help describe market-based interventions and their sensibilities: phased political negotiations in the EU ETS and moment-to-moment interactions in the REF. This focus provided an opportunity in the last chapter to explore how a market-based intervention is continually remade through the practices of negotiated technocracy, while here we explored the practices through which the consequences of the REF were composed. But what we can also see in our opening chapters is that something is always at stake – the environmental future, the prospects of UK HE research and European or UK competitiveness. We will need to remain attuned to these stakes in subsequent chapters. What we have seen so far is these stakes expressed among a limited range of actors – mostly regulators and institutional actors. We have not seen much yet of how subjects of market-based interventions are made. In the next chapter, in switching attention to the market sensibility of property and ownership and the problem of privacy, our focus will broaden. We will turn attention to the ways in which the individual is reconceived as both consumer and newly equipped data subject by market-based interventions into the data industry. What will become clear is that acquiring the necessary competences required to be a market participant is central to ensuring that market-based interventions achieve their effects.

References

Brown, R. (2014) *The Marketisation of Higher Education.* Available at: www.uwl.ac.uk/sites/default/files/Departments/Research/new_vistas/vol1_iss1/vol1_iss1_art1_23April2015.pdf (last accessed 3 April 2019).

Brown, W. (2015) *Undoing the Demos: Neoliberalism's Stealth Revolution.* Brooklyn, NY: Zone Books.

Callon, M. (1986) Some elements of a sociology of translation: Domestication of the scallops and the fishermen of St Brieuc Bay. In J. Law (ed.), *Power, Action and Belief: A New Sociology of Knowledge?* London: Routledge, pp. 196–223.

Chubb, J. and Watermeyer, R. (2017) Artifice or integrity in the marketization of research impact? *Studies in Higher Education* 42(12): 2360–72.

Davies, W. (2017) *The Limits of Neoliberalism.* London: Sage.

de Rijcke, S., Wouters, P., Rushforth, A.D., Franssen, T.P. and Hammarfelt, B.M.S. (2016) Evaluation practices and effects of indicator use: A literature review. *Research Evaluation* 25(2): 161–9.

Espeland, W. and Sauder, M. (2007) Rankings and reactivity: How public measures recreate social worlds. *American Journal of Sociology* 113(1): 1–40.

Foucault, M. (2004) *Security, Territory, Population.* London: Palgrave.

Garfinkel, H. (1967) *Studies in Ethnomethodology.* Englewood Cliffs, NJ: Prentice-Hall.

Gray, R. (1992) Accounting and environmentalism: An exploration of the challenge of gently accounting for accountability, transparency and sustainability. *Accounting, Organizations and Society* 17(5): 399–425.

Latour, B. (2004) Why has critique run out of steam? From matters of fact to matters of concern. *Critical Inquiry* 30: 225–48.

Mallard, A. (1998) Compare, standardise and settle agreement: On some usual metrological problems. *Social Studies of Science* 28(4): 571–601.

Neyland, D. (2007) Achieving transparency: The visible, invisible and divisible in academic accountability networks. *Organization* 14(4): 499–516.

Peck, J. (2010) *Constructions of Neoliberal Reason*. Oxford: Oxford University Press.

Power, M. (1999) Research assessment exercise: A fatal remedy? Knowledge for what? The intellectual consequences of the research assessment exercise. *History of the Human Sciences* 12(4): 135–7.

Sacks, H. (1972) Notes on police assessment of moral character. In D. Sudnow (ed.), *Studies in Social Interaction*. New York: Free Press, pp. 280–93.

Sayer, D. (2014) *Rank Hypocrisies: The Insult of the REF*. London: Sage.

Schatzki, T. (2001) Introduction: Practice theory. In T. Schatzki, K. Knorr Cetina and E. von Savigny (eds.), *The Practice Turn in Contemporary Theory*. London: Routledge.

Stern, N. (2016) *Building on Success and Learning from Experience: An Independent Review of the Research Excellence Framework*. Available at: https://assets.publishing.service.gov.uk/government/uploads/system/uploads/attachment_data/file/541338/ind-16-9-ref-stern-review.pdf (last accessed 3 April 2019).

Strathern, M. (2002) Abstraction and decontextualisation: An anthropological comment. In S. Woolgar (ed.), *Virtual Society? Technology, Cyberbole, Reality*. Oxford: Oxford University Press, pp. 302–13.

Suchman, L. (1993) Technologies of accountability: Of lizards and aeroplanes. In G. Button (ed.), *Technology in Working Order: Studies of Work, Interaction, and Technology.* London: Routledge, pp. 113–26.

Wall, S. (1996) Public justification and the transparency argument. *The Philosophical Quarterly* 46(184): 501–7.

Watermeyer, R. (2012) From engagement to impact? Articulating the public value of academic research. *Tertiary Education and Management* 18(2): 115–30.

Watermeyer, R. and Chubb, J. (2018) Evaluating "impact" in the UK's Research Excellence Framework (REF): Liminality, looseness and new modalities of scholarly distinction. *Studies in Higher Education.* Available at: https://doi.org/10.1080/03075079.2018.1455082 (last accessed 3 April 2019).

Watermeyer, R. and Hedgecoe, A. (2016) Selling impact: How is impact peer reviewed and what does this mean for the future of impact in universities? Available at: http://blogs.lse.ac.uk/impactofsocialsciences/2016/05/05/selling-impact-peer-reviewer-estimations-of-what-counts-and-what-is-needed-in-ref-impact-submissions/ (last accessed 3 April 2019).

Wilsdon, J., Allen, L., Belfiore, E., Campbell, P., Curry, S., Hill, S., Jones, R., Kain, R., Kerridge, S.R., Thelwell, M., Tinkler, J., Viney, I., Wouters, P., Hill, J. and Johnson, B. (2015) *The Metric Tide: Report of the Independent Review of the Role of Metrics in Research Assessment and Management.* Available at: www.researchgate.net/publication/279402178_The_Metric_Tide_Report_of_the_Independent_Review_of_the_Role_of_Metrics_in_Research_Assessment_and_Management (last accessed 3 April 2019).

Woolgar, S. and Neyland, D. (2013) *Mundane Governance.* Oxford: Oxford University Press.

4

Property and Ownership

Opening

In both Chapters 2 and 3 we noted the significant regulatory framework required to introduce and hold in place market-based interventions into fields where a significant public matter was at stake: the environment (through the EU ETS) and UK higher education (through the REF). In both cases we had to carefully scrutinise the market sensibility at work: trade and exchange only accomplished its effects in Chapter 2 through a convoluted negotiated technocracy and the REF navigated complex practices of representation, accountability and consensus in introducing a specific form of competition. This chapter will be no different to the extent that, in studying *property and ownership* as the market sensibility in focus, we will encounter a significant bureaucratic infrastructure and will need to pay close attention to the form this gives to the matters at stake. But through looking at property and ownership as a means to regulate the problem of privacy – in particular, privacy as a means to resolve concerns with ever-changing forms of digital data and its use – we will also encounter some very different kinds of intervention and market participants.

Alongside the significant regulatory infrastructure of the EU General Data Protection Regulation (GDPR) we will also find a non-regulatory form of intervention that is nonetheless market-oriented. This derives from oversight by the Federal Trade Commission in the US of an emerging market for privacy products as a consumer-oriented solution to digital privacy. Along with regulators, then, we will also find a distinct market participant: the individual consumer or data subject. The comparison we offer between the regulatory and non-regulatory intervention will enable us to shed light on distinct attributions that each intervention depends upon in characterising the individual data subject, the role of regulation and industry. For example, attributing responsibility for problem-solving, on whose behalf the problem is solved and the extent, interest in, and feasibility of oversight are each different. Despite these differences, both interventions seek to solve a problem with privacy and define the problem in specific ways. They each depend on data having a market orientation in order to enable intervention. In order to achieve this orientation, both interventions look to property and ownership as a market sensibility through which data can take on specific economic characteristics and around which a solution can then be organised.

But what is property and ownership as a market sensibility and why is it drawn in to regulating privacy? Here we are faced with 2,000 years of thinking and rethinking around privacy, what this could and should mean, and what ought to provide a regulatory impetus. Property and ownership has been fundamental to this history. In ancient Greece, privacy was understood in relation to property rights, with the private realm indistinguishable from that which was owned, controlled and secreted from view (although Plato was seemingly against such privacy, noting a connection between concealment and society's ills). In the eighteenth and nineteenth centuries, privacy was still understood in terms of property rights, with English courts deciding on infringements of privacy through the attribution of ownership rights in the entity infringed (Chlopecki, 1992). In the US, court decisions regarding privacy tended to draw on the 3rd, 4th, 5th and 14th amendments to the Constitution as a basis for safeguarding property against invasions of privacy.

It was only with Warren and Brandeis' influential *Harvard Law Review* article of 1890 that a loosening of property rights and privacy was initially proposed (they considered privacy more broadly in relation to, for example, newspaper gossip). Nonetheless, property rights and privacy continued their close connection throughout the twentieth century. Notable interventions, for example by the economist Posner (1977–78: 393), although seen by many as against privacy at least in an individualistic sense, still noted the importance of "organisational privacy" and the rights that follow from owning such matters as a trade secret. The development of the Data Protection Directive in Europe in the 1990s established a set of principles around the proportionality and necessity of data collection and use that went beyond property and ownership. But the central problem was still conceived in terms of an invasion of privacy. This metaphor was itself a little misleading as privacy problems were generally regarded in terms of an invasion across a recognisable boundary from which data is extracted and then used to reconnect to the original source of data. Invasion, extraction and reconnection might capture the concern for privacy more accurately. Despite these metaphorical issues, what we can note is that these concerns had a proprietary orientation: the home as a proprietary space should not be invaded, rights to access the body were owned and controlled by the individual, and broad disclosures of sensitive data could only be made with the consent of the data subject as owner of that data.

Property, ownership and privacy, then, have a long history of entanglement. To make sense of these, we need to know something more of property. As the most basic introduction will suggest, property is not solely focused on a specific entity (such as a house or a car that one might own).[1] Instead, property relates to an entity (such as a house) combined with a set of relations, such as property rights, through which ownership designates some specific matters (use, profit, rent) that can be made from the entity. Digital data as we will see in this chapter, depends on some very specific relations of property that enable what is said to be a free flow of data, to then be owned, monetised and used. Attempts to renew the regulation of data also pose new concerns around privacy and how privacy ought to be understood and regulated.

Digital data we will suggest is conceived in terms of property and ownership by regulators in order to render it amenable to legislation. Without this move, data might appear beyond the grasp of regulators. But, as we will see, the basis for regulating data and attendant privacy concerns can no longer be organised around the traditional invasion metaphor. This is because data is now said to operate on an unprecedented scale, moving at a speed and across distances not previously possible, mined, scraped and utilised in ways previously unimaginable (Kitchin, 2014). Monetising data now takes place in myriad ways, with behavioural advertising, data brokers, social media giants, conventional firms and consumers engaged in ever-changing data relationships (Milyaeva and Neyland, 2016). Figuring out who owns data, who controls it, how it ought to be regulated has become, by the second decade of the twenty-first century, a challenging task. The proprietary-based invasion of privacy

---

[1] See, for example, Suvorova and Romanov's (1986) *ABC of Social and Political Knowledge: What is Property?* For more on property and markets, see Swedberg (2005); Davies (2012).

metaphor no longer seems relevant, as most data seems more or less public (although even the meaning of that term is now complex; Neyland, 2006), data flows more or less freely (at least up to a point) and data is reconnected to its source frequently (sometimes this is welcomed, sometimes not so much). And the relevance of notions such as proportionality and necessity in data collection and use seems to have been swept away. What we will see in this chapter is that two different responses to these contemporary challenges of data and privacy look to reimpose property rights on data in different ways. Through the GDPR we will see property rights and privacy re-engaged through a new regulatory framework. Through the Federal Trade Commission and the nascent US market for privacy products, we will see data ownership – and in the process, privacy – reconceived. And in both cases, the expected role of the individual market participant as consumer or data subject differs. We will begin with an introduction to the data market.

Digital Privacy: The Visible Hand of Markets

The rapid increase in quantities of data, their means of movement, interconnection, mining, scraping and monetising has been termed a "data revolution" (Kitchin, 2014). This apparent revolution has depended on a surge in "datafication" wherein everything has become data – words, locations, interactions and more (Mayer-Schonberger and Cukier, 2013). One means to grasp this ever-changing data landscape is to treat data as a footprint of human and non-human digital interaction. This has the advantage of moving away from data as a neatly bounded entity, owned or used by a single source, under the aegis of a single person, organisation or technological system. It also usefully moves away from the notion of data as deliberatively or knowingly created, as much data emerges through traces left behind by digital encounters. Search engine enquiries and shopping histories become part of a user's digital footprint, their devices made identifiable through, for example, cookies[2] stored on users' devices by a web browser.

These developments have been noted as economically important by a wide range of actors, particularly at a time of little economic growth elsewhere. Data footprints and devices are said to have enabled a "data-driven economy" (EC, 2014) to emerge with its global flows of personal data now proclaimed "the new oil of the Internet and the currency of the digital world" (EC, 2009). This reference to personal data as "oil" captures something significant in the way these arguments are made about data monetisation and its importance. The argument suggests that if the nineteenth and twentieth centuries can be characterised by their fossil economy (Malm, 2016), perhaps the twenty-first century will be characterised by the economic centrality of data.[3] By using oil as a metaphor, personal data is positioned as a natural resource that could be mined to extract economic value. This metaphor is not entirely without merit, as data mining is a technique that involves the algorithmic composition of patterns in data, and once patterns have been composed they are monetised through, for example, behavioural advertising, which targets individual online users with a product offer based on digitally generated assumptions of their value, identity and online activity.[4] At the same time,

---

[2] A cookie is a small piece of data that is sent from a website and enables a device to be recognised.

[3] Although, as Chapter 2 shows, reducing dependency on carbon/fossil fuels is not straightforward.

[4] For a more detailed account of data mining see Milyaeva and Neyland (2016), but also Andrejevic and Gates (2014) and Cohen (2017). The same process of data mining

oil as a metaphor risks oversimplifying the nature of data. Most critics of the data industry suggest data flows more freely than oil,[5] is open to capture and simultaneous use by multiple parties, one use does not necessarily inhibit or damage another and multiple different outcomes can be composed from the same source depending on what data is combined with what, using what algorithm, with what reconnection to the original source and for what purpose.

Although the oil metaphor may be imperfect, we cannot dismiss the scale of data use and its economic worth. And as we shall see, this kind of activity is at the heart of the problem around which concerns of privacy are expressed. Personal data and its use is noted as the "foundation of the data economy" (Schweidel, 2015), and data-driven innovation is presented as "a key pillar in 21st century sources for growth" (OECD, 2015). The European Commission estimates the value of the European data economy will be over €700 billion in 2020 and worth 4% of EU GDP (EC, 2017). In May 2017, the US Chamber of Commerce issued a statement arguing that the data economy is "increasingly indistinguishable from the worldwide 'brick and mortar' economy", and unfettered flows of data

---

provides a means to create not only economic but political value; although less researched, the techniques of creating political value recently appeared in the media with regard to the US presidential elections and the UK EU referendum of 2016 (Booth, 2017; Hern, 2017; Cadwalladr and Graham-Harrison, 2018).

[5] Critics recognise that data does not flow freely without the vast data infrastructures of the Internet but these do not need to be invented anew by each data firm. Firms can straightforwardly capture the data that the Internet makes available.

are "essential for companies of all sizes and sectors" (US CC, 2017). In subtle ways, this statement plays a part in the back-and-forth discussion of the data economy. The US Chamber of Commerce statement is a response to the new data legislation developed in Europe – the GDPR that we will meet below – and to the ever-growing criticism of the data economy in its current configuration. Hence for some, the data economy is vital to economic growth while for others the process of generating economic value from personal data is increasingly viewed as the basis for "surveillance capitalism" (Zuboff, 2015) or "platform capitalism" (Srnicek, 2017).

In these critiques, value generation and capital accumulation depend upon inequitable relations between the data industry who monetise data at the expense of individuals who only supply (or produce) digital data (Fuchs, 2014; Dwoskin, 2014; Andrejevic, 2014). Here the value of personal data and its inequitable distribution is discussed in the context of the political economy of privacy (Campbell and Carson, 2002; Gandy, 2011; Aquisti, John and Loewenstein, 2013; Sevignani, 2013; Crain, 2016) and the "surveillance economy". Such an economy is said to depend on a form of "informational capitalism [that] produces wealth" (Cohen, 2017) based on the alienation and exploitation of personal data (Andrejevic, 2011). It is this inequitability and associated forms of exploitation that are said to urgently require a legal solution to address the question of "who *owns* our data" (Rees, 2014, emphasis added).

In this way, despite huge changes in technology, data, its use and relations of data production, concerns are still couched in terms of ownership: proprietary concerns and privacy are as entangled now as they were for Plato. However, whereas for Plato the private realm was a cause for concern, contemporary critiques of the data economy seem to suggest that the problem now lies with the very possibility of privacy, who owns and controls data. In the following sections we will explore how digital data is being used to rethink the notion of privacy through new kinds of property rights and forms of control. We will suggest these ways of (re)thinking underpin the development of the two distinct market-based interventions we will consider in this chapter: the GDPR as a regulatory framework and attempts to develop a market for privacy products. The two interventions we will discuss seek to embed the notion of ownership through control in digital personal data in very different ways.

Facilitating a Market for Privacy Products: Shifting from Value Capture to Data Service through a Data Vault

Discussions regarding markets and privacy have been ongoing for several decades (Laudon, 1996; Hagel and Rayport, 1997; Hagel and Singer, 1999). Within these discussions, traditional regulatory approaches have been critiqued and a more market-oriented intervention envisaged. For example, Laudon (1996: 93) put forward the idea of "a regulated national information market" that would facilitate the sharing of personal information.

When individuals claim that information about them is private, they generally mean they do not want the information shared with others or they personally would like to control the dissemination of this information, sharing it with some but not with others. (Laudon, 1996: 93)

Within these discussions and the development of early data protection legislation, Davis (1997: 143) further observed that privacy had been turned into a "consumer issue". In these contributions to the privacy debate, the market is noted as playing a part in solving the problem of privacy – at least in the sense of designating where responsibility for data lies and how problems might be rectified (as a consumer matter).

This stands in contrast to other contributions to the privacy debate, mainly from economists who point to the role of privacy in constraining economic growth. For Posner (1977–78, 1979, 1981, 2008) the free flow of data is what renders markets efficient, whereas "concealment of information" in the form of individual (but not organisational) privacy is an impediment to economic growth. In interviews we conducted with US data firms, these economic views were further emphasised. The sharing of personal data is at the forefront of these firms' views on what will stimulate economic growth:

If you think you can stop somebody from tracking you, you're crazy; instead of saying, "You can't track me", it's "I must see whatever you track." (Interview with a data start-up founder, New York, 4 November 2013)

We recognised early on that if we [...] block everything by default, it would keep things from working on the web like people expect them to work. [...] Blocking is not meaning more private. (Interview with a senior product manager, New York, 5 November 2013)

We can see these debates echoed in discussions from 2010 onwards in the US around the potential for privacy legislation. The data industry utilised the work of economists like Posner to align with the view of the US President's Council of Advisors on Science and Technology report (PCAST, 2014). Here data regulations of any form were understood as "inhibiting economic growth" (PCAST, 2014: xi). Indeed, data brokers insisted that data sharing was a prerequisite for economic growth, with "third-party data use and sharing ... essential for business success in today's information economy" (Wooley, 2013: n.p.). The apparent need for data regulation was said by the data industry to be "unfounded". Within this atmosphere that seems to support the data industry and insulate that industry against all costs, regulators interested in privacy protection have had to seek a different path forward (at least in comparison to European data protection that we will encounter below). In the US, digital privacy has been taken up as a public problem by the Federal Trade Commission. This positioning is important: the Federal Trade Commission has a responsibility for consumer rights and, hence, privacy and any form of data protection must be couched in these terms. But managing privacy through consumption is not straightforward. Consumption practices are at least part of the problem here, with online consumer activity being used to create vast data footprints for the data industry. And given the protection of the data industry in the US, any approach to privacy regulation that appeared to limit consumption, and as a result limit economic growth, would be likely to fail. Instead, the Federal Trade Commission has sought to use consumption as a means to redress the kinds of imbalances and asymmetries that were previously critiqued in the distribution of control over data, between user-producers and the data industry (Brill, 2013).

One upshot of this regulatory position in the US has been that the Federal Trade Commission (FTC) has sought to emphasise the role of consumers in privacy protection. This has emerged in conjunction with the FTC's oversight of a potentially emerging market for privacy products. If privacy is going to be a consumer issue, then "regulation" will have to come from consumers either purchasing apps and devices or using services that enable privacy on their behalf. But this is far from straightforward.

When we began our research in 2013, the idea that aggregated personal data was a new and highly profitable economic or political resource was not in the news as it is now.[6] But what had begun to attract public attention was a concern with ubiquitous and intrusive online commercial tracking (Angwin, 2010; Constine, 2013; Bachman, 2014; Chon, 2014; Goel, 2014). The notion of "privacy" was now visibly and publically linked to commercial as well as state surveillance; what's more, privacy was at least becoming discussed as "web's hot new commodity" (Angwin and Steel, 2011). The Federal Trade Commission's approach to regulating privacy as a consumer matter might come to something. Media excitement about the nascent "privacy market" was growing, including coverage of emerging start-ups and interviews with the start-ups' founders (Brustein, 2012; Sullivan, 2012; Brewster, 2014). Online calculators for personal data worth (Steel, Locke, Cadman and Freese, 2013) had started to appear, alerting consumers to the possibility that their data had value. And start-up firms had started to produce privacy products.[7] Could consumerism create a market for privacy?

This perhaps oversimplifies the scene. As a New York-based data entrepreneur explained to us, creating a market for "privacy" involved the development of a very specific composition

---

[6] Although academic awareness and analysis of commercial surveillance had been present for some time: see, for example, Lyon and Zureik (1996), Staples (2000), Lyon (2001) to name just few. Concerns about government surveillance – the so-called NSA leaks scandal – were, of course, very prominent in the media at the time, with the UK *Guardian* breaking the story (Greenwald, 2013)

[7] Personal data management products cover various technical (including software) solutions to enable consumers and businesses to accumulate and share (or manage) personal data.

of what privacy might entail. This was not the traditional metaphor of the invasion of privacy that we previously encountered, wherein an individual owned and hence controlled access to a space or body from within which data ought not to be collected. However, this was a form of privacy that did involve at least a sense of ownership – in this case data ownership:

> The way the media presents privacy has nothing to do with how people really think about privacy. [...] And when people talk about the privacy problem, I don't really think there is a problem except for the fact that people are unable to capture the value for themselves. (Interview conducted in New York, 4 November 2013)

These kinds of speculative claims from start-ups seeking a market for a new form of privacy abounded in our interviews at this time. A strong sense of optimism seemed to carry through these discussions that a privacy market might be just around the corner. There seemed genuine expectation (or at least a convincing sales pitch by entrepreneurs) that the value of personal data could be captured by individuals. Personal data could be worth something and the monetary equivalent of this worth could be paid to individuals who produced data. The technical implementation of this redistribution of data control through the sale of one's own data would be achieved via various kinds of data vault.

One version of a data vault would enable the individual to capture their personal data and secure its value by storing data and allowing data sharing, but only for a return.[8] The start-up would derive income from selling, in the words of its founder,

---

[8] At the time of writing this chapter, there are start-ups that are launching the same business idea of monetising personal data for users using Blockchain technology.

"aggregated insights on population and segments of people", combining personal data from social network platforms (such as Twitter, LinkedIn, Google+, Facebook and YouTube) with individual's financial transaction data. The data received and stored in the vault would be anonymised, analysed, repackaged and sold to data purchasers. According to the start-up founder, the only difference with the conventions of the data industry – and the most crucial one – would be that the individual gets to profit from the sale of data, as the start-up provides the individual with a monthly return on her personal data:

Those guys [data brokers] the exact antithesis to what we are. Right? Their livelihood is predicated on mining and harvesting without us [individuals] getting anything for it. Whereas what my livelihood [as a start-up] is predicated on is not mining and harvesting but letting the user dictate everything that happens with their data. (Interview conducted in New York, 5 November 2013)

Six years after this interview took place, the start-up and its business idea have not proved to be commercially successful. Initial optimism dissipated as it turned out that firms did not want to pay the start-up for data, particularly when it flowed so freely elsewhere. These warnings were already apparent in 2013 when a rival New York-based entrepreneur, reasoned that this idea most likely would not work "because businesses won't pay for it":

There are three problems when you try to help somebody sell their data. The first problem is scale. In order for an advertiser to want to buy data from you, you have to have data of millions of people. Right? So any start up that comes out to help people sell data, they won't work because they need two million people that overlap with that advertiser's audience. [...] There are two other problems. The other one is keeping the data up-to-date. It cannot be like, you know, where somebody goes in and types in all of their information about what they want to buy and what they are in a market for. And that is the third problem, which is the accuracy and validity of the data. (Interview conducted in New York, 4 November 2013)

However, data vaults produced by other firms that work in different ways have proved more enduring. In other examples, the data vault would operate more like a data service than a single product. As a service, the way a consumer encounters the vault, the extent to which they even know about the vault, the way in which data is monetised and value accomplished were all distinct from our previous example. Since these are data vaults they keep

the types of data that [the individual] feels safe and comfortable trading, and they also understand what an advertiser wants, and can [trade] it automatically, they can verify the authenticity of the data, [and] once they've reached scale, they can be successful.[9] (Interview with a New York-based entrepreneur, 4 November 2013)

The way this service works in practice is the personal data vault would collect and store data on consumer preferences for different services, for example, a specific type of mortgage. Once the vault had a database of consumers with the same preferences, it would approach mortgage providers to obtain the cheapest cost for such mortgages, but would not give the

---

[9] And indeed, in the UK vaults have achieved this scale through having a data vault as part of price comparison sites such as Moneysupermarket.com with 17 million users. Here the vault can take advantage of a "readymade" market of price comparison site users rather than having to build a market of privacy-concerned consumers.

mortgage provider data on the interested consumers. Instead the data service would take the offers from the mortgage provider and offer these to its customers. As a result: "the consumer should decide who sees their data, and how much of it they see and when they see it, who they trust" (interview conducted 11 October 2013).

The data service also sets up direct relations with suppliers who are keen to move away from broad and untargeted advertising and are willing to pay a small fee to send their products directly to consumers who have expressed a potential interest. Only at the point of sale does a consumer's data move to the firm from which they are buying a product. For consumers, privacy becomes the default option and many may not even be aware of the vault through which their data is managed; in place of a consumer having to continually express preferences, privacy is the assumed consumer preference.

Transforming privacy into a consumer matter, a product or service to be utilised, shifts us away from the straightforward proprietary features of the invasion of privacy metaphor. Instead of the individual directly owning and as a result controlling access to the data contained in a bounded space or owning and controlling access to their body, the data vault acts as a digital intermediary. Some data is shared under the control of the consumer, a product may still be purchased, but only with data shared on the terms of the consumer. In place of a substantial regulatory framework that appears unlikely in the current political climate in the US, this may provide a feasible way forward. Although as we saw with the initial example, building a viable market for privacy is not straightforward. Central to the transformation of privacy into a consumer matter, a product or service to be engaged, is a shift in the dominant metaphor used to describe privacy matters. From invasion we have moved to control. And control is underpinned by new relations of property and ownership. The consumer is now the data producer who also gets to manage the terms of data movement (at least to a degree, in a small way, with those few services that provide a data vault. Having privacy by default is still a long way from being ubiquitous).

This stands in some contrast to our preceding chapters. Whereas Chapters 2 and 3 required extensive engagement with large-scale regulatory frameworks, in the US the data market and consumer choice were assumed to be the appropriate vehicle for intervention. As we will see in the next section, in Europe a significant regulatory infrastructure for privacy (at least in terms of data protection) has been developed. This works on a scale far beyond the small field of privacy-inclined data start-ups. However, this infrastructure does not sit outside the market, seeking to simply impose limits on the data industry. It is a market-enabling piece of legislation. Just like a data vault, it utilises control as the central metaphor for privacy.

Enabling a Privacy Market through Regulation: The GDPR

By contrast with the US focus on privacy as a consumer matter, in Europe over the past 20 years the focus for privacy protection has been on large-scale regulatory intervention. The EU Data Protection Directive of 1995 established a set of principles for the management of data and provision of data protection as a proxy for privacy protection. Data minimisation, only collecting data necessary for a specific task, only stored long enough for the completion of that task, only collecting data proportional to the task and strict management of the transfer of data outside the EU were all basic principles of data protection that continue to exist. However, the legislation developed in 1995 had begun to seem outdated by the second decade of the twenty-first century. A piece of legislation preoccupied with such matters as what happens to VHS tapes stored by CCTV systems was ill-equipped to deal with the data landscape, forms of datafication, data footprints, the growth in digital devices and the data industry that we have witnessed in this chapter. Furthermore, as a Directive, the 1995 legislation provided nothing more than a set of regulatory principles to be implemented and given effect by national authorities. This had led to the development of a patchwork of distinct levels and forms and interpretations of the legislation across European member states. What was required was legislation that could cope with the new data landscape that would be uniformly introduced across Europe. As Viviane Reding (vice-president of the European Commission) suggested: "The current EU Data Protection laws date from 1995, from pre-Internet times [whereas the new Regulation] will make the Digital Single Market more accessible for both businesses and consumers, which will make Europe more competitive" (Reding, 2012).

At the same time, the European Union was not free from the constraints of the debate we saw flourishing over the data industry in the US. The data industry lobby was alive and well in Europe and vociferously critiqued the emerging legislation if it seemed like an imposition on their trade. US legislators, keen to kill off any momentum behind calls for the European legislation to cross the Atlantic, joined in with this critique. The US commerce secretary Wilbur Ross opined in 2018 that the freshly implemented European General Data Protection Regulation (GDPR) is "likely to create barriers to trade". In response, Viviane Reding tweeted that "Data privacy is a fundamental right, not a trade barrier!" After many years of negotiation, discussions, lobbying, critiques and moves to defend the legislation, the GDPR was eventually enacted by the European Parliament on 14 April 2016, and implemented on 25 May 2018.

Unlike in the US where consumers would be left to purchase (or not) privacy protection, European citizens would now have rights to data protection that were the same in every member state. To achieve this regulatory feat, the legislation had to be presented as market-enabling. This is made clear in the full title of the statute: "Regulation (EU) 2016/679 of the European Parliament and of the Council of 27 April 2016 on the Protection of Natural Persons with Regard to the Processing of Personal Data and on the *Free Movement of Such Data*, and Repealing Directive 95/46/EC" (EU GDPR, 2016, emphasis added). As a legal tool, the Regulation would try and protect EU citizens' personal data (Article 1(2)) at the same time as facilitating personal data flows across member states within the EU (Article 1(3)) (EU GDPR, 2016). This move to create a market-enabling piece of legislation was designed to assuage doubts among members of the data industry but was also a legal necessity. European Union rules only allow for Regulations (that impose a single legislative text across all member states) for matters of market-enabling standards. The very existence of the Regulation thus had to combine legal protection against the data industry with market facilitation of the same data industry.

Producing, further developing and agreeing on a single piece of data legislation to be enforced uniformly across the European Union, enabling and regulating the data market, was no easy task. According to the European Commission, the creation of the Digital Single Market could only be achieved by "tearing down regulatory walls and moving from 28 national markets to a single one" (EC, 2018). As a head of one of the European Data Protection Authorities explained:

The European Commission certainly claims one of the big motivations behind their reform of the Directive is to boost cross border trade within the single market. [...] Different member states have transposed the [previous data protection] Directive in different ways. They are very jealous of their own systems. (Interview, 8 April 2014)[10]

Aware of the possible controversies involved in pushing forward a pro-market piece of legislation, continual efforts were made to emphasise the positive benefits a Regulation could bring. Positive statements abounded, such as the GDPR:

provides for a single set of rules, valid across the EU and applicable both to European and non-European companies offering online services in the EU [which] avoids a situation where conflicting national data protection rules might disrupt the cross-border exchange of data. (CEU, 2016)

Yet these kinds of statement did not pave the way for a smooth enactment of the legislation. To impose a single legal form of data protection across Europe, to combine market enabling and data protection principles in the same text, was: "a massive shock to the system, to data controllers":[11]

The [Regulation] proposal tried to re-establish the balance between [...] the protection of the individual on the one hand, and the facilitation of the market on the other. And it did in a way that markets did not like very much [...]. The industry immediately saw its margin of

---

[10] To keep the source anonymous we do not reveal the interviewee's location.

[11] Data controllers are entities collecting personal data, data processors are entities processing personal data (EU GDPR, 2016, Chapter 4).

discretion being taken away. (Interview with a legal scholar focusing on online privacy, 30 April 2015)

Even as an apparently market-enabling piece of legislation, the data industry was strongly critical of the GDPR and lobbied European Parliamentarians on this basis (BBA, 2012; ICDP, 2013). For example, following consultation on early proposals for the legislative text, the Parliamentary Committee on Civil Liberties, Justice and Home Affairs received 3,999 proposed amendments to the GDPR draft:

I think of Jan Philipp Albrecht [the MEP and rapporteur of the European Parliament for the GDPR] ... 4,000 amendments from his colleagues in the Parliament alone. I am following EU law for a long, long time – I don't think I've ever seen anything like it. (Interview with a legal scholar focusing on online privacy, 30 April 2015)

Once the draft passed the Parliament in March 2014, it had to be ratified by the Council of the European Union, that together with the Parliament constitutes the EU legislature and consists of member states' ministers (governments) articulating their joint position on legal matters. There, the change in legal form from a Directive (as a set of data protection principles to be implemented by member states) to a uniform Regulation, along with the attempt to enable the data market and regulate that market, was also a cause of consternation. In the words of the UK negotiator at the Council:

We absolutely accepted the argument that harmonised rules would have been pro-business, but at the same time we felt that the Regulation itself was so prescriptive that it wasn't pro-business. [...] I think on a political level there is this whole issue around EU competence and subsidiarity; you know, we are shackled to this huge Regulation, which is being administered by a central European authority, where the European Commission has all these powers to issue delegated acts. (Interview, London, 28 April 2016)

Market enabling features of the legislation included new data protection concepts, such as a "one-stop shop" for data regulation. Through this concept, data controllers operating across Europe would now be supervised solely by the data protection authority (or "supervisory authority") of the country where their "main establishment" is located. All the supervisory authorities would then collaborate under a single European Data Protection Board (EDPB) (EU GDPR, 2016, Articles 46–55). This would be market-enabling in the sense that the number of authorities with whom a data controller would have to work and the number of different interpretations of data protection principles they had to work with would be radically cut. But for EU member states, this was a significant imposition. They needed to know that a uniform set of rules would be equally enforced in every member state, that data controllers would be equally treated and data subjects experience fair and equal rights. This delayed the Regulation significantly:

because [member states] had very long discussions [...], and this is where member states have more intrinsic motivations to get it right, because it affects their national authorities, the way they cooperate and so on. It was not such a big issue for us in the Parliament. (Interview with a technical expert from the European Parliament, Brussels-London, 20 April 2016)

Or, as the UK negotiator at the Council witnessed it:

The UK point of view was "Let's keep this one-stop shop simple; let's keep this single main establishment". Some of the other countries said "Well, our countries had to have a say; we need serve our citizens" [...] But I think to some extent this was the idea that it's not acceptable for a data protection authority of one member state to make a judgement on behalf of the other member state. So it went through endless rounds of rewriting [...] and then finally it was agreed and the compromise was it was this very complicated system where member states can intervene, they can take a local case if the legal authority says it's a local case. Also if it's got a cross-border effect, so it's a complaint involving data subjects from different member states those data authorities become concerned authorities [and] then if it happens then it goes to this new thing called the European Data Protection Board. (Interview, London, 28 April 2016)

The Council negotiated these most contentious elements of the draft for two further years, throughout 2014–15, finally reaching a consensus in December 2015. This painstaking and lengthy negotiation to (arguably) reconcile market enabling and data protection legislation within the same Regulation would now form a new European Digital Single Market (Neyland and Milyaeva, 2017). As we will see, this still required a (modified) combination of privacy and property rights, instituting a sense of control that, in a similar manner to the nascent US privacy market, might replace 'invasion' as the dominant metaphor in privacy discussions.

To make sense of this modification of privacy and property rights through control, we need to turn away from the controversy inspired by the legislative process towards its content. Unlike the US approach to privacy through consumer choice, the GDPR introduced a set of legal rights that data subjects could now exercise. Having rights "provides for many lawful grounds for processing & transfers" of personal data.[12] In this sense, the rights were market-enabling – allowing the data industry to pursue data analytics, move data around and monetise that data. However, the lawful grounds for processing

------

[12] https://twitter.com/VivianeRedingEU/status/100186610074 3733248

and transferring data also enabled data subjects to exercise their rights, for example, to data portability or to be forgotten. Among data firms these rights were not uniformly seen as a limitation, and for some were even heralded as an opportunity. An industry offering GDPR compliance services has emerged and online marketing firms have even begun to promote their compliance as a form of competitive advantage. For example, one firm recently suggested that "no major paradigm shift [is] required" as data-driven businesses "can embrace the values of permission-based marketing that the GDPR is heralding, showing the rest of the pack what leaner, cleaner data-driven marketing can do" (from Duncan Hendy (2018), Content Strategy Manager of the online marketing platform Kentico).

Rights as a form of control, then, are perhaps less absolute than forms of privacy discussed under the metaphor of invasion. Whereas the latter presupposed that privacy depended upon a more or less fixed set of boundaries across which access would not be permitted, rights-based legislation enables data transfers to happen and enables the online marketing industry to continue (and even develop GDPR compliance as a promotional tool). Controlling data through legal rights is then designed to enable the data subject to have some (but not exclusive) ownership of their data. This may sound complex, given that traditional models of property and ownership tend to distribute a fixed set of rights over what can be done to that property. But the form of control that the GDPR introduces, with its less certain proprietorial rights, might be well-suited to data given its peculiar properties of non-exclusivity (multiple parties can make something of the same resource, see earlier discussion of the misleading oil metaphor) and legislators' concerns not to limit the data industry's potential for expansion.

Investigating these new European data rights in more detail can help flesh out this initial picture of control. The *right to be forgotten* (or the right to erasure) is the right of a data subject to request that personal data about them and links to that data that are outdated or irrelevant, should be deleted. In a re-emphasis of the traditional data protection notion of necessity, the GDPR states that a request can be made to delete data when: "the personal data are no longer necessary in relation to the purposes for which they were collected or otherwise processed" (EU GDPR, 2016, Article 17). Although the right was already present in the first 2012 draft of the Regulation, it became more widely publicised with the complaint filed against Google by a Spanish citizen. With the European Court of Justice ruling in favour of this data subject, the Court asked Google to remove specific links from its searches (BBC News, 2014). Control over data has thus been rebalanced with this right, with data subjects now able to exert a limited sense of ownership over their data. Previous concerns that such rights would limit the data industry mostly seem to be unfounded. As one European data protection regulator pointed out:

So okay, the difference [is] that [Terry] now enters his name in the search bar, and has successfully got something de-linked. Well, then Google doesn't have the full picture to make the judgement as to what ad is most likely [Terry] to click on. So therefore, arguably, that's impeding the market. But I suspect given that you've got to request, item by item, removal of links, and frankly, given the types of links you're likely to remove are things like links to press reports about criminal activity or socially unacceptable activity, what's the relevant ad you can serve to them? If you are a politician who's been involved in some indiscretion, what ad is relevant to that? (Interview, 8 July 2014)[13]

---

[13] To keep the source anonymous we do not reveal the interviewee's location.

Following the terms of this argument, the data industry is unlikely to find itself limited by the right to be forgotten, as what is forgotten represents a tiny fragment of our data footprint. The deletion requests are also likely to encompass stories entailing some reputational risk, which data analysts would struggle to monetise, as there are few relevant adverts to send, for example, a politician caught in a scandal. The redistribution of control over data and the partial redistribution of ownership rights leads to few restrictions on the data industry. What we can also note in this interview excerpt is the limited nature of these rights. Although the nascent privacy market in the US was limited in scale, the services offered by privacy start-ups did tend to focus on privacy by default. The data service would automatically protect a user's data and users would be protected however much or little interest they had in privacy. By contrast, the GDPR utilises a combination of minimal privacy by default, for example when website users are asked to consent to the use of cookies, and privacy rights that need to be invoked by data subjects. These rights enshrined in the GDPR often require, as we will see below, an active and knowledgeable data citizen, aware of and enthusiastic about their data rights, their (limited) control over data and how this operates through a set of modified property rights that they themselves must pursue.[14] The concerned data citizen must identify all the links they want to be deleted and apply for that content to be deleted. Alongside a small amount of privacy by default, comes a rights-based privacy, only achievable through great effort.

---

[14] At least in the rights we will look at here: the right to be forgotten and the right to data portability. Issues of consent do place a bit more emphasis on the data industry's responsibilities.

Perhaps unsurprisingly, the initial reaction of data brokers and data-driven advertisers to this rights-based Regulation has been focused on how "thriving in the new regulatory environment" is possible because "the GDPR should be seen as a chance to transform a business [...] to enforce best practices that can only improve relationships with customers [in] finding an effective way of integrating the new behaviours, processes and roles" (Experian, 2017).

Contrasting the right to be forgotten with *the right to data portability* places a stronger emphasis on control derived from a less obtuse sense of ownership. This right guarantees that:

the data subject shall have the right to receive the personal data concerning him or her, which he or she has provided to a controller, in a structured, commonly used and machine-readable format and have the right to transmit those data to another controller without hindrance from the controller to which the personal data have been provided. (EU GDPR, 2016, Article 20)

Even the most sceptical of national regulators at the time the GDPR was a draft found the right to data portability commendable:

Given the fact that the proposed regulation is far too long and far too detailed, what do we need to hang on to? Well, we do need to the arrangements for data portability, because it is making a very important point - my data is my data; it remains my data. I may have provided it to you, so you can provide a service to me. [...] That's why I like the idea of personal data stores, because it is saying, "You are in charge of this very valuable information, and it is valuable to you." It may be valuable to somebody else but is your information. So you use it for getting best deals. (Interview, 8 April 2014)[15]

---

[15] To keep the source anonymous we do not reveal the interviewee's location.

Unlike the right to be forgotten and the limited sense of control and ownership that right enabled, data portability seems to facilitate something more akin to the data vault we saw made available by US privacy start-ups. The GDPR acts here as an "enabling legal construct" (Cohen, 2017) by economising data in a different way. Instead of relying on the data industry to mine, scrape and monetise data through, for example, behavioural advertising, the GDPR insists upon the packaging up of data for data subjects, in order that it is movable, transferrable, and reusable by other data services on the terms of the data subject. The right enables the data subject to pursue the best deal through their portable packets of data. Ownership is redrafted again, with control partially redistributed back toward the data subject who can move data from one firm to another for their own economic gain. Data subjects are, a little like the US model, consumers who are newly enabled to share their data for "lawful" collection and processing. Privacy is now reworked from forms of concealment central to the invasion of privacy metaphor, to forms of control over sharing.

Reconciling the legislative needs of the GDPR to be market-enabling at the same time as regulating that market, requires this kind of broad reworking of the entities involved: data is changed, the data industry is changed (a little bit), the data subject has new rights, privacy becomes a matter of control and sharing maintains its position at the centre of the data economy, albeit with the data subject able to oversee this sharing in new ways. This may seem distinct from the right to be forgotten, yet the right to data portability still relies on an active data citizen, making informed choices about who and what to share, aware of their rights and interested in expressing those rights for economic or other reasons. Users of digital devices are now composed as a complex hybrid of data-subject-citizen-consumer.

Conclusion

In Chapter 2 we used the EU ETS to explore the ways in which a market-based intervention organised around a sensibility of trade and exchange could give shape to a specific means to define and (attempt to) solve a problem: CO_2 emissions. What we found in place of a straightforward sensibility that drove a ruthless and singular economic rationale through the intervention was a negotiated technocracy. Endless and convoluted discussions, forms of lobbying, claims and counterclaims regarding the positive and negative features of legislation and the need for intervention, were all at times brought to the fore, accommodated in the policy-making process or carefully pushed to one side. The Brussels ecosystem was a small world within which this negotiated technocracy could continue to flourish. In this chapter, particularly through the GDPR, we have seen some similar lines of research emerging. Just as the ETS gave carbon a particular shape through devices that enabled the creation of tradeable allowances, here data has been drawn into a new set of economic relations.

The GDPR constituted a large scale, convoluted, negotiated legislative framework. Unlike the EU ETS, this framework was not oriented toward trade and exchange, but instead a modified form of property and ownership. We could multiply the points of comparison between the two EU interventions. For example, while the climate policy was seen as a threat to the competitiveness of European industry and a special mitigation measure had to be put in place (the carbon leakage question), the data protection legislation ought, from the onset, to combine effective regulation of the industry with protection or even enhancement of Europe's competitiveness. A major difference we would like to foreground here concerns the relevant market actors: with the GDPR, individual data subjects were as much a feature of the intervention as (the data) industry. This particular form of legislative juggling took years and created much controversy. In place of moderately disputed number-based rules (for example, the cap on CO_2 emissions in the ETS), data was subject to the development of new rights-based legislation. These rights required active data citizens to know their data rights and police the data industry on their own behalf. Despite these differences in market participants, one similarity is clear: just like ETS compliance, this data protection legislation also enabled a flourishing industry of GDPR compliance.

What we have also noted in this chapter is that an extensive piece of legislation was not the only option. The US was pursuing its own consumer-based solution that imagined privacy being purchased-into-existence. These distinct approaches to privacy, what it might be and how it might be resolved in the EU and the US, created two situations in which the state as a kind of political infrastructure took very specific forms. In the US, the political infrastructure took a back seat in an environment that was seemingly hostile to privacy legislation and keen on promoting the economic advantages of the data industry, as extolled by industry lobbyists and some legislators. What then needed to be sorted out was the precise way in which privacy could be consumed – a matter of practice envisaged through majoritarian choice. If enough people wanted privacy, then a market for privacy products and indeed the products and services themselves would come into being. Consumers would accommodate privacy into their purchasing practices and privacy would be satisfactorily accomplished.

In the EU, political infrastructure occupied the driving seat in the action, with legislators continually working over several years with the data industry, politicians and pressure groups to produce a text that could reconcile all their different interests. The structures and processes of EU decision-making framed expectations of individuals' new practices, with rights-based legislation giving people privacy in the form of control, but only if they were sufficiently active and informed and willing to practice it. Looking at the different ways in which privacy as a form of control was envisaged in the privacy services market of the US and the EU GDPR tells us something about the differential effects of market-based interventions on the "same" problem. While privacy in the US, at least for some start-ups, was a matter of default controls that limited consumers' exposure to the data industry through a data vault that they might not even know about, privacy in the EU involved a combination of minimal privacy by default along with an expectation that data citizens would pursue their newly acquired rights.

Property and ownership continued its entangled relationship with privacy within both the EU and US approach. Whereas historically privacy has been understood as a matter of protecting privacy from invasion (and extraction and the reconnection of matter extracted with the original source), in the US and EU, approaches to privacy now take the form of control via a modified sense of ownership. This ownership reflects that data flows freely up to a point and is available to be used by multiple individuals and firms and then monetised. This newly modified notion of ownership involves property rights that are less exclusive (they are distributed among parties) and require varying degrees of effort (the consumer in the US must choose to purchase a product and the EU rights holder must pursue the enforcement of their entitlements).

What we will see in the following chapters is that this movement from a general concern (in this chapter, privacy) to a particular intervention (through utilising a market sensibility to give a very specific shape to a market-based intervention) continues, along with some of the entanglements of political infrastructure and specific practices we have witnessed here.

In the next chapter we will consider a relatively new form of market-based intervention – a Social Impact Bond for children at risk of going into residential care – designed to address the problem of financing social care. What we will see here is that investment and return is the crucial market sensibility for shaping an intervention, on which the aspirations of private investors have strong purchase, while the concerns of the individual subject of care are mostly absent. In Chapter 6, we will continue investigating the question of financing. The market sensibility of incentives will be explored through an Advance Market Commitment for vaccines. Here contracts and a global partnership are put in place to ensure that populations in low-income countries receive vaccination. And in Chapter 7, the focus will be on the market sensibility of selling and in particular the sale of UK higher education student loans by the government to rebalance public spending. These sales are also focused on property, but in the case of student loans, what is at stake is the composition of properties required in the loans and a new set of practices that are needed in order to achieve their sale.

References

Andrejevic, M. (2011) Surveillance and alienation in the online economy. *Surveillance & Society* 8(3): 278–87.

Andrejevic, M. (2014) Big data, big questions: The big data divide. *International Journal of Communication* 8(1): 1673–89.

Andrejevic, M. and Gates, K. (2014) Big data surveillance: Introduction. *Surveillance & Society* 12(2): 185–96.

Angwin, J. (2010) The web's new gold mine: Your secrets. *The Wall Street Journal*, 30 July. Available at: www.wsj.com/articles/SB100014 24052748703940904575395073512989404 (last accessed 3 April 2019).

Angwin, J. and Steel, E. (2011) Web's hot new commodity: Privacy. *The Wall Street Journal*, 28 February. Available at: www.wsj.com/articles/ SB10001424052748703529004576160764037920274 (last accessed 3 April 2019).

Aquisti, A., John, L.K. and Loewenstein, G. (2013) What is privacy worth? *Journal of Legal Studies* 42(2): 249–74.

Bachman, K. (2014) Confessions of a data broker. *Adweek*, 25 March. Available at: www.adweek.com/digital/confessions-data-broker-156437/ (last accessed 3 April 2019).

BBC News (2014) EU court backs "right to be forgotten" in Google case. Available at: www.bbc.co.uk/news/world-europe-27388289 (last accessed 3 April 2019).

Booth, R. (2017) Facebook employs ex-political aides to help campaigns target voters. *The Guardian*, 8 May. Available at: www. theguardian.com/technology/2017/may/08/facebook-political-aides-campaigns-target-voters (last accessed 3 April 2019).

Brewster, T. (2014) Meet Datacoup – the company that wants to help you to sell your data. *The Guardian*, 5 September. Available at: www. theguardian.com/technology/2014/sep/05/datacoup-consumer-sell-data-control-privacy-advertising (last accessed 3 April 2019).

Brill, J. (2013) Demanding transparency from data brokers. *Washington Post*, 15 August.

British Bankers' Association (BBA) (2012) BBA position on proposed EU DP regulations. Available at: www.bba.org.uk/policy/ retail/managing-customer-data-and-information/data-protection/ bba-position-on-proposed-eu-dp-regulations/ (last accessed 3 April 2019).

Brustein, J. (2012) Start-ups seek to help users put a price on their personal data. *The New York Times*, 12 February. Available at: www. nytimes.com/2012/02/13/technology/start-ups-aim-to-help-users-put-a-price-on-their-personal-data.html (last accessed 3 April 2019).

Cadwalladr, C. and Graham-Harrison, E. (2018) Revealed: 50 million Facebook profiles harvested for Cambridge Analytica in major data breach. *The Guardian*, 17 March. Available at: www.theguardian.com/news/2018/mar/17/cambridge-analytica-facebook-influence-us-election (last accessed 3 April 2019).

Campbell, J. and Carlson, M. (2002) Panopticon.com: Online surveillance and the commodification of privacy. *Journal of Broadcasting & Electronic Media* 46(4): 586–606.

Chlopecki, M. (1992) The property rights origins of privacy rights. *Foundation for Economic Education*. Available at: https://fee.org/articles/the-property-rights-origins-of-privacy-rights/ (last accessed 3 April 2019).

Chon, G. (2014) FTC calls for clampdown on data brokers. *The Financial Times*, 27 May. Available at: www.ft.com/content/61ba15aa-e5c2-11e3-aeef-00144feabdc0#axzz3BPoUcN7G (last accessed 3 April 2019).

Cohen, J. E. (2017) The biopolitical public domain: the legal construction of the surveillance economy. *Philosophy & Technology* 31(2): 213–33.

Constine, J. (2013) Facebook lets advertisers tap purchase data partners to target customers, categories like car-buyers. *Techcrunch*, 27 February. Available at: https://techcrunch.com/2013/02/27/facebook-ad-data-providers/?guccounter=1 (last accessed 3 April 2019).

Council of the European Union (CEU) (2016) Data protection reform: Council adopts position at first reading. Available at: www.consilium.europa.eu/en/press/press-releases/2016/04/08-data-protection-reform-first-reading/ (last accessed 3 April 2019).

Crain, M. (2016) The limits of transparency: Data brokers and commodification. *New Media & Society* 20(1): 88–104.

Davies, W. (2012) Ways of owning: Towards an economic sociology of privatisation. *Poetics* 40(2): 167–84.

Davis, S. (1997) Re-engineering the right to privacy: Hoe privacy has been transformed from a right to a commodity. In E. Agre and M. Rotenberg (eds.), *Technology and Privacy: The New Landscape*. Cambridge, MA: MIT Press, pp. 143–67.

Dwoskin, E. (2014) Podesta urges more transparency on data collection, use. *WSJ Blogs – Digits*. Available at: http://blogs.wsj.com/digits/2014/03/21/podesta-urges-more-transparency-on-data-collection-use/ (last accessed 3 April 2019).

EU General Data Protection Regulation (GDPR) (2016) *Regulation (EU) 2016/679 of the European Parliament and of the Council of 27 April 2016 on the Protection of Natural Persons with Regard to the Processing of Personal Data and on the Free Movement of Such Data, and Repealing Directive 95/46/EC*. Available at: https://eur-lex.europa.eu/legal-content/EN/TXT/?qid=1528874672298&uri=CELEX%3A32016R0679 (last accessed 3 April 2019).

European Commission (EC) (2009) Keynote speech of Meglena Kuneva at the Roundtable on Online Data Collection, Targeting and Profiling. Available at: http://europa.eu/rapid/press-release_SPEECH-09-156_en.htm (last accessed 3 April 2019).

European Commission (EC) (2014) Making the most of the data-driven economy. Press release issued on 2 July. Available at: http://europa.eu/rapid/press-release_MEMO-14-455_en.htm (last accessed 3 April 2019).

European Commission (EC) (2017) Final results of the European data market study measuring the size and trends of the EU data economy. Available at: https://ec.europa.eu/digital-single-market/en/news/final-results-european-data-market-study-measuring-size-and-trends-eu-data-economy (last accessed 3 April 2019).

European Commission (EC) (2018) Priority: Digital Single Market – bringing down barriers to unlock online opportunities. Available at: https://ec.europa.eu/commission/priorities/digital-single-market_en (last accessed 3 April 2019.)

Experian (2017) *Defining the Data Powered Future: An Experian Guide to EU GDPR*. White Paper. Available at: www.experian.co.uk/assets/gdpr/brochures/defining-the-data-powered-future.pdf (last accessed 3 April 2019).

Fuchs, C. (2014) *Social Media: A Critical Introduction*. London: Sage.

Gandy, O. (2011) The political economy of personal information. In J. Wasko, G. Murdock and H. Sousa (eds.), *The Handbook of Political*

Economy of Communications. Malden, MA: Wiley-Blackwell, pp. 436–57.

Goel, V. (2014) With new ad platform, Facebook opens gates to its vault of user data. *The New York Times*, 28 September. Available at: www.nytimes.com/2014/09/29/business/with-new-ad-platform-facebook-opens-the-gates-to-its-vault-of-consumer-data.html (last accessed 3 April 2019).

Greenwald, G. (2013) NSA collecting phone records of millions of Verizon customers daily. *The Guardian*, 6 June. Available at: www.theguardian.com/world/2013/jun/06/nsa-phone-records-verizon-court-order (last accessed 3 April 2019).

Hagel, J. and Rayport, J. (1997) The coming battle for consumer information. *Harvard Business Review* 75: 53–65.

Hagel, J. and Singer, M. (1999) *Net Worth: Shaping Markets When Customers Make the Rules.* New York: McKinsey & Company, Harvard Business School Press.

Hendy, D. (2018) Right to be forgotten: The death of data-driven marketing? *Fourth Source*, 4 April. Available at: www.fourthsource.com/data/right-to-be-forgotten-the-death-of-data-driven-marketing-22675 (last accessed 3 April 2019).

Hern, A. (2017) How social media filter bubbles and algorithms influence the election. *The Guardian*, 22 May, Available at: www.theguardian.com/technology/2017/may/22/social-media-election-facebook-filter-bubbles (last accessed 3 April 2019).

Industry Coalition for Data Protection (ICDP) (2013) Industry concerned over negative impact of Albrecht draft report. Press release.

Kitchin, R. (2014) *The Data Revolution: Big Data, Open Data, Data Infrastructures and Their Consequences.* London: Sage.

Laudon, K. (1996) Markets and privacy. *Communication ACM* 39(9): 92–104.

Lyon, D. (2001) *Surveillance Society: Monitoring Everyday Life.* Buckingham: Open University Press.

Lyon, D. and Zureik, E. (1996) *Computers, Surveillance and Privacy*. Minneapolis: University of Minnesota Press

Malm, A. (2016) *Fossil Capital: The Rise of Steam Power and the Roots of Global Warming*. London: Verso.

Mayer-Schonberger, V. and Cukier, K. (2013) *Big Data: A Revolution That Will Transform How We Live, Work, and Think*. London: John Murray

Milyaeva, S. and Neyland, D. (2016) Market innovation as framing, productive friction and bricolage: An exploration of the personal data market. *Journal of Cultural Economy* 9(3): 229–44.

Neyland, D. (2006) *Privacy, Surveillance and Public Trust*. Houndmills, Basingstoke and New York: Palgrave.

Neyland, D. and Milyaeva, S. (2017) Brexit and the failure of pre-emptive reconciliation: A study of the general data protection regulation. *Sociological Review*. Available at: www.thesociologicalreview. com/journal/rapid-responses/article/brexit-and-the-failure-of-pre-emptive-reconciliation-a-study-of-the-general-data-protection-regulation.html (last accessed 3 April 2019).

Organisation for Economic Co-operation and Development (OECD) (2015) *Data-Driven Innovation: Big Data for Growth and Well-Being*. Paris: OECD Publishing. Available at: www.oecd.org/sti/ieconomy/ data-driven-innovation.htm (last accessed 3 April 2019).

PCAST (2014) Big data and privacy: A technological perspective. Executive Office of the President President's Council of Advisors on Science and Technology. Available at: https://bigdatawg.nist.gov/ pdf/pcast_big_data_and_privacy_-_may_2014.pdf (last accessed 3 April 2019).

Posner, R. (1977–78) The right of privacy. *Georgia Law Review* 12(3): 393–422.

Posner, R. (1979) Privacy, secrecy, and reputation. *Buffalo Law Review* 28(2): 1–55.

Posner, R. (1981) The economics of privacy. *American Economic Review* 71(2): 405–9.

Posner, R. (2008) Privacy, surveillance, and law. *University of Chicago Law Review* 75(1): 245–60.

Reding, V. (2012) *The EU Data Protection Reform 2012: Making Europe the Standard Setter for Modern Data Protection Rules in the Digital Age*. Speech Innovation Conference Digital, Life, Design – 22 January, Munich, Germany. Available at: http://europa.eu/rapid/press-release_SPEECH-12-26_en.htm (last accessed 3 April 2019).

Rees, C. (2014) Who owns our data? *Computer Law & Security Review* 30(1): 75–79.

Schweidel, D. (2015) *Profiting from the Data Economy*. New Jersey: Pearson Education.

Sevignani, S. (2013) The commodification of privacy on the Internet. *Science and Public Policy* 40: 733–9.

Srnicek, N. (2017) *Platform Capitalism*. Cambridge: Polity.

Staples, W. (2000) *Everyday Surveillance: Vigilance and Visibility in Postmodern Life*. Lanham, MD: Rowman & Littlefield.

Steel, E., Locke, C., Cadman, E. and Freese, B. (2013) How much is your personal data worth? *Financial Times*, June 12. Available at: https://ig.ft.com/how-much-is-your-personal-data-worth/ (last accessed 3 April 2019).

Sullivan, M. (2012) Personal data vaults put you in control of your data online. *TechAdvisor*, 13 July. Available at: www.techadvisor.co.uk/feature/internet/personal-data-vaults-put-you-in-control-of-your-data-online-3369859/ (last accessed 3 April 2019).

Suvorova, A. and Romanov, B. (1986) *ABC of Social and Political Knowledge: What is Property?* Moscow: Progress Publishers.

Swedberg, R. (2005) Towards an economic sociology of capitalism. *L'Année Sociologique* 55: 419–49.

US Chamber of Commerce (US CC) (2017) *Promote Digital Trade and the Data-Driven Economy*. Available at: www.uschamber.com/issue-brief/promote-digital-trade-and-the-data-driven-economy (last accessed 3 April 2019).

Wooley, L. (2013) DMA responds to op-ed attacking commercial data use. *Direct Marketing Association.* Available at: http://blog.thedma.org/2013/08/19/dma-responds-to-op-ed-attacking-commercial-data-use/ (last accessed 3 April 2019).

Zuboff, S. (2015) Big other: Surveillance capitalism and the prospects of an information civilization. *Journal of Information Technology* 30: 75–89.

5

Investment and Return

Opening

In Chapter 4 we contrasted the US approach to privacy as a consumer matter with the EU focus on building a significant regulatory infrastructure – the GDPR. The latter picks up on one of the themes also present in Chapters 2 and 3: that bureaucratic and management functions of the state are not replaced by the invisible hand of the market. Neither do these interventions lead to a neoliberal reduction of the state or indeed a promotion of the free market in places where the state once operated. Instead, what we see are a variety of struggles to align the significant governance infrastructures developed to introduce and manage market sensibilities with the emerging action that takes place once an intervention is implemented. What tends to happen in these interventions is not a reduction of bureaucratic infrastructure with an attendant reduction in costs, but the emergence of ever-changing infrastructural requirements as different ways to understand the nature of the problem intervened upon come to light and as the intervention itself appears to create further problems that require resolution. The US approach to privacy in this context may seem more like an exception. However, in this chapter we will turn attention to a distinct sensibility for thinking about and organising a market-based intervention that has been introduced more explicitly to reduce the bureaucratic infrastructural requirements of governance, giving form to the sensibility of investment and return.

Recent writing on investment and return provides us with a number of ways to explore this market sensibility. One entry point is to consider the very basis upon which investment-return relations are made. In order to do so, Birch suggests we need to understand how things: "are turned into assets (i.e., resources that generate recurring earnings) and then capitalized (i.e., discounting future earnings in the present)" (2017: 463). In this way, an investment–return relationship is fundamentally characterised by an assessment of the risk and viability of achieving a greater amount back from money put into a scheme. Making something into an asset and capitalising on that asset are thus key. The promotion of an asset class would provide an opportunity to entice investors to make financial commitments within a structure that would help calculate the risks involved and manage investments and returns, as one asset could be compared to others in the class and different histories of performance could be comparatively invoked. Such matters as discounted cash flows would then enable a potential investor to judge the present value of a future income stream (Muniesa et al., 2017). Future income streams are conventionally "discounted" to reflect the risk that the return might not be achieved, at least not in its entirety. Importantly, composing a value in the present for the future income enables a form of liquidity to be established: the investment can be cashed in now if potential buyers are willing to accept the present value composed by the investors or other parties. For this to work as the basis for a market-based intervention into a public problem, the constitution of a particular kind of investment–return relation is required: a position needs to be established from which investors could judge the feasibility of entry into a set of financial commitments, potential risks and returns, and likely liquidity offered by an intervention underwritten by the state. If such a position was construed, we might even be tempted to suggest that the costs of an intervention into a public problem would be capitalised (to use the term of Doganova and Muniesa, 2015; Muniesa et al., 2017).

These ideas are useful for alerting us to the need to explore the basis on which investment–return relations are built, costs and risks assessed, and investments made and potentially sold. But retuning these analyses toward market-based interventions into public problems raises further specific questions. Chiapello (2015) suggests that these investment–return relations are becoming prominent as ways to solve public problems as "forms of analysis and calculation specific to finance are spreading, and changing valuation processes in various social settings" (13). Through government austerity measures, Chiapello suggests, states are not covering all the costs of expensive interventions into social, cultural and environmental issues. Instead, they are dedicating smaller, but focused budgets toward attracting in private investors "who propose to use the mechanisms of finance to do good, and are also on the lookout for new asset classes to expand their activities" (32). The interventions that are then generated through new relations between state and private investors produce a new range of investments: "The commodities that are created are financial assets related to new intangible commodities such as ecosystem services or social impacts and these intangible products exist purely because of the financialised valuation techniques that brought them into being" (32).

Following on from this, key questions for understanding the nature of this form of market sensibility relate to the types of investment–return relationships put in place, how these are held in place and the new devices of quantification that give these relations a series of effects. For Warner (2013), such relations are held in place by a troubling and outdated mode of intervention designed to fix in place investment positions that

harken back to a rigid concept of contracting that trusts evaluation and profit mechanisms to ensure contract compliance while the contracting literature has found those mechanisms to be inadequate and shifted its attention to studies of relational contracting and networked governance. (304)

These issues of inflexibility, and dependence on calculative devices to measure effects, are exacerbated by further concerns, for example, that setting up forms of investment as a basis for addressing public problems leaves the state facing interest costs on repayments to investors (Dowling and Harvie, 2014). These interventions also raise the possibility that investors will seek to control interventions to protect their investment capital (Bryan and Rafferty, 2014) and that the state will struggle to use investment based mechanisms to cut costs when it is forced to ring-fence budgets to underwrite the risks involved in these new relations with private investors (Mitropoulos and Bryan, 2015).

In place of any counter-expectation that building an asset class and introducing investment–return relations to entice in private money can act as a basis for straightforwardly solving public problems come a series of challenging questions. Questions of the nature of investment–return relations and their costs, how these are composed and held in place, dependent on calculative devices, contracting and the constitution of effects through which repayments are made, each need to be explored. Furthermore, issues of discount cash flows, composing a present value of a future return, liquidity and the ability to cash in an asset, seem to raise further questions regarding the precise nature of the relationship between state and investor. In this chapter we will address these questions through a particular market-based intervention, the Social Impact Bond. After an initial introduction to these Bonds, we will focus in on a Social Impact Bond for children at risk. The Bond was introduced and operated by Essex County Council, a regional political authority on the east coast of England. This will enable us to move between the general and the particular in different ways. In contrast to the GDPR and EU ETS we will be focusing in on a more local intervention, but one that might prove to be a useful example for others to copy. This also offers us a chance to reconsider the devices, relations and practices of market-based interventions. Whereas in Chapter 2, calculative devices engaged with such matters as capping emissions and the future price of allowances, here the focus will be on calculations built into fixed contractual devices. Although in Chapter 3 we explored the practices that compose the competitive consequences of the REF, here we will see how market-based practices can also prove exclusionary (particularly of the subjects of care). And in contrast to Chapter 4, wherein we witnessed the regulatory relations through which the individual data subject is expected to become a market participant, here we will explore the ways in which investors directly shape the relations of intervention.

We will end the chapter with a consideration of the temporal structure of investment and return, and how this is held in place by contractual relations that produce a different kind of unanticipated consequence in comparison with our preceding market sensibilities. Instead of focusing on the ongoing challenges of bureaucratic infrastructures, we find ourselves drawn to the notion of providence as a means to make sense of who benefits from investment–return relations, who faces risks and in what timeframe.

Social Impact Bonds

An Austerity Measure

According to Schram (2014), the genesis of Social Impact Bonds can be traced to a presentation by an economist from New Zealand called Ronnie Horesh in 1988, under the name of Social Policy Bonds. The central idea was to create an investment-return structure through which the costs of state intervention could be replaced by private investment that would only attract a return on investment, underwritten by the state, if certain commitments were met. In other words, a public problem could become the basis for building new relations of investment and return and public money could be shifted from a straightforward pay-out to a future income stream for investors depending on the level of success achieved in solving a specified problem. Horesh's vision was for these Bonds to be traded on a secondary market, introducing a form of liquidity by opening up opportunities for capitalising on future income streams. Horesh's suggestion was that the value of a Bond would increase as an intervention got closer to success or produced more and more successful outcomes, incentivising the Bond holder to solve as much as possible of the public problem at stake, at a cost as low as possible.

Under the revised name and with a slightly different focus, Social Impact Bonds[1] continued to be discussed by academics and policy-makers through the 1990s. These discussions were given greater policy impetus by the nominally left-of-centre UK New Labour government of Prime Minister Tony Blair and

[1] The term *Social Impact Bond* is attributed to Geoff Mulgan of the Young Foundation.

Chancellor Gordon Brown who instituted the Social Investment Taskforce in 2000. Under the leadership of Ronald Cohen, a key advocate of social investment's ability to provide new ways to intervene in public problems, Social Impact Bonds continued to retain a prominence in the policy discussions of the Taskforce. Eventually the UK Taskforce became the G8 Social Investment Taskforce also under the leadership of Cohen and Bonds were discussed on a global stage. Meanwhile in the UK, Social Impact Bonds were one of a number of policy devices with a clear basis derived from economics that were strongly supported by Gordon Brown that also included Private Finance Initiatives, various forms of Public–Private Partnerships and schemes such as the Advance Market Commitment (see Chapter 6). Whereas, traditionally, Labour Party policies had sought collective bases for solving social problems and promoting greater justice, at least since the Thatcher-led party of the late 1970s, the Conservatives had advocated for a greater focus on the individual and the reduction of the state through privatisation and greater market freedom. Now these New Labour initiatives proposed a remixing of political traditions, seeking collective justice and a solution to public problems at least partially outside the state and very much within markets.

Despite these ongoing discussions and high-level support, sufficient momentum to transform talk about Social Impact Bonds into a written policy that might pass through Parliament only materialised in direct relation to the financial crisis of 2008 onwards. It is crisis, as Roitman (2014: 59) suggests, that "secures the grounds for witnessing and testing" a range of new ways to intervene. Austerity could become a means to problematise (Callon, Lascoumes and Barthe, 2009; Callon, 1986; see also Chapter 8) public-sector budgets and costs, opening up for discussion the possibility of new and more radical measures of intervention. Of particular interest from 2008 onwards were questions of apparently irreducible costs for government in specific fields of policy around, for example, homelessness, vulnerable children or crime. Here problems and costs seemed to endure in tandem with whatever intervention was made.

Social Impact Bonds could then be presented as a viable, but experimental, basis for a different kind of approach. Such Bonds could be experimental by focusing in on a particular problem, geographical area (typically under the auspices of a specific local or regional political authority) and for a fixed time (usually five to eight years). These parameters provided a grounds for witnessing and testing, and then rolling out or changing, Social Impact Bonds. In their most general form, these Bonds involved drawing up a recognisable problem to be intervened upon. The nature of the problem had to be recognised by all participants in the intervention, along with a method for solving the problem, a desirable impact that, if achieved, would demonstrate that the problem was solved, and an agreed measure of that impact. Such measures were crucial for the composition of an investment–return relationship. Investors would be given the opportunity to cover the costs of the intervention – that would form their investment. Returns would then be paid that covered those costs and a fixed percentage on top of those costs, depending on the extent to which a problem was solved. If the measures demonstrated great results, higher returns would be paid to investors, typically capped at 10–13% annually on top of their investment. If low results were achieved, lower returns would be paid. In theory, if the measures suggested a minimum impact had not been met, investors would not only stand to miss out on a percentage return, but also lose their initial investment.

The Social Impact Bond was thus said to provide a vehicle to help manage impacts and measurements, but also to provide a structure through which investments and returns could be made and (mostly financial) risks assessed and distributed.[2] Central to the structure of Bonds would be contracts that could help set in place who would invest and how much, how outcomes would be measured and the level of outcome to be achieved. Yet under these proposals, the method used to solve the problem itself would be left to a localised competition whereby different service providers could compete and seek to replace incumbent providers if targets were not being met. A special purpose vehicle would be set up, incorporating representatives of various participants to oversee these arrangements and manage the local form of competition between service providers. Social Impact Bonds in this idealised form would thus attempt to transform intractable social problems into an asset class whose intractability would be addressed through funds provided by investors, with efficiency and effectiveness ensured by localised market competition.

In terms of investment, Social Impact Bonds attempt to utilise the finance and enthusiasm of participants in the social investment market (see Barman, 2015) who suggest that they can save government money, correct poor incentives, unlock new funding, promote evidence-based action, transfer risk away from public finances, and generate returns (Mulgen, Reeder, Aylott and Bo'sher, 2011). Corporate entities such as Goldman Sachs have been important here in identifying Social Impact Bonds as a type of social investment that provides a new and distinct means to leverage private finance and innovative thinking, while also earning returns.[3] These returns have become closely tied to government austerity measures where spending

---

[2] See https://data.gov.uk/sib_knowledge_box/

[3] See www.goldmansachs.com/our-thinking/pages/social-impact-bonds.html

cutbacks have become a financial opportunity. As one of the key financial vehicles in social investment, Big Society Capital[4] suggest "government austerity" has become one of the key drivers of interventions like Social Impact Bonds.[5] Another financial institution that draws together interested investors into social funds, Social Finance, argues that such Bonds "present an opportunity to provide support to reduce the strain on acute services".[6] This focus on austerity goes beyond the investors. For the G8 Social Investment Task Force: "The financial crash of 2008 highlighted the need for a renewed effort to ensure that finance helps build a healthy society"; a goal they suggest is only achievable through social investment.[7] And the UK government Centre for Social Impact Bonds consider that Bonds:

enable commissioners to capture the expertise of social ventures in tackling complex problems by providing them with the upfront capital to deliver... In addition to this, they enable social investors to use their money to achieve both a social impact and a financial return.[8]

From the invisible hand of markets, we now have social investors providing the "invisible heart of markets".[9] A combination of austerity, finance, private-sector expertise, ongoing

---

[4] Initially funded through dormant bank accounts.

[5] See www.biglotteryfund.org.uk/.../social_investment_workshop_slides

[6] See www.socialfinance.org.uk/services/social-impact-bonds/#sthash.xLCC4MQm.dpuf

[7] See www.socialimpactinvestment.org/reports/Impact%20Investment%20Report%20FINAL[3].pdf

[8] See https://data.gov.uk/sib_knowledge_box/home

[9] See www.socialimpactinvestment.org/reports/Impact%20Investment%20Report%20FINAL%5B3%5D.pdf

competition among service providers, and contracts that enable the management of investment–return relations and risks is pushed forward as an innovative way to solve problems. Through this combination of relations, devices and practices, Social Impact Bonds appear to promote a set of market-like interventions nested within each other. Within the social investment market, Social Impact Bonds appear to generate a smaller, more localised investment market and localised competition to provide a solution. The market as a concept is presented as both an important feature of the intervention – with enthusiastic investors propelling particular interventions – and a means to govern and regulate the intervention – with market competition between service providers designed as a means to ensure the efficiency and effectiveness of the Bond.

Initial Experiences with Social Impact Bonds

In line with our previous chapters, expectations of the intervention are presented in a positive light. In this instance, such positivity is partly designed to manage the passage of this new proposal – Social Impact Bonds – through the vagaries of the UK political system where it will need to accrue support. Partly this positive presentation is also intended as a means for central government to encourage local and regional government to introduce these new initiatives (which, as we shall see, require some effort and risk). Yet in practice, this positive presentation seems to slip from view as various significant questions have been raised. The first example of a Social Impact Bond was launched in 2010–11 in Peterborough in the UK to reduce recidivism rates.[10] It involved drawing together £5 million of

---

[10] The rate at which recently released prisoners reoffended.

investment from 17 investors who worked with the probation service to establish a set of outcome measures. The intervention would involve three cohorts of 1,000 prisoners and if the rate of recidivism within those cohorts dropped by at least 7.5% more than a control group, the government would pay back the £5 million investment plus interest. The bigger the drop in recidivism as the key outcome measure, the bigger the annual rate of return in interest, up to a cap of 13%. If the outcome threshold of a comparative drop in recidivism of at least 7.5% was not met, investors would lose both their initial investment and their return.[11]

In this Social Impact Bond, the service providers were paid upfront for their interventions from the £5 million fund and it was investors who faced financial risk. Measurement of recidivism was subcontracted to an independent third party as the government had now effectively become a vested market actor; interested in paying for outcomes or saving public money if the intervention failed. The Social Impact Bond was due to last eight years and some payments could have been received as early as 2013 depending on results. Peterborough for a time became the centre of interest for proposed and emerging Social Impact Bonds as local governments around the UK and local and national governments in the US, Australia, New Zealand and even France looked with increasing interest at emerging results.

Yet the Peterborough recidivism intervention launched to great acclaim and watched closely around the world, was cancelled in 2015. Private investment could no longer fund

---

[11] See https://data.gov.uk/sib_knowledge_box/ministry-justice-offenders-released-peterborough-prison

the probation service to deliver new interventions as the probation service effectively disappeared[12] when national government, in the form of the Home Office, developed contracts for the provision of prisoner rehabilitation services with private-sector firms in 21 regions of the UK. It seemed that one market-based intervention – a national contracting out of probation services – effectively led to the cancellation of another – a local, experimental Social Impact Bond. Although it was only a small scheme, subject to the vicissitudes of government policy, the Peterborough Bond had been intended as an exemplar (see Chapter 8). Cancelling the exemplar raised questions of government commitment to these types of intervention. Further questions were raised regarding practical aspects of the intervention. For example, the much-heralded local market competition for solutions whereby participants could choose between different service delivery organisations never emerged. In place of dynamic market-based competition between providers designed to provide effective and efficient solutions came a seemingly rigid and fixed intervention that was then cancelled.

These early Social Impact Bonds have inspired multiple further questions, leading Silver and Clarke (2014) to suggest: "The reach of financial capitalism is increasing through the development of SIBs. Marginalised people are converted into commodities and re-packaged as derivatives by investors plying their trade in the new marketplace of inequality." Questions have also been raised regarding the ways in which Social Impact Bonds tend to focus on the easiest to solve cases, ensuring high returns for investors, while hard cases

---

[12] See www.theguardian.com/voluntary-sector-network/2014/may/01/social-impact-bonds-funding-model-sibs-future

are abandoned,[13] ensuring enduring problems for those most in need. Fox and Albertson (2011) have suggested that measurement difficulties arise in Bonds making it difficult to definitively attribute change to any particular intervention, with measures being used to trigger pay-outs to investors. Further concerns have been raised regarding the narrowness of measurements used (Lottery Fund, 2014). An OECD report suggests that Bonds are part of a: "financialisation or commodification of social services" (OECD, 2015: 13) that can lead to an erosion of trust in public services. And Oxfam suggest these interventions stifle innovation by reducing opportunities to respond to situations as they arise by contracting everything into place for a fixed period and by diverting charitable and third sector foundations' funds that might be used for grants into fixed investment schemes (Oxfam, 2013). The overall effect, according to Cooper, Graham and Himick, is to transform the most vulnerable into an investment proposition "for the profit of those most able to pay" (2014: 36).

These multiple concerns have also begun to spread to financial assessments of the public worth of Social Impact Bonds as market-based interventions. Existing Social Impact Bonds appear to be resource-intensive in their set-up, with contractual negotiations proving complex, time-consuming and unfamiliar to most participants (PIRU, 2015). Such set-up costs suggest these Bonds simply shift the costs of intervention back from the delivery of a measure to its initial set-up.[14] We

---

[13] See www.theguardian.com/commentisfree/2013/feb/20/work-programme-success-creaming-parking

[14] Although the costs of an intervention might only be met once a positive result has been achieved, the initial infrastructural set up costs have to be met upfront.

are back to the issue raised in our preceding chapters: market-based sensibilities require significant and costly bureaucratic apparatus to support their implementation. In this way, Bonds may not be very efficient for local and regional government agencies looking to reduce spending. Austerity seems to provide the grounds for witnessing and testing an intervention that has its own significant costs. But what of the investors? The Peterborough intervention and a US equivalent involving prisoners recently released from Rikers Island,[15] suggest that Bonds are not a straightforward proposition for investors. The latter might lose a significant proportion of their funds. However, rather than assume that this applies to all Bonds or that we know all we need to regarding investment and return in Social Impact Bonds by reading their publicised results, we will now turn attention to a particular intervention and the investment–return relations it brought into being. Here we will examine a Social Impact Bond for children at risk of going into care launched by Essex County Council in England.

A Social Impact Bond for Children At Risk

According to the UK national government Centre for Social Impact Bonds,[16] since the Peterborough initiative began, there have been 30 more UK Social Impact Bonds launched.[17] Each

------

[15] The Social Impact Bond for recidivism in the US, also collapsed and led to a $7.2 million loss for investors Goldman Sachs and Michael Bloomberg (with the latter taking on most of this loss). See www.ft.com/cms/s/0/5eee5f46-293e-11e5-8613-e7aedbb7bdb7.html

[16] See https://data.gov.uk/sib_knowledge_box/

[17] See www.civilsociety.co.uk/finance/news/content/19304/cabinet_office_launch_seven_new_social_impact_bonds

of these has involved investors marking out a recognisable problem with local and national government, delivery agencies, and producing outcome measures of intervention. These parties are active participants in the development of Bonds, creating different structures for intervention according to the problem in focus. Despite this differentiation among Bonds, efforts have been made to standardise to an extent their form and function through an approval mechanism managed by the national government's Centre for Social Impact Bonds.[18] To achieve approval, interventions must follow prescriptive instructions from the Centre, and are provided with template contracts and guidance on using the templates. No two Social Impact Bonds are quite the same, then, but looking in detail at one Bond can reveal how these general prescriptions have been put to work in a particular context.

In Essex, the County Council (a regional political authority with responsibility for such matters as roads and at-risk children) looked to set up a Social Impact Bond as a means to cut costs, but also improve the effectiveness of their actions. Local expectations of efficiency and effectiveness would need to work with national expectations and guidelines on the shape the Bond should take. Key to the development was setting up a contract to establish the different commitments involved and to demonstrate adherence to national government prescriptions. However, in line with existing studies of Social Impact Bonds that have raised concerns regarding the length and costs of contractual negotiation (PIRU, 2015), in Essex from first pursuing the idea in 2010, through negotiations, to then issuing a contract took around 29 months. This lengthy and costly set-up

---

[18] Once again, government bureaucratic structures are required to hold the intervention steady.

period included establishing a special purpose vehicle to oversee the Bond and deciding on the appropriate form of therapy, how it would be measured and the types of outcome payment made to investors.

The agreed aim of the Social Impact Bond was to deliver a type of therapy that could prevent children from being taken away from their families and placed in residential care operated by the County Council. Such care was costly to the local authority and also frequently led to children experiencing further issues in education, crime and life opportunities. The Council and investors agreed that choosing an appropriate therapy should be evidence-based to ensure the viability of the scheme and to provide a basis for triggering payments to investors. The only approach that the parties agreed upon as providing a sufficiently compelling evidence base had been developed in the US; Multi-Systemic Therapy (MST).[19] MST Inc. could provide training for UK therapists to engage with children identified as at risk of going into care. A charity called Action for Children was awarded the Service Provider Agreement to manage the trained therapists in delivering MST through two teams of four therapists, a team manager and business administrator, dealing with four cases at a time on a rolling basis. MST would involve in-home or school therapy to try and get at the root of problems faced by the children. For children it would involve 60 hours of contact over four months.

---

[19] In a US MST intervention on those who committed sex crimes, 89% of participants who completed the study had 83% fewer arrests for sex crimes and 70% fewer arrests for other crimes in comparison to a control group. See: www.mstuk.org/evidence-outcomes and: www.ncbi.nlm.nih.gov/pubmed/19170451

The local authority as commissioner, investors, Action for Children as service provider working with MST Inc., and the new special purpose vehicle had to contractually agree on specific outcome measures. These would take the evidence base that MST routinely produced and retune it to the needs of a Social Impact Bond investment structure. Establishing the outcome measure was also one way that the parties to this Bond could give specific shape to the prescriptions of the national government Centre for Social Impact Bonds. One of the Centre's prescriptions was that the local political authority responsible for the Bond must project a cashable saving.[20] This is equivalent to the amount that would have been spent on an intervention that would now not be spent as a result of the Bond. Cashable savings could include lower staffing costs, for example; if children did not enter a home, fewer staff may be required. They could also include lower estates costs; fewer children in care might enable care homes to be closed. The cashable savings must then be of sufficient value that it could underwrite the investors' initial contribution, to cover repayments to investors. The savings must also be able to cover subsequent payments to investors on top of their initial investment (if targets were met and these needed to be paid) and usually a surplus that could in theory be banked by the local

---

[20] These are not the only criteria to fulfil. Others suggest Social Impact Bonds must satisfy five criteria: sufficiently high net benefits to allow both taxpayers and investors to come out ahead; measurable outcomes; well-defined treatment populations; credible impact assessments; and safeguards against harming the treatment population. See http://siblab.hks.harvard.edu/files/siblab/files/social-impact-bonds-lessons-learned.pdf?m=1419347692

authority. Cashable savings are in effect a business-as-usual counterfactual (see also Chapter 9). They set out a projection of what spending would have been incurred if no intervention was made.

However, within the UK government's approval mechanism, cashable savings cannot be the result that triggers payments to investors. Instead, the trigger-measure has to be something more immediate, which offers an indication of a future saving, such as the level of success of MST, rather than the closure of residential care homes. This separation of measures that trigger returns and savings that must be projected, but do not trigger payments, is designed to reassure investors. The separation is designed to encourage investors that their rate of return will be tied to the success or failure of the intervention funded, rather than its future savings that might be reduced or eliminated by other factors beyond the intervention, including changes in government policy or an increase in other areas of costs. The choice of therapy, the choice of outcome measure and the design and implementation of the Bond can thus be seen in relation to aspects of the investment-return relation: how much money will be put in, how much investors will receive as a return, with specific measures used to trigger returns. One key target was that over five years, 380 families should be taken through MST in 20 cohorts in order to try and prevent 110 children from going into care. The specific measurement that would tie this target to a successful outcome that indicated a potential cashable saving and trigger a payment to investors involved calculating "days of care averted". This required that a cost was attached to each day of care, monitoring those children who went through MST and did (and did not) enter care, then tracking those children over the lifetime of the Bond. Calculating how many children went into care set against the prevention target and calculating "days of care averted", were central to the contractual set-up of the Social Impact Bond – effectively tying together financial risks and returns.

The lengthy contract negotiation produced the following financial structure: £3.1 million would be provided by investors; Essex County Council projected a cashable saving of £17 million in total through a reduction in costs of children going into care, of which they would retain £10 million and pay out up to £7 million to investors; £120 was attached to each "day of care averted" as a payment to investors, and this figure was achieved by calculating the average cost of care (in the range of £20,000 to £180,000 per child per year, depending on the level of care required) and a distribution of savings that would enable Essex County Council to achieve its £10 million savings target and pay investors around an 8% to 12% annual return on investment. Unlike other Social Impact Bonds where payments could only be made after a number of years upon successful outcomes, the "days of care averted" calculation enabled payments to be "frontloaded", meaning that investors could start to see a return immediately. Further forms of measurement were derived through comparing the success of the MST-based intervention quarterly to a "control" group based on a business-as-usual counterfactual derived from historical data and the whole scheme would be evaluated by the Office of Public Management, an independent research organisation, focused on social outcomes.

The contract was thus an important site of negotiation for setting in place the terms of the market-based intervention, the impact to be achieved, how the impact would be measured and how returns to investors would be triggered. However, at this stage, these are investment–return relations on paper and in theory. To see how these relations played out, we need to get close to the action. We need to go to some well-heeled offices in London where investors make their decisions, some slightly shabby looking offices above a retail unit in Chelmsford where the local authority operate, return to central London to enter the Centre for Social Impact Bonds and we need to invite various intermediary experts to come and visit us as they don't seem to have fixed offices. It is among all these locations that investment–return relations take shape and take place.

Investment–Return Relations

The Essex Social Impact Bond for children at risk involved a number of investors, including a "high net worth" individual, Bridges Ventures (an investment fund specialising in social and impact investment) and Big Society Capital.[21] They each took part, along with the local authority, in contract negotiations that established the initial investment–return relation, the upfront costs to be paid by the investors, the level of return they could achieve, the outcome measure that would trigger repayments, the timing of repayment and the risks to which investors were exposed. Initially at least, the investment–return relation might appear high risk: investors might stand to lose all their upfront investment and miss out on any returns if an intervention did not succeed. However, this investment–return relation and its attendant risks were somewhat modified. Within the UK government Centre for Social Impact Bonds' approval mechanism, we noted that cashable savings could not be the outcome measure that triggered payments to investors.

----

[21] Both Bridges Ventures and Big Society Capital have been set up by Sir Ronald Cohen, the leading proponent of Social Impact Bonds and a member of the UK and then G8 Social Investment Taskforce whom we met earlier in this chapter.

Instead, the trigger-measure had to be something more immediate – in this case based on the "days of care averted" measure.
Risk was thus redistributed from government to investors, but
within structured terms designed to limit investors' exposure.

According to Liebman (2011) and Warner (2013), Social
Impact Bonds require this kind of structure to create conditions that might prove attractive to investors (in a similar manner to the preparation of bundles of student loans for sale, see
Chapter 7). The UK government has attempted to enhance
such conditions for investors through Social Investment Tax
Relief. Since April 2014 investors "can deduct 30% of their
investment from their income tax liability".[22] The distribution of
risks shifts again here. Although investors' capital might be at
stake in a Social Impact Bond, a proportion of that risk can be
deducted from tax liabilities that they would have paid anyway.
Adding in the possibility that investors can actively promote
their involvement in attempting to reduce recognised social
problems, what might initially appear a significant financial
risk could be recast as a tax offset, publicity opportunity and a
chance to make a return on investment.

The Essex Social Impact Bond for children at risk went
further. The investment return-relation became more attractive once it was agreed that "days of care averted" could act
as the measure of the success of the intervention and that this
could trigger payments to investors. This meant that as soon
as a child entered into MST, money could begin to accumulate
and returns to investors could be made. Rather than waiting
on a lengthy and uncertain outcome, as investors have had

---

[22] Up to £270,000 on investments up to £1 million in actions
and organisations qualified by HMRC pre-assurance schemes.
See HMRC (2016).

to do in other Social Impact Bonds, in Essex the returns were quite immediate. Also, frontloading the payments from the moment when a child entered into therapy ensured the investors received a partial return immediately, regardless of longer-term future outcomes. The investors could even use returns received in the first phase of the intervention to cover the costs of their investment in later phases, introducing a kind of real-time recycling of funds that reduced the total amount of money the investors were required to find.

This set up seemed to introduce two issues with regard to the nature of the investment–return relation. First, there were in this Bond a number of what one interviewee termed *perverse incentives*:

One of the great perverse incentives in a thing like – Essex was a very good example of it, but it happens in all Payment by Results things. We want to make sure the children who should go into care do go into care, not that they're kept out of it because then they [the investors] get a payment. (Interviewee 7, philanthro-capitalist)

In place of a high level of financial risk to investors came financial security for investors created through a "perverse incentive" that might rank the need to give investors a guaranteed return ahead of assessments of the appropriateness of keeping children out of residential care. Indeed the interests, concerns and voice of the children involved and their families appeared entirely silent throughout this research.

Second, this reduction of risk for investors seemed to lead to a shift in financial risks onto the local authority. In place of the social investment market seeking returns through high risks, came the threat of the local authority having to cover the costs of the intervention through frontloaded payments to investors. This concern became particularly acute as frontline workers in children's services noted that MST was only suitable as an intervention for a fixed number of children:

One of the things we've found with MST there are a number of exclusions with MST ... for example young people on the autism spectrum are excluded from it. ... it actually isn't an intervention designed for crisis edge of care work [if you had an urgent problem] MST can't deliver that. (Interviewee 1, local authority)

As a result, Essex County Council faced what a former UK Treasury advisor called "a double-spend" problem: having to maintain children's services for cases where MST was not suitable or failed, and having to make frontloaded payments to investors. Cashable savings were thus drastically reduced (as all children's homes and staffing had to be maintained) at the same time as the costs of the Social Impact Bond remained steady (with frontloaded payments to investors steadily accumulating). Maintaining the idea that days of care averted were equivalent to a cashable saving also depended on various assumptions being held in place. For example, if a child did not enter care, their housing, food and clothing might remain the responsibility of their family (resulting in one type of saving), but to save on the estates costs of residential care would require that sufficiently high numbers of children were kept out of care to reduce staffing levels in care homes or even close care homes. To account for a third type of saving – the costs involved if children went into care and then followed a predicted transition from problematic (and costly) childhood to problematic (and costly) adulthood – would have required monitoring well beyond the life of the Social Impact Bond.

One outcome of this activity is that even advocates of Social Impact Bonds who took part in this research were cautious in noting the forms of efficiency and effectiveness that

Bonds might introduce. For example, the Centre for Social
Impact Bonds suggested cashable savings remain a "question
to answer" and an investment "facilitator" suggested that for
the local authority most savings were actually quite "theoretical". Drawing these issues together, it seems that the intervention in Essex raised significant questions of efficiency and
effectiveness that were inseparable from the form given to the
investment–return relation by the contract structure, its negotiation and enactment. It is in the very nature of the contract,
its negotiation and fulfilment that concerns arise for many of
the participants that are given voice (the council management
and social workers) or are side-lined for those not given voice
(the children).

Providence

One means to organise a reflection on the concerns raised
by this market-based intervention is provided by the notion
of providence. The Oxford Concise English Dictionary
(1999: 1151) defines *providence* as "timely preparation for
the future". In this sense, a provident investment would be
one through which a future has been well prepared (also see
Chapter 9 for more on futures). Among the participants in the
Essex County Council Social Impact Bond, the ability to confidently establish a future through which the investment–return
relation could be envisaged and brought into being seemed to
be unevenly distributed. In particular, the Bond appeared to
bring together parties into the same space with differential calculative agency (Callon and Muniesa, 2005). This uneven distribution of capacities to calculate, seemed to result in certain
parties (such as the investors) being able to forecast and enact
their preferred future with certainty. Meanwhile, for other parties (such as the local authority), their ability to calculate the

future with any certainty or come close to enacting the future they initially anticipated, retrospectively certainly seems to have been limited, meaning their projections of, for example, cashable savings, were later opened to question as the Social Impact Bond began operating. The investment was only provident for some parties.

We can see this calculative asymmetry and differential confidence in projecting and enacting future effects in quite straightforward ways. MST was not cost-free. In the US, the marginal cost of using MST was $4,246 (approximately equivalent to £3,418).[23] Investors knew their fixed costs. Yet returns, which formed the principal cost for the local authority, were less fixed, being based on "days of care averted" – the more days averted, the higher the cost for the local authority. At the same time, the local authority had to cover further costs, including, for example, a high turnover of staff during the intervention leading to extra recruitment and training costs. These extra costs to be met by the local authority had not been foreseen. Although it is unclear to what extent an uneven distribution of calculative agency meant that one party (the investors) could foresee potential general categories of costs (such as staff training) and contractually avoid them while another party (the local authority) did not foresee such costs and was stuck with them, the contract certainly instituted these terms. The contract effectively ensured that the provident terms sought by the investors would be enacted as the costs for investors were fixed. At the same time, the provident terms anticipated by the

---

[23] Marginal cost here is the cost of treating one more person, which might be slightly higher than the average cost, but still provides a reasonable reflection of its expense. This evidence was used to justify the selection of MST in the UK.

local authority through cashable savings were not fixed, were separated from the returns paid to investors by the rules established through the Centre for Social Impact Bonds and their costs were increased as they became responsible for unanticipated matters.

These calculative difficulties seemed to pervade the intervention. The initial decision from the local authority to enter into a Social Impact Bond in order to bring extra finance into edge of care services was part of a package of measures to try and improve service delivery following an "inadequate" assessment from the government inspector OFSTED.[24] However, by the time the Bond had started to offer MST to children, the service had improved significantly and this was recognised by OFSTED. Essex Children's Service had been placing large numbers of children in care as a risk-averse, safety-first measure in the immediate aftermath of receiving their initial inadequate assessment. However, in the time it took to set up the Social Impact Bond much had changed (including investing in more and better-trained staff) and that made it difficult to attribute a definitive effect to the MST-based intervention. The business-as-usual counterfactual based on historical data, depended on a "business" (sending large numbers of children into residential care) that was no longer "usual" (as the form and practice of intervening in children at-risk had changed). For the local authority, other interventions that they had already put in

---

[24] OFSTED is the government inspector, assessor and regulator of schools in the UK and children's services. OFSTED assessments of schools provide league tables of best and worst performing schools. A good performance impacts on student recruitment, teacher recruitment and even the local housing market (as parents seek to move into an area wherein their child will be eligible to enter the school).

place could be just as likely to lead to a decline in the residential care population. In this way, the local authority seemed to be stuck with a set of Bond-related costs and without the kinds of benefits they had anticipated or without an ability to clearly collate evidence that attributed a benefit to the Bond rather than to other actions. Meanwhile, the investors seemed to face costs and receive returns directly in line with their forecasts. The uneven distribution of ability to accomplish providence was quite stark: the future anticipated by investors was contractually assured while the future prepared by the local authority continually slipped from their grasp.

According to those tasked with delivering children's services, these problems stemmed from frontline staff being excluded from contract negotiations.

There is a disconnect between the strategic needs and the operational needs of the county council. They [central managers who took part in the negotiation] don't understand [edge of care needs], just as I don't understand many of the nuances of their practices. They assumed that edge of care evidence [provided by MST] was fine. It doesn't do that, it can't do that ... So they can make assumptions that an ordinary person would make – "you just refer someone to MST" – but no you can't. (Interviewee 1, local authority)

Calculative asymmetries between investors and the local authority in contract negotiations could partly be explained by this absence of frontline workers, with county council managers assuming that MST was well-suited to all children at risk. The investors were happy to see the contract built around MST as it enabled them to clearly project their costs (the level of investment based on costs of MST and the likely number of children that would go through MST) and their return (based on frontloaded payments of days of care averted that accumulated as soon as children entered MST). Perhaps it is more accurate to say that the future did not slip from the grasp of the local authority but instead that providence was always out of reach from the contract negotiation onwards.

However, given that the parties in the Bond recognised the double-spend problem encouraged by perverse incentives and the narrow effectiveness of MST, a switch should be feasible to place children in a different, more suitable intervention. And indeed once the Social Impact Bond was up and running, an initial response from those delivering services to children at risk was to not refer children to MST, eliminating half of the double-spend. Instead, those on the frontline sought to take advantage of the money that had already been spent on equipping children's services following their inadequate assessment by OFSTED and place children on alternative pathways of intervention. If it had continued, this position may have shifted significantly the investment–return relation (and its costs to the local authority) as fewer "days of care averted" would have been amassed. MST may have been reduced in scope to a specialist option for a small number of children, the providence of this smaller investment more or less guaranteed by ensuring its relevance to this smaller cohort of children.

Yet not sending children through MST led to antagonism in meetings of the special purpose vehicle set up for the Bond, between children's services, local authority managers and the investors keen to start building up frontloaded payments. This resulted in a reversion to sending higher numbers of participants into MST in order to meet targets for the number of children that would go through therapy during the life of the Bond. Meeting these targets meant the investment–return relation remained secure for the investors: the costs for each child remained fixed and returns began to build up for each child in a predictable manner as soon as they entered into MST, regardless of the therapeutic outcome. Perverse incentives and an uneven distribution of providence became a contractual obligation. But this is not a form of contractual determinism; the investors' provident position was not achieved through the contractual obligations simply and singularly accomplishing their own effects. Instead, the existence of the special purpose vehicle, investors' presence and the pressure they put on the commissioners to meet agreed targets were all required in order for the obligations to be enacted and for the investors' position to be provident, to plan for and enact the prepared future.

As a result, Essex County Council's frontline delivery team made a mostly negative assessment of costs and savings:

Would Essex County Council look at this intervention and say this is saving us money? It probably wouldn't at the moment. It would probably not do that. At the moment it would probably say "would we buy MST if the SIB was not here?" which is the key question, is it that important? – and the answer is probably not. (Interviewee 1, local authority)

Conclusion

In the Essex County Council Social Impact Bond for children at risk, of 60 families that went through MST initially, 20% (12) disengaged and 10% (six) of children still went into care. The children of the remaining families did not go into care where there had been a risk this would happen. It should be noted, then, that despite the range of concerns raised regarding Social Impact Bonds, in this instance there were children who were not taken from their families and placed in care when this had been expected.

What can we say about the investment–return relation? It seems that the Social Impact Bond is only a Bond in name and promotes no tradable element. It is not an investment that can be easily capitalised (Muniesa et al., 2017) as it cannot be cashed in a Bond market. Although in its very first public outing as a Social Policy Bond, it was envisaged that there would be a market for such Bonds through which investors would be able to cash their positions, this has never emerged. Partly this is because investors form part of, and lend expertise to, special purpose vehicles (along with commissioners) to oversee interventions. To cash in their investment position would require a change in the membership of the intervention and the kind and quality of expertise on offer. Furthermore, as policies, Social Impact Bonds were given stimulus and a practical shape during 2008–09, emerging through austerity government and as a response to the financial crisis. As investors were still being publicly chastised at this time for lending without responsibility and then cashing their investment positions, possibly causing the crisis, it may have been difficult for the nominally left-of-centre Labour Party to gain sufficient support for a new market for social problems within which investors might similarly be given an opportunity to shed their responsibilities. As a result, there is in effect no liquidity for investors in these Bonds in the sense that an investment position cannot be cashed.

Furthermore, the risks involved in the investment–return relation are certainly modified by the availability of social investment tax relief, the outcome measure with its partial dislocation from cost savings, and the frontloaded payments to investors. The asymmetrical distribution of calculative abilities also seems to suggest that rather than facing investment risk, potential future problems for investors are recognised during the contract negotiations and protections against these risks are built into the contract. In the absence of risk, there is no need to discount future earnings (Doganova and Muniesa, 2015). While both parties (the investors and commissioners) anticipate very specific futures (returns on investment and cashable savings respectively), only the investors seem able to prepare and enact a provident future.

The Social Impact Bond hence seems to provide an example of what Bear terms: "the hidden rentier regimes through which political and economic influence is maintained by the tiered brokering of access to resources" (2013: 394). However, reversing the conventional logic of a rentier state that enables external parties to pay rent to access public resources, the rentier in Social Impact Bonds is the investor. The contract negotiation operates as the basis for investors to take part in solving social problems and as a form of brokerage, deciding who will take up what position on costs and risks within a tax and incentive structure that seems to lean heavily towards the investors. The latter are paid rent by the commissioner to access their resources, with the rent drawn from tax income.[25] In this way the central components of the investment market (liquidity, discounted cash flows and risk) seem to be rendered irrelevant by the protections for investors built into the contract. In a similar manner to trade and exchange in Chapter 2 and competition in Chapter 3, once up and running, the market sensibility at the heart of this intervention – investment and return – seemed to slip from view.

If the aim of the investment–return relation is to introduce an effective and efficient means of intervening in a public problem, the Social Impact Bond for children at risk seems to be only partially effective (it suited certain children in certain circumstances) and not very efficient (it did not allow the County

---

[25] There is not the space here to say more about rent and this is not primarily a chapter about rentier-ship, but for more on rent, see McGoey (2017).

Council to make the kinds of cashable savings they projected or that would be apparent if, for example, they could close residential care units). At the same time, the Bond seemed to enable investors to avoid most forms of risk associated with conventional forms of investment. It shifted these risks onto the local authority, through the double-spend problem, and eventually to the children, through perverse incentives that encouraged their entry into therapy that would only ever be suitable for a proportion of the population entered.

Although Warner (2013) might be correct in her assertion that Social Impact Bonds rely on a rigid model of contracting that might have problematic consequences, it seems too straightforward to refer to Social Impact Bonds as a new asset class (Chiapello, 2015). The extent to which they are asset-like and the investment–return relations on which they depend are precisely the matter that needs investigation. Further issues raised regarding the complexities of who faces what cost and how much of this cost might ever be saved through these interventions (Dowling and Harvie, 2014; Bryan and Rafferty, 2014; Mitropoulos and Bryan, 2015) can then be addressed through studying the investment–return relation. To stay within the language of investment and return, rather than assume these investments are provident, we have instead explored how providence is brought into being and for whom.

In contrast to the significant scale of the EU ETS, REF and GDPR, the Social Impact Bond we have studied is a relatively local matter. Yet its importance lies in its potential to act as an exemplar for others to follow (see Chapter 8): it provides a future-oriented beacon of how investment and return relations might be utilised to manage a market-based intervention. Through this chapter's focus on Bonds, we have now seen calculative devices put to different use (in securing favourable and less favourable contractual positions), relations mediated in different ways (via national government guidance, through a special purpose vehicle and via the contract) and further new practices emerging (with local authorities now having to become expert in contract negotiations and new forms of investment). What remains clear is that things are at stake in this intervention. Following the environment in Chapter 2, the future of higher education in Chapter 3, and privacy in Chapter 4, we now see at-risk children, with all their attendant vulnerabilities, subject to market sensibilities. Although we continue to move between general and particular, from the political infrastructure to the practices of individuals, it is important that we do not lose this sense that matters are at stake. In the next chapter we will turn attention to an Advance Market Commitment and the market sensibility of incentives. But we will also retain a concern for those intervened upon, which in the next chapter will comprise populations of low-income countries, their health problems and their need to access vaccines.

References

Barman, E. (2015) Of principle and principal: Value plurality in the market of impact investing. *Valuation Studies* 3(1): 9–44.

Bear, L. (2013) The antinomies of audit: Opacity, instability and charisma in the economic governance of a Hooghly shipyard. *Economy and Society* 42(3): 375–97.

Birch, K. (2017) Rethinking value in the bio-economy: Finance, assetization, and the management of value. *Science, Technology and Human Values* 42(3): 460–90.

Bryan, D. and Rafferty, M. (2014) Financial derivatives as social policy beyond crisis. Sociology 48(5): 887–903.

Callon, M. (1986) Some elements of a sociology of translation. In J. Law (ed.), *Power, Action and Belief: A New Sociology of Knowledge?* London: Routledge, pp. 196–223.

Callon, M., Lascoumes, P. and Barthe, Y. (2009) *Acting in an Uncertain World: An Essay on Technical Democracy*. Boston: MIT Press.

Callon, M. and Muniesa, F. (2005) Economic markets as calculative collective devices. *Organisation Studies* 26(8): 1229–50.

Chiapello, E. (2015) Financialisation of valuation. *Human Studies* 38: 13–35.

Cooper, C., Graham, C. and Himick, D. (2014) *Social Impact Bonds: Can Private Finance Rescue Public Programmes?* Available at: https://strathprints.strath.ac.uk/45845/ (last accessed 3 April 2019).

Doganova, L. and Muniesa, F. (2015) Capitalization devices: Business models and the renewal of markets, in M. Knornberger, L. Justesen, A. Madsen and J. Mouritsen (eds.), *Making Things Valuable*. Oxford: Oxford University Press, pp. 109–25.

Dowling, E. and Harvie, D. (2014) Harnessing the social: State, crisis and (big) society. *Sociology* 48(5): 869–86.

Fox, C. and Albertson, K. (2011) Payment by results and Social Impact Bonds in the criminal justice sector: New challenges for the concept of evidence-based policy? *Criminology & Criminal Justice* 11(5): 395–413.

HMRC (2016) *Social Investment Tax Relief Factsheet*. Available at: www.gov.uk/government/publications/social-investment-tax-relief-factsheet/social-investment-tax-relief (last accessed 3 April 2019).

Liebman, J. (2011) *Social Impact Bonds*. Available at: www.americanprogress.org/issues/general/report/2011/02/09/9050/social-impact-bonds/ (last accessed 3 April 2019).

Lottery Fund (2014) *Commissioning Better Outcomes and Social Outcomes Fund*. Available at: www.biglotteryfund.org.uk/global-content/programmes/england/commissioning-better-outcomes-and-social-outcomes-fund (last accessed 3 April 2019).

McGoey, L. (2017) The elusive rentier rich: Piketty's data battles and the power of absent evidence. *Science, Technology and Human Values* 42(2): 257–79.

Mitropoulos, A. and Bryan, D. (2015) Social benefit bonds: Financial markets inside the state. In G. Meagher and S. Goodwin (eds.),

Markets, Rights and Power in Australian Social Policy. Sydney: Sydney University Press, pp. 153–68.

Mulgen, G., Reeder, N., Aylott, M. and Bo'sher, L. (2011) *The Opportunity and Challenge of Social Impact Bonds*. Available at: http://youngfoundation.org/publications/social-impact-investment-the-opportunity-and-challenge-of-social-impact-bonds/ (last accessed 3 April 2019).

Muniesa, F., Doganova, L., Ortiz, H., Pina-Stranger, Á., Paterson, F., Bourgoin, A., Ehrenstein, V., Juven, P.-A., Pontille, D., Saraç-Lesavre, B. and Yon, G. (2017) *Capitalization: A Cultural Guide*. Paris: Presses de Mines.

OECD (2015) *Social Impact Investment: Building the Evidence Base*. Available at: www.oecd.org/sti/ind/social-impact-investment.htm (last accessed 3 April 2019).

Oxfam (2013) *Development Impact Bonds and Impact Investing: Genuine Impact or Snake Oil?* Available at: https://oxfamblogs.org/fp2p/development-impact-bonds-and-impact-investing-genuine-impact-or-snake-oil/ (last accessed 3 April 2019).

Oxford Concise English Dictionary (1999) Oxford: Oxford University Press.

PIRU (2015) *An Evaluation of Social Impact Bonds in Health and Social Care*. Available at: www.piru.ac.uk/assets/files/Trailblazer%20SIBs%20interim%20report%20March%202015,%20for%20publication%20on%20PIRU%20siteapril%20amendedpdf11may.pdf (last accessed 3 April 2019).

Roitman, J. (2014) *Anti-Crisis*. London: Duke University Press.

Schram, S. (2014) The appeal and limitations of Social Impact Bonds. *Scholars Strategy Network*. Available at: www.scholarsstrategynetwork.org/brief/appeal-and-limitations-social-impact-bonds (last accessed 3 April 2019).

Silver, D. and Clarke, B. (2014) *Social Impact Bonds: Profiting from Poverty?* Available at: www.the-sarf.org.uk/social-impact-bonds/ (last accessed 3 April 2019).

Warner, M. (2013) Private finance for public goods. *Journal of Economic Policy Reform* 16(4): 300–19.

6

Incentive

Opening

Following on from our consideration of trade and exchange, competition, property and ownership, and investment and return, in this chapter we will focus on the provision of incentives. We will explore how this market sensibility is given form through an intervention – an Advance Market Commitment – designed to address international inequalities in access to healthcare, in particular vaccines. In previous chapters we have come across incentives on a number of occasions; for example, when we suggested that the EU ETS seemed to fail to provide incentives for industrial investment in low-carbon production processes (Chapter 2) or when we questioned the incentivising implications of impact case studies in the REF (Chapter 3). Here we will explore the practices, relations and devices through which incentives are given effect.

By analysing the development of a market-based intervention designed to stimulate the supply of vaccines to populations of low-income countries, we will also have the opportunity to move once again between the general and the particular. We will capture something of the general aspects of anticipatory futures that are imagined through incentives and the broad contours of global health. At the same time, we will also attend to the particular challenges of developing pneumococcal vaccines and the requirements that emerge from the need to deal with the demands of various political administrations and the idiosyncrasies of two large pharmaceutical firms. This will further develop our picture of market-based interventions into public problems by providing a different kind of focus on regulation. Whereas we have seen rather coercive modes of regulation (for example, the EU ETS and GDPR), incentives seem predicated on intervention at arm's length. This market sensibility anticipates a regulatory form wherein political actors set a goal and try to induce market participants to respond. In theory the direct involvement of the former with the latter is not required. As we will see, in practice, this regulatory distance does not materialise in any straightforward manner.

In order to make sense of the incentive and its role in the Advance Market Commitment we need to know something of public health: the improvement of the physical and mental well-being of populations. This has become a major expenditure for international cooperation and the transfer of financial and technical resources from wealthy economies to countries with a low GDP per capita. It is estimated that overseas aid spending on health increased from a total of $7.2 billion in 1990, to $11.7 billion in 2000, to $36.4 billion in 2015 (Dieleman et al., 2016), a trend discussed at length within the social sciences. Scholars have noted its simultaneous emergence with global public–private health partnerships supported by substantial funding from philanthropic donors, in particular the Bill & Melinda Gates Foundation (Birn, 2009).[1] These partnerships are expected to operate more efficiently

---

[1] In the first half of the twentieth century, philanthropic organisations, such as the Rockefeller Foundation, were already active in international health initiatives but the amount of funding currently provided by the Gates Foundation

than the heavy bureaucratic apparatus of the World Health Organization (WHO). In order to do so, they often integrate some form of corporate management and metrics to assess the value for money of their activity and justify their expenditure (Adams, 2016; Reubi, 2018). Global health partnerships also aim to engage more closely with the pharmaceutical industry, yet without infringing on their proprietary claims (McGoey, Reiss and Wahlberg, 2011). As we will see throughout this chapter, the relationship fostered with private-sector companies is one of economic inducement rather than coercive regulation, hence our focus on incentives. Our objective will be to examine what it means in practice to provide incentives, what problem(s) is targeted through such a market sensibility, and what consequences follow.

Displaying a shared humanitarian ideal, according to which all humans across the globe ought to have access to healthcare (see Lakoff, 2010), global health partnerships can take different forms. In this chapter, we will explore how a market-based intervention, referred to as the pilot Advance Market Commitment (hereafter AMC) for pneumococcal vaccines, has been implemented by one of the pioneer global health partnerships called the GAVI Alliance. Both the AMC and GAVI came into existence around 2000 in response to problems experienced in low-income settings where mortality and morbidity rates were high and suitable vaccines were not available. The problem was framed in market terms as low-income countries and their populations were suffering from an absence of adequate purchasing power and an inability to satisfy the commercial interests of pharmaceutical companies.

---

and the policy influence it seems to exert is incomparable (McGoey, 2015).

Trying to provide these companies with the right incentives, as we will see, was then presented as the solution.

In what follows, we will show how the AMC aimed to give the pharmaceutical industry an incentive to produce large volumes of pneumococcal vaccines, agree on a pricing structure fixed in advance and enter long-term supply agreements, in order to reduce the vaccine's price and make it quickly available to poor populations in great need. The Geneva-based secretariat of GAVI and the international collective of civil servants, economists, lawyers, epidemiologists and business experts who we have met in studying the AMC dedicated a great deal of work to enacting the market sensibility in focus here; that is, the provision of an incentive. What this work entailed, including financial diplomacy, risk, compromise and product shortages, will be examined in this chapter.

Incentives to Address International Health Inequalities

As a preventative measure, the use of vaccines to secure healthy national populations is the epitome of governmental action (see Foucault, 2007). Historically, in Europe and the United States, the development and production of vaccines were entangled with state (e.g., military) action, and involved a mix of public institutions and local private manufacturers (Blume, 2017). Now, however, vaccine production is mainly in the hands of a few multinational companies, while vaccine development tends to occur within start-ups financed through venture capital. A gradual "privatisation" of vaccine development and production has taken place from the 1980s onwards with the rise of academic research on biotechnologies and the introduction of stronger protection for proprietary claims allowing for the commercialisation of the outcomes of this research (Blume and Geesink, 2000). Privatisation was also further fostered by increasing costs associated with the clinical testing and large-scale manufacturing of what have become highly regulated and standardised products.[2] The time of publicly funded clinical research and state-run production has come to an end, with vaccines being treated as technological innovations with market prospects.[3] One result has been that when, in the 1980s, pharmaceutical companies developed new vaccines, against the Hepatitis b virus notably, the envisioned markets were North America and Europe, with prices set accordingly high (Huzair and Sturdy, 2017). It took nearly 20 years for these vaccines to become affordable and then used to protect populations in poorer parts of the world where the disease burden (liver and respiratory diseases respectively) was much higher.[4]

However, the systematic vaccination of infants against a series of pathogens has received international support since the mid-1970s. The WHO and the United Nations Children's Fund (UNICEF) were channelling funds towards child

---

[2] In contrast to the neoliberal advocacy of deregulation in the pharmaceutical industry (Nik-Khah, 2014; see Chapter 1).

[3] Only a few public institutions are still manufacturing vaccines, for example the Butantan Institute in Brazil. In Europe, the Netherlands Vaccine Institute, which used to produce vaccines for the Dutch population and played a major role in developing a new polio vaccine (Blume, 2005), was put on sale in 2009 and sold to the private sector three years later (Blume, 2017).

[4] A similar delay was witnessed for the vaccine against the flu virus Haemophilus influenza type b also licensed in the 1980s (Greenwood, 2014).

immunisation programmes in countries with low GDP per capita. Vaccination coverage in poorer regions was increasing and this was celebrated in the overseas aid milieu (Hardon and Blume, 2005; Roalkvam, McNeill and Blume, 2013). UNICEF acted as the main procurement agency of this international effort. It had regularly been issuing tenders through a competitive system that proportionally awarded supply contracts to the lowest bidders.[5] The vaccines requested and offered were rather old technologies, such as the oral polio vaccine. They had become fairly cheap as companies were willing to sell them at their production cost, around a few cents a dose, to use up their excess capacity. Immunisation was consistently praised for its cost-effectiveness. Relying on public resources (overseas aid and government budgets) to finance this health measure remained unquestioned even when international organisations advocated for pro-market reforms and a reduction of public debt (World Bank, 1993). Nevertheless, in the early 1990s, the amount of overseas aid directed towards immunisation decreased, vaccination coverage stagnated and UNICEF did not purchase the new, more costly vaccines marketed in wealthy countries (Mitchell, Philipose and Sanford, 1993).

This situation, characterised by international inequalities in access to vaccines resulting from a lack of public resources and high prices, triggered endless discussion. In Geneva and beyond (particularly in the United States) discussions involved health experts and policy-makers within international organisations and think tanks (Hardon and Blume, 2005; Muraskin,

---

[5] The rule was in principle to award the lowest bidder with two-thirds of the total requested volume and then to award the successive bidders with a third of the remaining demand (Mitchell, Philipose and Sanford, 1993).

1996). From the accounts available, one gets the sense of a general "skepticism about market solutions to immunization", where market solutions were understood as letting the private sector make "decisions about vaccine research, development, production, and distribution" (Freeman and Robbins, 1991). This scepticism called for a stronger role for "public institutions" which could "offer well-structured plans incorporating industry and market forces" (Freeman and Robbins, 1991). Task forces were established, conferences organised, reports written, all with little tangible effect before the creation in 1999 of the Global Alliance for Vaccines and Immunization (Roalkvam et al., 2013). GAVI was set up by a well-acquainted group of people working for the WHO, UNICEF, the World Bank, the International Federation of Pharmaceutical Manufacturers & Associations and the Rockefeller Foundation (which had been involved in campaigning for immunisation since the mid-1980s). Thanks to a five-year $750 million grant from the Gates Foundation (swiftly complemented by pledges from national governments such as the UK, Norway and the United States), GAVI could establish itself. This financial influx was instrumental. It enabled the procurement of large quantities of vaccines, whereas previous attempts to address vaccine supply had been deprived of such a purchasing capacity.[6]

GAVI was meant to be a partnership to coordinate the financing of immunisation and improve access to old and new

---

[6] The organisations (and even the individuals) at the origin of the creation of the Global Alliance for Vaccines and Immunization, which then became the GAVI Alliance, had established in the early 1990s the Children's Vaccine Initiative, which was supposed to draw attention and resources towards vaccines.

vaccines in low-income countries. Its organisational structure was, at first, rather minimal. It was composed of a non-profit association in the United States managing the money, a small secretariat located within UNICEF's building in Geneva and a decision-making board with a diverse membership. This included representatives from the founding partners (WHO, UNICEF, World Bank and Gates Foundation), donor and beneficiary governments and the pharmaceutical industry.[7] While UNICEF continued to operate as a procurement agency – issuing tenders, signing purchase contracts with vaccine manufacturers and overseeing the logistics of exchange and delivery – GAVI soon became its main financier, focused on raising and pooling overseas aid for vaccines.

In the early years, this financial activity made it possible to introduce in low-income countries the now not-so-new Hepatitis b and Haemophilus influenza vaccines. But GAVI was expected to also act on vaccine prices, and its achievements in this respect were, at first, rather disappointing. The vaccines cited above had become affordable because companies were selling them at cost price and new manufacturers from so-called emerging economies (e.g., India) had entered the market. The creation of GAVI played no role in this process and the secretariat of the partnership started thinking that its "model" of action was too simplistic.

[The assumption was that] if you had a large amount of money that is spent on something and you pull demand, then price would drop, pretty clear neo-Keynesian curves of supply and demand [...]. But I think what they [at GAVI] realized is that they neglected the complexities of vaccine production and what are the incentives needed to reduce cost. (Interview, former GAVI staff member 1)

---

[7] Plus civil society organisations and research institutions.

The consultants tasked with evaluating the partnership's first five years of existence arrived at a similar conclusion (Chee, Molldren, His and Chankova, 2008). However, at the same time as this diagnosis was made, a significant change in how vaccine prices were approached by overseas aid donors and GAVI was already emerging in the form of an innovative purchase mechanism: a pilot AMC for vaccines. The AMC was developed to help procure and distribute second-generation pneumococcal conjugate vaccines manufactured by the multinational companies Wyeth (acquired by Pfizer in 2009) and GlaxoSmithKline (GSK). This vaccine represented a major achievement in vaccine production in the 2000s. The bacterium pneumococcus was a major cause of respiratory diseases across the world, while efficacious vaccines proved hard to manufacture given the existence of multiple bacterial strains, sufficient number of which had to be covered in order to have a significant impact. A first-generation pneumococcal vaccine offering protection against a limited number of pneumococcal strains had been marketed in the United States in 2000 and sold at more than $50 a dose (at least three doses were needed to ensure protection). Second-generation products were designed to provide wider protection and their price was expected to be even higher. Yet, as soon as they were licensed in North America and Europe in 2010, these new vaccines were almost simultaneously bought by GAVI at a comparatively low price ($3.5 a dose) and introduced into the immunisation programmes of countries such as Nicaragua and Kenya. And this was said to be thanks to the AMC.

The AMC took place among a succession of international actions that gradually concretised a market-oriented conception of what the problem was with new vaccines. It can be summarised as follows. The pharmaceutical industry holding the means of vaccine production has *a priori* no economically sound reason to consider the needs of poor populations in countries with strained governmental budgets. These needs do not appear sufficiently solvent to bear the cost of novel, expensive products and ensure companies will receive the return on investment they can obtain from wealthier populations and states. Hence, new vaccines tend to remain unavailable until firms agree to sell excess production at a low or cost price. In response to this state of affairs, GAVI and the AMC remobilised donors and international organisations in order to make them take a much more active role in the market transactions through which vaccines are bought. This more active role did not translate into renationalising vaccine production or abandoning patents and private ownership. Rather, the idea was to "make the market", to borrow the words of commodity traders reported in Çalışkan (2010).[8] This meant obtaining transaction terms (price, volume and payment conditions) attuned to the interests of poor populations.

Before turning to the specifics of the AMC for pneumococcal vaccines, let us pause for a moment and examine the notion of incentive at work here more closely. The notion is both a formalised economic concept and a word commonly used in policy (for example, when the European power lobby says that the EU ETS does not provide incentives to invest in clean production processes, see Chapter 2). Talking of incentives is a way of making sense of economic behaviours and of devising deliberate interventions designed to act on these behaviours (Dix, 2016). These interventions usually aim to encourage someone to follow a certain path in order to change a problematic situation. The problem itself is partly transformed: the central focus is now on a lack of incentives to do the right thing or the

---

[8] GAVI secretariat now actually talks about "shaping markets".

existence of incentives to do the wrong thing. The idea then is to create an alignment of potentially divergent interests oriented towards an objective, set unilaterally. Monetary rewards ought to have this motivational effect and help in achieving the desired effect if they are distributed according to carefully conceived conditions. It is anticipated by regulators that incentives intervene on behaviour without the requirement for a direct form of regulation. Those incentivised will choose to act in the ways they deem appropriate in order to meet the incentive. In contrast to several of our preceding examples where we explored interventions that entailed legislative obligations (the EU ETS, REF and GDPR), focusing on incentives provides an opportunity to look more closely at the challenges involved in inducing rather than coercing behaviour.

Incentives are thus mapped out and designed, and legal tools can be employed to translate these economic expectations into measurable codes of conduct. In the case we are interested in here, the AMC, the legal form is a conditional purchase guarantee setting a specific pricing mechanism expected to incentivise the supply of a new vaccine. To better understand what it means to provide incentives, we need to examine the legal work through which the terms of the guarantee were formulated. We also need to consider the theoretical formalisation, the political mobilisation and the evidential actions that went into preparing for and enforcing the agreement in order to accomplish the expected incentivising effect.

From Economics to Financial Diplomacy

The idea of an AMC for vaccines, which, like emissions trading, originated within academic economics, was not initially supposed to be a response to the lack of access in poor regions of the world to the pharmaceutical industry's latest (and too expensive) vaccines. Rather, the market-based intervention had been conceptualised to stimulate biomedical research and radical innovation. Tracing how this shift from incentivising innovation to incentivising cheap supply occurred will prove useful to get a sense of the political constraints imposed on the market-based intervention.

In the documentation of the AMC for pneumococcal vaccines and according to our interviewees, the market-based intervention can be traced back to the academic work carried out in the late 1990s by Michael Kremer, a development economist at MIT (before joining Harvard University). His initial idea was that of vaccine purchase commitments to encourage innovation. A response to "failures in the market for vaccine research" (Kremer, 2000: 11), purchase commitments would be able to "create incentives for vaccine research and help ensure that if vaccines were developed, poor countries could afford them" (1). The diseases Kremer had in mind were malaria, tuberculosis and HIV and his economic reasoning around the market sensibility of incentive was as follows: although a vaccine against malaria (the main example in Kremer's work) would be particularly cost-effective, as it would prevent a widespread, chronic disease and save on treatment expenditure, companies have little incentive to invest in research and development. This is not only due to the apparent lack of purchasing power of the populations most affected, but also because "governments are often tempted to use their powers as regulators and large purchasers to hold down vaccine prices after firms have sunk their research investments and developed a vaccine" (16). Health administrations and overseas aid donors would announce they will buy the vaccine but, once the product is available, they might have changed their minds, given priority to other expenditure and require very low prices. Promises made by public authorities to spend money

in a distant future are considered unreliable and, in anticipation of this "time inconsistency" (16), companies "invest less
in research than they otherwise would" (17). The core idea of
a purchase commitment is that "sponsors" (e.g., governmental
donors) commit to purchase a malaria vaccine in advance of
its development and marketing by private firms, and are then
bound to honour the commitment when the vaccine becomes
available. Time consistency (rather than inconsistency) is
assured and provides an incentive for action.

In light of policy discussions in the 1990s, Kremer's understanding of why donors and UNICEF used to buy vaccines at a
few cents a dose exaggerates the existence of strategic behaviour. Low prices, it seems, resulted from companies selling
excess production after returns and profits had been secured,
rather than from coercive actions taken by public authorities
(Mitchell et al., 1993). Valid or not, the economist's diagnosis
of the situation nevertheless had enduring effects as it prepared the ground for an AMC. In particular, the notion of time
inconsistency (decision-makers changing their preferences
over time) assumed the existence of a certain political volatility
that a legally binding commitment would constrain by forcing
donors to live up to their promises.

The economistic reasoning formalised all behaviour as a
matter of incentive, from donors' actions to the motivation for
doing research. Indeed, given their objective to stimulate biomedical innovation, purchase commitments were expected to
also act on the behaviour of scientists and "pull" innovation
instead of "pushing" it as with research grants. For the economist, under public grant-based financing, academics have an
incentive to be overly optimistic about possible outcomes in
order to secure and maintain funding. In contrast, a purchase
commitment would create an incentive to "self-select promis-
ing projects [and] focus intently on developing a marketable

vaccine, rather than on other goals", for example "fundamental science", which tends to be more rewarding "intellectually" and for academic careers (Kremer, 2000: 26). A vaccine purchase commitment would make research more useful because it would be engaged in the development of marketable products through partnerships between universities, start-ups and vaccine manufacturers (and we have already seen the pressure put on universities to be impactful; see Chapter 3). The intervention would then complement the incentivising effect of intellectual ownership by further guaranteeing a market return to patent owners.[9]

These fairly abstract suggestions on how to encourage research on new vaccines through the provision of incentives progressively made their way into overseas aid policy. This occurred, first, via the Center for Global Development, a think tank on development issues based in Washington, DC.[10] With a grant from the Gates Foundation, a working group was set up in 2003 that included Michael Kremer, alongside other US-based academic economists, health experts, biotech executives, World Bank officials, the finance director of the newly created GAVI and two British government officials. The group's aim was to "explore the feasibility of advance guarantee

---

[9] Although patents are discussed in relation to incentives, Kremer suggests the assumed incentivising effect of market exclusivity derived from patents alone is actually weak given that it is often possible to "design around vaccine patents" (Kremer, 2000: 16), especially in jurisdictions offering little protection to intellectual ownership.

[10] The Center for Global Development had been created only a few years before, in 2001, by a former US official and Silicon Valley philanthropist called Edward Scott.

agreements as a tool for stimulating research, development and production of vaccines for neglected developing-country diseases" (Levine, Kremer and Albright, 2005: 80). The process involved consultation with representatives from the pharmaceutical industry, the writing of a report published in 2005 and dissemination activities across the world. The term "Advance Market Commitment" was coined and the possible design of the market-based intervention fleshed out.

The central idea of what would, from now on, be called an AMC was that donors would provide a legally binding commitment to buy a vaccine that meets certain requirements (efficacy rate, etc.) according to the following pricing structure: for a fixed number of vaccine doses a subsidised price would be offered and, in exchange, manufacturers would agree to supply the vaccine at a second, lower price in the longer term. The report insisted on the use of the term "market commitment" in place of "purchase commitment" because donors would pay for the vaccine only if the latter met certain requirements and if countries benefitting from overseas aid support decided to introduce it into their immunisation programmes. Thus, donors' political volatility would be constrained and time inconsistency would be mitigated, while the freedom of choice of vaccine consumers would be preserved.

The idea of an AMC continued to gain political momentum. It became a matter of financial diplomacy, "negotiated finance minister to finance minister" at G7/G8 summits in London, Saint Petersburg and Rome from 2005 to 2007, as recalls a former staff member of the British Treasury (interview, former staff member of the British Treasury 1, now at the Department for International Development, DFID). Indeed, the UK chancellor at that time Gordon Brown had, according to another former staff member, a strong interest in "policy innovation around international development" and, together with the Italian minister of finance, is said to have been a main advocate of an AMC for vaccines.

> The Treasury was leveraging its experience of financial markets and international economic factors and very importantly its place at the table at the G7, G8 Finance Ministers' meetings, to try to create both the ideas and then the political space for [the AMC] to be adopted. (Interview, former staff member of the British Treasury 2)

Besides the broader enthusiasm for market-based interventions of the UK's (new) Labour government (see for example the Social Impact Bond, Chapter 5), the Treasury's involvement in making an AMC happen was further motivated by "a strong tradition of internationalism in the Labour Party" and a commitment to take UK spending on overseas aid up to 0.7% of its gross national product (GNP), in line with a 40-year-old target agreed on at the UN (interview, former staff member of the British Treasury 2).[11] While meeting the percentage remained an unfulfilled promise for many countries (donors' time inconsistency once again), in the UK the moral obligation was even translated into law in 2015.

This financial diplomacy at global summits took place at a time when political momentum surrounding interventions such as the AMC could gather as these initiatives seemed financially feasible. The pre-crisis and pre-austerity state of the economy in the mid-2000s, according to our interviewees, meant there simply was much more public money to spend than in subsequent years. The high profile championing around the set-up of an AMC for vaccines ended up with the launch of a pilot AMC for pneumococcal vaccines in Rome in February 2007. The governments of the UK, Italy, Norway,

---

[11] www.oecd.org/dac/stats/the07odagnitarget-ahistory.htm

Canada and Russia and the Gates Foundation together pledged a total of $1.5 billion that would be spent over the lifetime of the AMC (which might last up to two decades).[12] The management of this commitment would involve well-established development and health organisations working together (the WHO, the World Bank and UNICEF) with GAVI occupying a central, coordinating position.

A Low-Risk, High-Gain Pilot

With the choice of pneumococcal vaccines, the objective of the market-based intervention shifted from stimulating innovation in new vaccines to encouraging investment in production capacity (through new and bigger plants). This shift in economic objectives mirrored a shift in the health problem under consideration, from malaria to pneumococcus.

In 2006, donors and international organisations interested in the AMC established an independent expert committee responsible for choosing the targeted disease among six candidates (malaria, rotavirus, pneumococcus, HIV, human papilloma virus and tuberculosis). Composed of public health officials (e.g., from the Ministry of Health of Malawi), WHO experts and managers of scientific funding bodies (e.g., the president of the Medical Research Council of South Africa), the committee made its decision to focus on pneumococcus.

---

[12] According to one of our interviewees who used to work for the British Treasury at the time, representatives of the Gates Foundation were not particularly enthusiastic about the AMC, as GAVI might already play this role of vaccine procurement. Their relatively small contribution to the AMC reflected this concern.

The report concluded that "pneumococcal vaccines are the most suitable candidate for a demonstration/pilot AMC both because of their ability to demonstrate quickly that the AMC concept works and their potential impact on the health of the target populations" (Independent Expert Committee Recommendation for AMC Pilot, 2006).

The AMC for pneumococcal vaccines was thought of as a pilot, a real-world experiment, which nonetheless "had an awful lot of political capital behind it", as recalls a former civil servant from DFID. It was an experiment that needed to work:

This was politically a big deal at the time. It did need to work because there was some political reputation at stake. They could have decided to go for something more difficult like malaria, at that point there was no vaccine, and really the AMC was designed not just, not originally related so much to encourage manufacturers to install production capacity to supply developing countries, it was much more about pulling innovation through the R&D pipeline [...]. But they decided not to do that because they thought that was a bit risky for the first time this was attempted. So they chose something that was pretty well at the end of the R&D pipeline which was the pneumococcal vaccine, which had been produced with another market in mind, the western world basically. (Interview, former DFID civil servant 1)

Trying out an AMC to tackle malaria was considered too "risky" because, despite many years of research, the possibility of an efficacious vaccine was still surrounded by many scientific uncertainties (see Neyland and Simakova, 2015). During consultations carried out for the 2005 report of the Center for Global Development, pharmaceutical representatives, from biotech companies in particular, had expressed their doubts about the capacity of the market-based intervention to stimulate research. These doubts were relayed by vaccine experts and economists who put forward how hard it would be to specify the biomedical performance of a malaria vaccine (e.g., efficacy rate) and design a set of incentives attuned to the pace and financing of innovation (Farlow, Ligh, Mahoney and Widdus, 2005). Given the level of scepticism and donor's willingness to quickly demonstrate that the AMC could have an incentivising effect, the focus shifted from innovation to production. A vaccine was chosen that was not yet on the market but close to licensure and for which manufacturing investment decisions were being made.

The suitability of second-generation pneumococcal vaccines for a pilot AMC was established through strong evidence of the public health problem caused by the pneumococcus bacterium and the promise of the nearly licensed products. From the 1980s onwards, epidemiological investigations consistently indicated the existence of a large burden of disease in poor regions of the world benefitting from overseas aid (Ehrenstein and Neyland, 2018). When, in 2000, the firm Wyeth commercialised a first-generation pneumococcal vaccine, it did so in limited quantities because the manufacturer considered the American population as its main market.[13] The first-generation vaccine had been designed to target the strains causing diseases within the American population and, although it fitted the needs of European populations as well, it did not match the strains dominant in sub-Saharan Africa, for example, where much of the potential demand represented by countries in receipt of overseas aid was located.

---

[13] Wyeth had also expected competition from other companies with comparable vaccines under development (interview, former head of PneumoADIP team). But for about ten years, its product remained the only pneumococcal vaccine available because the biotechnology turned out to be very complicated to produce at a large scale.

When the AMC was discussed among G8 finance ministers, the development of second-generation pneumococcal
vaccines was already at the centre of attention of GAVI's board
and secretariat. The new partnership was gradually becoming the main financier of immunisation in poor regions of the
world. It complemented the procurement activity carried out
by UNICEF by raising overseas aid money, pooling requests
from health administrations and investigating the industry's
vaccine pipelines. In 2003, GAVI secretariat had launched a
five-year evidence-gathering initiative called PneumoADIP
(ADIP for Accelerated Development and Introduction Plan).
Under the leadership of epidemiologists at Johns Hopkins
University in the United States, the initiative aimed to "lay out
the investment case" for pneumococcal vaccines by enquiring
into their industrial development and reaching out to policy-
makers in low-income countries (interview, former head of
PneumoADIP team). In partnership with the WHO, meetings
were organised in low-income countries that brought together
"the health policy community" to communicate around pneumococcal diseases (interview, former head of PneumoADIP
team). The rationale driving this epidemiological advocacy
was market-based and demand-focused.

So [with Hepatitis b vaccines, for example] you see how the market
dynamic leads to this vicious cycle. There is high prices which keeps
demand low, demand is low so supply is constrained which keeps the
prices high and the demand low. So when we went into PneumoADIP
we said "we are going to break that vicious cycle, if we can create predictable demand they can scale up the capacity, which will actually
improve demand and bring down the prices" [...] From the beginning
we were clear this is what PneumoADIP is out to do, it's to figure out
"can we go from a vicious cycle to a virtuous one?", where clarity and
predictability about demand is linked to greater supply capacity and

lower prices which will enforce the demand. (Interview, former head of PneumoADIP team)

The market thinking at the core of PneumoADIP and the evidential work done by its team of epidemiologists was also oriented towards donors, who would provide the financial resources for the demand represented by low-income countries to become solvent. Cost-effectiveness analyses were carried out by testing out a range of vaccine prices against the anticipated health outcome, if improved vaccines were widely used. Given a very high burden of disease, these estimates tended to consistently justify the purchase of pneumococcal vaccines up to $12 a dose, which remained, however, much lower than the price of first-generation pneumococcal vaccines when they had been released in the United States (at around $50 a dose).

The accumulation of evidential material and active attempts to create a large demand were instrumental in making pneumococcal vaccines seem like a low-risk, high-gain investment option for overseas aid. Investment here was talked about rather metaphorically, as the spending of public money on an intervention that would yield substantial return in the form of a health impact (for more on the complications of investment-return, see Chapter 5). The announcement of the pilot AMC to the general public in 2007 then emphasised the severity of pneumococcal diseases killing 1.6 million people every year and the number of children (5.4 million by 2030) whose lives could be saved thanks to the AMC making pneumococcal vaccines widely available so quickly.[14]

---

[14] See GAVI's online press release: www.gavi.org/library/news/press-releases/2007/five-nations-and-the-bill-and-melinda-gates-foundation-launch-advance-market-commitment-for-vaccines/

Advocacy work prepared the grounds for an incentive-based intervention – the AMC – to be established. A vaccine was close to manufacture. Low-income countries had been informed of the potentiality of the new vaccine. Donors had expressed their willingness to fund an intervention. A structure was on the table for overcoming the usual problems of time inconsistency. The AMC and its guarantees could provide an incentive for pharmaceutical firms to scale-up their production and offer each dose at a low price for low-income countries. The market sensibility was thus moving out into the world, but the grounds for its unfolding were being carefully prepared. A significant challenge was how to legally secure the financing and design the pricing mechanism that would underpin the incentive.

The Organisation of Financial Flows and the Design of a Pricing Mechanism

Financial diplomacy and the prioritisation of pneumococcal vaccines were followed by discussion on how to legally structure the financial management of the pilot AMC in order to create an incentive structure. Ad hoc groups were set up, legal and economic experts were brought together, face-to-face meetings, email exchanges and phone conversations took place and formal consultations were organised (Cernuschi et al., 2011; Dalberg Global Development Advisors, 2013). Legal obligations were required to avoid time inconsistency that might undermine the incentivising features of the intervention. It took two years, from 2007 to 2009, for the market-based intervention and its incentive to become operational.

While the idea of donors committing to spend $1.5 billion might have appeared straightforward when finance ministers proudly announced the pilot AMC, finding the adequate legal terms proved to be hard work. The *raison d'être* of the intervention was to create a credible (because it was legally binding) commitment to buy a vaccine if specific conditions were met (a suitable product demanded by health administrations). Donors seemed to have unquestionably accepted the idea of their own time inconsistency being a problem and the AMC was expected to "give vaccine firms enough confidence that they would be rewarded in the way that they were promised", explains a former British civil servant (interview, former DFID civil servant 1). But making a legally binding commitment for overseas aid funding was very unusual, certainly for DFID.

[At] DFID, whenever we make a financing commitment, we write into it that, [...] basically that we are in a political environment, ministers can change their mind anytime about anything and we reserve that right. So even when we make a commitment to GAVI we will set up a memorandum of understanding in which it says "we'll pay you X hundreds millions each year" and "we reserve the right to cease this agreement". (Interview, DFID staff member 1)

Instead of this conditional commitment, the financial commitment required in an AMC was made bankable and would enable companies to sue donors for not living up to their promises. UK commercial law was chosen as a basis for writing the agreement because, according to the adviser who helped set up the legal arrangement, it "is predictable and well used in more commercial transactions than probably other laws". It would thus provide manufacturers with enough certainty they could enforce the commitment if needed (establishing similar contractual expectations to those of investors in Social Impact Bonds; Chapter 5). Certainty was a key feature of the incentive: knowing finance was there and would be reliably paid was considered important by the AMC's participants.

Alongside these legal concerns, additional guarantees were given to the pharmaceutical industry to ensure that the AMC was perceived as credible. In particular, the World Bank was tasked with managing the $1.5 billion funding. The triple A-rated financial organisation even agreed to put the entire commitment on its balance sheet. This meant that even if some governments were late or defaulted on their payment, the money would still be made available to companies according to the terms and conditions of the AMC. Such a decision resulted from lengthy negotiations between donor representatives and the World Bank's staff. According to a former member of the British Treasury (interview, former member of British Treasury 2), the "World Bank wanted to be a neutral actor" and didn't want to take the risk of having to pay for the vaccine without having received enough funds from donors. But, from the latter's perspective, the World Bank could provide a "buffer zone" because the timing of the payments were uncertain (it depended on when the vaccines would be made available and when they were requested) and the organisation's balance sheet was composed of money that would "come from the regular donors to the bank anyway" (interview, former member of British Treasury 2). As the treasurer of the $1.5 billion commitment, the World Bank entered into grant agreements with the six donors to the AMC, the terms of which were attuned to various national budgeting practices. These practical issues were arranged in order to ensure the AMC's credibility, its financial management and its incentivising effect. Without a reliable structure in place for such matters as making payments, it was assumed that the pharmaceutical firms would be disinclined to produce the vaccines at the required scale.

But mitigating the time inconsistency of politicians' promises would not be enough to enact the market sensibility and incentivise the pharmaceutical industry to produce and supply large quantities of pneumococcal vaccines. Parallel to the legal formalisation of the financial management of the commitment, the pricing mechanism of the AMC also had to be carefully designed. Donors to the AMC convened a group of experts, this time in economics (including Michael Kremer again), to formulate recommendations. In initial sketches of the AMC, the idea was that companies could obtain a subsidised price for a fixed number of doses in exchange for agreeing to supply the vaccine in the longer-term at a lower price. The subsidised price was supposed to allow manufacturers to quickly recover the cost incurred by investing in additional production capacity to satisfy a newly solvent demand (among low-income countries), while the long-term price would ensure reliable and affordable supply.

The economists of the expert group dedicated a great deal of effort to calculating possible values for the long-term price and the subsidy. Economic modelling was used to "try to get the feel for how did different assumptions about [industry's] costs and about demand sort of fit together", as recalls a former member of the group (interview, economist of the expert group).

I'm just going to make up some numbers. Suppose that we thought it will cost $300 million to build a plants and suppose we thought you would be able to sell 15 million doses a year, and suppose that once you've built the plant, it would cost $2 to produce a dose. How high would we need to set the price so that over, say, a ten-year period, you would be able to recover enough money to justify spending the $300 million depending, you know, on how you discount future cash flows and so forth? (Interview, economist of the expert group)

These analyses were meant to pre-test the incentivising effect of a range of values for the subsidy and the long-term price.

The modelling of industry's behaviour in response to these values was based on a series of assumptions about investment decisions and manufacturing costs. For this purpose, numbers were needed. A central piece of information was provided by the consultancy work carried out at the request of the PneumoADIP initiative. Based on interviews with scientists and patent holders, consultants had estimated an average "cost of goods" of slightly more than $2 per dose, a rather high production cost mainly due to the technical challenge of manufacturing a molecule targeting several bacterial strains at once. There was also talk of the two companies (GSK and Wyeth) with vaccines under development and close to commercialisation having quite different costs. Gathering together these kinds of insights ought to provide donors with some kind of calculative power to prepare for a legal commitment (see Chapter 5). But overall, little information was available, as pharmaceutical firms tend to be very secretive about their business.[15] For the legal adviser who eventually wrote the legal documents, the whole process amounted to "soft testing the market" in contrast to "a normal commercial transaction [where] you are negotiating with someone" (interview, DFID legal adviser).

The pilot ended up working as follows. GAVI was tasked with publishing regular demand forecasts for pneumococcal vaccines at least 15 years into the future. Companies with vaccines meeting the AMC's technical requirements (e.g., the vaccine's efficacy against specific strains) were invited to register and formally agree to the terms and conditions of the market-based intervention, especially its pricing mechanism. By entering the AMC, they would commit themselves

---

[15] For an overview of the debate triggered by the pricing mechanism of the AMC see McGoey (2014).

to a ten-year-long supply offer of at least ten million doses per year, starting not later than five years after the issuance of the call. The pricing applied in the offer was a price cap of $3.5 a dose that would be topped up by a subsidy of $3.5 a dose in the first years of supply for a fixed number of doses. The total subsidy received by one manufacturer was calculated based on the supplied quantity of doses. The latter was compared to an indicative annual demand target of 200 million doses that GAVI and UNICEF had estimated in the mid-2000s to be the volume needed in the long term by countries benefitting from their support. The percentage of that target demand of 200 million doses covered by the offer made by each pharmaceutical firm gave the percentage of the $1.5 billion subsidy they would receive for that offer.

Compromises

The incentive was about legal structure and payment terms, underpinned by modelling the future intervention and estimating demand. Designing the pricing mechanism by "soft testing the market" involved economic reasoning and calculation as well as industry consultations. From these, additional insights into the possible behaviour of companies – how they would respond to what level of incentive with respect to capacity investment – could then be developed. Indeed, the success of the high-profile pilot was dependent on the pharmaceutical industry being receptive to the AMC.

For the AMC to have the expected incentivising effect, the subsidy and long-term price were envisioned in relation to supply obligations. But company executives voiced some concerns about these obligations. By linking the amount of subsidy to supplied volumes, firms were encouraged to sell large quantities of vaccine doses in exchange for a greater share of the subsidy. This created a risk: manufacturers might invest huge amounts in building a significant capacity to manufacture vaccine doses that might not be required if only a few countries decided to use pneumococcal vaccines in their immunisation programmes. Indeed, the terms and conditions of the intervention specified that UNICEF, acting as the procurement agency, was not bound to honour the ten-year supply offer when placing its annual purchase orders to organise delivery. The vaccines had to be requested by health administrations first. The demand forecasts produced by GAVI based on various insights (expressions of interest from countries, past introduction rates, birth cohorts, wastage, etc.) and used to issue calls for offers would not be binding. To mitigate the risk of surplus capacity generated by the uncertainty surrounding future actual demand, donors agreed to include a small purchase guarantee (firm order) in each supply agreement. This concession together with the awareness-raising conducted around pneumococcal vaccines by the PneumoADIP initiative seemed to comfort AMC participants.

But other demands from the pharmaceutical industry were not taken into account in the design of the market-based intervention. Company executives from Indian and Chinese companies had called for the creation of a legal means to keep some of the $1.5 billion commitment aside in order to wait for additional manufacturers to become able to participate. For a former DFID staff member, such a "credential mechanism" would have created the "risk [of] being in a situation where companies have vaccines available that we know are cost-effective, but we are not going to vaccinate children and wait for other companies to develop their vaccines, which they may not succeed in doing" (interview, former DFID staff member 2). Donors had moved away from trying to encourage the development of a malaria vaccine in order to avoid the uncertainty around R&D. Although the AMC was supposedly also "trying to incentivize the companies in emerging markets to invest in research and development" and stimulate competition within the pharmaceutical industry to further reduce prices (interview, former DFID staff member 1), the request to freeze some of the subsidy and wait for the commercialisation of new products was rejected.[16] The market-based intervention remained rather insensitive to this call for competition (see Neyland, Ehrenstein and Milyaeva, 2017).

In the legal arrangement of the AMC, the relationship between donors (providing the financial resources to subsidise the purchase of pneumococcal vaccines) and companies (producing the vaccines) was mediated through this distribution of exposure to financial harm (in other words, risk) and price levels. This mediating function relied on compromises. For a former staff member of DFID, the AMC and, at its core, the pricing mechanism had two competing aims.

It was to find a set of incentives that would represent good value for money but at the same time will make it very likely that industry would respond and install additional capacity for manufacturing pneumococcal vaccines. [...] I know that some have argued that [members of the economic expert group] were too generous to business, to the industry. But I think there was so much uncertainty about things like the cost of producing vaccines, which was central in setting the price that was acceptable to industry, and the risk of things like demand not materialising that they, the expert group, eventually came out with a pretty good

---

[16] The legal terms of the AMC authorised UNICEF not to award at once the full forecasted demand in order to manage the pace at which the subsidy was spent and hopefully leave enough time for new pneumococcal vaccines to be on the market, which has not happened yet.

compromise. Whether we could have had the same impact that we are currently having with less costs to the UK or to the tax payers, I guess we will never know for sure. (Interview, former DFID staff member 1)

As suggested in this excerpt, the final design of the AMC, its incentive structure and cost, was a matter of compromise and a contentious topic. The use of public resources to subsidise private activities was "an emotive subject", according to another former DFID staff member (interview, former DFID staff member 2). The market-based intervention also found little support during consultations organised with civil society organisations such as Oxfam and Médecins Sans Frontières. The latter vocally criticised the AMC for subsidising a vaccine, the sale of which in wealthy countries (at nearly \$130 a dose in the insurance sector in the United States) was already a major source of profit for these pharmaceutical firms.[17] The humanitarian organisation had also argued for a different approach to address the lack of access to new vaccines in poor regions of the world, namely constraining companies to surrender their intellectual property rights and support production by generic manufacturers in places such as India or Brazil. But the AMC with its arm's-length incentive-based mechanism, was never designed to operate as a coercive legal action of this kind. Whether or not a different kind of intervention would have greater or lesser success and how we might go about knowing is itself an ongoing issue in market-based interventions (see Chapter 9).

---

[17] See MSF's online opinion: https://msfaccess.org/gavi-money-welcome-could-it-be-more-wisely-spent. Vaccine prices in the United States are provided here: www.cdc.gov/vaccines/programs/vfc/awardees/vaccine-management/price-list/index.html.

Establishing the terms and conditions of the AMC, its legal agreements, how budgets would be managed, demand forecasted, supplies provided and future payments made were each required to give effect to its incentive mechanism. This was the work required to encourage manufacturers to invest in production capacity and supply low-income countries at a low price – while, at the same time, ensuring that the public cost of achieving this effect was in some sense justifiable.

All these efforts enabled the AMC to be operationalised in 2009 when, based on a demand forecast published by GAVI secretariat, UNICEF released a first call for offers. At the time, as expected, only two companies (GSK and Pfizer having bought Wyeth) had close-to-commercialisation second-generation pneumococcal vaccines. The volume that GSK and Pfizer agreed to supply in 2010 was the same: 30 million doses annually from 2012. This meant that each company initially obtained 15% of the $1.5 billion of available funding, an equivalent to $225 million of the subsidy. The incentive was in place, it was expected that vaccines would be issued at an unprecedented speed and volume and lives would (hopefully) be saved. While health administrations eagerly applied to GAVI's support to get the new vaccines, keeping up with the delivery of doses proved difficult. In the first years of implementation, there were shortages. Although both Pfizer and GSK reported on technical failures, the shortages could also suggest that the two companies might not have invested in manufacturing capacity in response to the intervention. The impact of the incentive thus seems limited.

As GAVI and UNICEF continued working with countries benefitting from their financial and logistical support, new calls were issued to meet changes in demand and new supply offers were signed in 2012, 2013 and 2018, with the same two companies. No new participants have entered the field of pneumococcal vaccines. With only 18.5% of its fund left ($262.5 million) in 2018, the AMC will probably not provide much of a future incentive for the commercialisation of new products. Yet, a major evaluation of the AMC carried out in 2015, suggested that the AMC "encouraged manufacturers with early-stage products to continue development by establishing that there would be significant demand for PCV [pneumococcal conjugate vaccine] after the conclusion of the AMC and phasing out of supply of initial contracts"; that is, from 2020 onwards (BCG, 2015: 28). In a way, one could say that the market-based intervention succeeded in creating (expectation of) a market.

Conclusion

In this chapter we have focused on the market sensibility of the incentive and its central role in orienting a specific market-based intervention: the AMC. In contrast to the coercive infrastructure of other market-based interventions that we have considered in previous chapters (such as the GDPR), incentives anticipate an arm's-length relationship between regulator (here governmental donors of overseas aid and GAVI) and regulated (here pharmaceutical companies). The incentive sets a particular, desired activity to be accomplished and the regulator simply has to check on its success; the means by which those targeted by the intervention achieve the target is left to the individual actors. In contrast to other interventions whereby the form of regulation will achieve efficiency and effectiveness through close regulation (for example in the REF's anticipation of an effective and efficient means of distributing government research funding by assessing every research-active academic in the UK), the incentive itself is supposed to be cost-efficient through minimal and indirect engagement.

Yet as we have seen in this chapter and in a familiar theme that emerges consistently throughout this book, futures that are anticipated through market-based interventions rarely come to pass without much work, much cost and some unintended consequences and changes in direction along the way.

Getting close to the practices through which an incentive was accomplished in a global health intervention was not a trivial matter. Once again we have the opportunity to witness what is at stake: in this chapter the health and well-being and even the lives of populations in low-income countries. Putting in place and holding in place the incentive at the centre of the AMC required specific acts of financial diplomacy, advocacy work that could stimulate interest among low-income countries in a new vaccine, the writing of appropriate legal terms and conditions and forecasts of future demand. These devices, practices and relations were directed towards stimulating the pharmaceutical industry into investing in more production capacity to manufacture a pneumococcal vaccine suitable for low-income countries at a large scale and affordable price. Even this required a lengthy prior discussion and negotiation to establish that pneumococcus was the appropriate target to build an incentive scheme around. None of these decisions were trivial, but selecting the health problems to be addressed through immunisation was key to also setting in place just how the incentive would anticipate the future. In place of malaria being the targeted disease, which would have required an incentive for innovative research and development with all the attendant uncertainty involved in scientific work, tuning the AMC to pneumococcal vaccines involved selecting a close to licensure product and incentivising industry to scale-up its production. To focus on pneumococcus was to choose a safer option at a moment when political commitments needed to be met with a successful intervention. The safe option was a means to save face.

However, in a similar manner to our preceding examples, this intervention created controversy. Questions were asked of the extent to which the AMC provided value for money, to what extent it subsidised already profitable private sector firms through public money, and whether or not a different kind of intervention could have been used. As we will see in Chapters 8 and 9, these questions over the success and failure of market-based interventions are not straightforward to address and often involve an entire industry of evaluations, metrology and consultancy reports. What we can say for now, besides doubts regarding its incentivising effect, is that the AMC as a pilot was not taken up. The testing of the market-based intervention did not lead to a range of different AMCs for different diseases.

In this chapter we have had a chance to move from the general features of global health, the pharmaceutical industry and incentives to the particular detail of one incentive scheme, its legal, financial and promissory complications. Among other things, this has provided an opportunity to consider the requirements and challenges faced by market-based interventions in anticipating and then trying to enact a specific future. In Chapter 7 we will now turn attention to a different way in which market-based interventions manage the passage of time by investigating the UK student loans market and its opportunistic and successive development over 25 years.

References

Adams, V. (Ed.) (2016) *Metrics: What Counts in Global Health*. Durham, NC: Duke University Press.

Birn, A.E. (2009) The stages of international (global) health: Histories of success or successes of history? *Global Public Health* 4(1): 50–68.

Blume, S. (2005) Lock in, the state and vaccine development: Lessons from the history of the polio vaccines. *Research Policy* 34(2): 159–73.

Blume, S. (2017) The erosion of public sector vaccine production: The case of the Netherlands. In C. Holmberg, S. Blume and P. Greenough (eds.), *The Politics of Vaccination: A Global History.* Manchester: Manchester University Press, pp. 148–73.

Blume, S. and Geesink, I. (2000) Vaccinology: an industrial science? *Science as Culture* 9(1): 41–72.

Boston Consulting Group (BCG) (2015) *The Advance Market Commitment Pilot for Pneumococcal Vaccines: Outcomes and Impact Evaluation.* Available at: www.gavi.org/results/evaluations/pneumococcal-amc-outcomes-and-impact-evaluation/ (last accessed 3 April 2019).

Çalışkan, K. (2010) *Market Threads: How Cotton Farmers and Traders Create a Global Commodity.* Oxford: Princeton University Press.

Cernuschi, T., Furrer, E., Schwalbe, N., Jones, A., Berndt, E.R. and McAdams, S. (2011) Advance market commitment for pneumococcal vaccines: Putting theory into practice. *Bulletin of the World Health Organization* 89(12): 913–18.

Chee, G., Molldren, V., His, N. and Chankova S. (2008) *Evaluation of the GAVI Phase 1 Performance (2000–2005).* Bethesda, MD: Abt Associates Inc.

Dalberg Global Development Advisors (2013) *The Advance Market Commitment for Pneumococcal Vaccines: Process and Design Evaluation.* Available at: https://marketbookshelf.com/wp-content/uploads/2017/05/the-advance-market-commitment-for-pneumococcal-vaccines-process-and-design-evaluation.pdf (last accessed 3 April 2019).

Dieleman, J.L., Schneider, M.T., Haakenstad, A., Singh, L., Sadat, N., Birger, M., Reynolds, A., Templin, T., Hamavid, H., Chapin, A. and Murray, C.J. (2016) Development assistance for health: Past trends, associations, and the future of international financial flows for health. *The Lancet* 387(10037): 2536–44.

Dix, G. (2016) A genealogy of the incentive. *Economic Sociology: The European Electronic Newsletter* 17(2): 24–31.

Ehrenstein, V. and Neyland, D. (2018) On scale work: Evidential practices and global health interventions. *Economy and Society* 47(1): 59–82.

Farlow, A.W.K., Ligh, D.W., Mahoney R.T. and Widdus, R. (2005) Concerns regarding the Center for Global Development report *Making Markets for Vaccines*. Submission to the Commission on Intellectual Property Rights, Innovation and Public Health, WHO, 19 April.

Foucault, M. (2007) *Security, Territory, Population: Lectures at the College de France 1977–78*. London: Palgrave Macmillan.

Freeman, P. and Robbins, A. (1991) The elusive promise of vaccines. *The American Prospect*. Available at: http://prospect.org/article/elusive-promise-vaccines (last accessed 3 April 2019).

Greenwood, B. (2014) The contribution of vaccination to global health: Past, present and future. *Philosophical Transactions of the Royal Society of London B: Biological Sciences* 369(1645).

Hardon, A. and Blume, S. (2005) Shifts in global immunisation goals (1984–2004): Unfinished agendas and mixed results. *Social Science & Medicine* 60(2): 345–56.

Huzair, F. and Sturdy, S. (2017) Biotechnology and the transformation of vaccine innovation: The case of the hepatitis B vaccines 1968–2000. *Studies in History and Philosophy of Science Part C: Studies in History and Philosophy of Biological and Biomedical Sciences* 64: 11–21.

Independent Expert Committee Recommendations for AMC Pilot (2006). *Executive Summary*. Available at: www.gavialliance.org/library/documents/amc/independent-expert-committee-recommendation-for-amc-pilot/ (last accessed 3 April 2019).

Kremer, M. (2000) *Creating Markets for New Vaccine, Part 1: Rationale*. NBER working paper series, working paper 7716, Cambridge, MA: National Bureau of Economic Research.

Lakoff, A. (2010). Two regimes of global health. *Humanity: An International Journal of Human Rights, Humanitarianism, and Development* 1(1): 59–79.

Levine, R., Kremer, M. and Albright, A. (2005) *Making Markets for Vaccines: Ideas to Action*. The report of the Center for Global Development Advance Market Commitment Working Group. Washington, DC: Communications Development Incorporated.

McGoey, L. (2014) The philanthropic state: market-state hybrids in the philanthrocapitalist turn. *Third World Quarterly* 35(1): 109-25.

McGoey, L. (2015) *No Such Thing as a Free Gift: The Gates Foundation and the Price of Philanthropy*. London: Verso Books.

McGoey, L., Reiss, J. and Wahlberg, A. (2011) The global health complex. *BioSocieties* 6(1): 1-9.

Mitchell, V.S., Philipose, N.M. and Sanford, J.P. (eds.) (1993) *The Children's Vaccine Initiative: Achieving the Vision*. Washington, DC: National Academy Press.

Muraskin, W. (1996) Origins of the Children's Vaccine Initiative: The intellectual foundations. *Social Science & Medicine* 42(12): 1703-19.

Neyland, D., Ehrenstein, V. and Milyaeva, S. (2017) Mundane market matters: On sensitive metrology and the governance of market-based interventions for global health. *Revue française de sociologie* 58(3): 425-49.

Neyland, D. and Simakova, E. (2015) The mosquito multiple: Malaria and market-based initiatives. In I. Dussauge, C. F. Helgesson and F. Lee (eds.), *Value Practices in the Life Sciences and Medicine*. Oxford: Oxford University Press, 136-51.

Nik-Khah, E. (2014) Neoliberal pharmaceutical science and the Chicago School of Economics. *Social Studies of Science* 44(4): 489-517.

Reubi, D. (2018) Epidemiological accountability: Philanthropists, global health and the audit of saving lives. *Economy and Society* 47(1): 83-110.

Roalkvam, S., McNeill, D. and Blume, S. (eds.) (2013) *Protecting the World's Children: Immunisation Policies and Practices*. Oxford: Oxford University Press.

World Bank (1993) *World Development Report 1993: Investing in Health*. New York: Oxford University Press.

7

Selling

Opening

Our final sensibility moves from incentives to open up an in-depth exploration of the nature of selling. Although selling has been apparent in several of our market-based interventions (for example, with data start-ups trying to sell new privacy sensitive products in Chapter 4 and polluters expected to buy and sell emissions allowances in Chapter 2), the complexities of selling specific entities require careful scrutiny to make sense of the nature of the problem being addressed. We will suggest that the form given to sales within the realm of market-based interventions into public problems is specific, with privatisation, sell-offs and trading involving their own formats and consequences. Selling here may draw on some of the terms used in more conventional sales (for example, incorporating talk of price, launches, and customers), but close inspection is required of the practices, devices and relations used to make things sellable (literally, to give some matter a set of characteristics that mean it can be sold), for relations of selling to be composed and for sales to be given effect. We will focus in this chapter on UK higher education student loans as our main illustration.

Whereas in Chapter 6, the AMC provided an incentive-based means to anticipate and establish criteria required for bringing a future into being, in this chapter we will suggest that student loans are only able to take the shape they do because of their history. We will argue that the policy for selling UK student loans is less directed toward the future, and instead gives new effect to the past. This suggests we will be able to engage in distinct, temporally inflected generals and particulars in this chapter, exploring the ways in which past policies become opportunities for new moments of exploitation. In order to achieve this analysis, we need to pay very close attention to the particular details of the policies through which loans have acquired their sellable characteristics.

UK higher education student loans have been the most recent act in an ongoing drama that gained momentum in the 1990s with increasing recognition of the difficulties in maintaining UK public financing of university teaching (particularly with rapid growth in the number of students). The apparent problem of the cost of expanding UK higher education was drawn into sharper focus by the financial crisis and a search for opportunities to cut public spending and reduce public financial deficits. The subsequent increase in tuition fees for students to be mostly covered by loans as a means to cut public spending, increased the number and amount of money involved on the student loan books on government accounts – students had to borrow more to cover the costs of higher fees. Successive governments also looked to position the loans as a fair cost – a cost that ought to be incurred by students who would go on to earn more as a result of their degrees and a cost that ought not to be borne by the general population of non-university admissions. The prospect of selling these loans seemed to provide a means to turn the loans from a cost into an asset and rebalance public spending. Yet controversy continues to plague the loan system, with income-contingent repayments, variations in interest rate, government bail-outs of the system, and political support for alternatives such as a graduate tax all vying for attention. At the same time and partly as a result of these controversies, making the loans an attractive prospect to buyers has been challenging.

Although as we noted in the privacy market of Chapter 4 "property" might be conventionally associated with notions of ownership as a precursor to making sales and transferring ownership, in the market-based intervention in focus here we will suggest that complications pervade the properties of the entities involved and how they might be accounted for, in this case the properties of specific tranches of loans. Repayment risks, loan book valuations, securitisation and the history of debt accumulated within bundles of loans were each technical matters that could be used to project a more or less generous future income stream and justify a more or less generous price for a bundle of loans. In line with the idea that markets involve the constant qualification-requalification of goods (Callon, Meadel and Rabehariosa, 2002), we suggest in this chapter that the activities of selling require a broader reconceptualisation, from a legalistic focus on the transfer of property, to also include the evidential actions needed to establish something as a sellable solution to a problem, a consideration of the properties of the entity being sold and a study of the practices of selling.

We begin this chapter with a brief consideration of one of the central practices of selling – what we will term the *preparatory imperative*. We will then introduce student loans as a means to illustrate the importance of paying attention to the properties of the entity being sold. In particular we will compare two tranches of student loans that were prepared for sale. The distinctions between the loans' form and function and the differential efforts required to prepare each tranche to make them sellable is illustrative, we suggest, of the importance and complications involved in preparing entities for sale. We conclude the chapter with an analysis of the temporal concerns managed through this preparatory imperative.

Selling and the Preparatory Imperative

As we saw in Chapter 3, academia can be subject to a range of market-oriented concerns, in that case with the competitive allocation of government research funding. Further discussions range broadly across English higher education and questions of marketisation (Molesworth, Scullion and Nixon, 2011), neoliberalisation (Canaan and Shumar, 2008), or financialisation (Holmwood, 2014). We can also find studies of the relationship between academia and industry (see, for example, the work of Popp Berman (2008) on universities and patents), changing notions of who owns ideas and what it might mean to profit from them. And in the work of Fuller (2016) we find analyses of the struggles of universities to prove their worth. By raising questions such as what the added value of the university is in "neoliberal times", the university is faced with an economic framing within which it might not prove valuable. Escaping this framing and producing new relations with the world beyond the institution might provide an alternative future (Fuller, 2016). These studies are useful for hinting at the range of ways in which a market imperative might enter into academic life. But these studies do not tell us much about the preparatory grounds required for selling off aspects of higher education, the careful work required or the consequences that follow. Markets enter the fray in these studies as a set of concerns to which universities must adapt. As we will see in the case of UK student loans, sales are carried out by the state, engaging investors (for example, pension funds), and involve a great deal of preparation that does not directly involve academic institutions (for more on the complexity of investment, see Chapter 5). Universities appear to be strategically limited by government in having any voice in these sales.

Following on from these concerns, we might anticipate that preparing loans for sale is a complex business. Against any counter-expectation (Smith, 1990), price does not materialise through its own agential force or through "the market" conceived as a price generating agent in its own right[1] (see Chapter 6 and the price of vaccine doses). Instead, in market-based interventions such as the student loan system, achieving a price through selling an entity, is something that must be produced. Producing a price requires careful preparation of the entity being sold, the building of relations through which the sale will take place, calculations via accounting rules, the establishment of a future value in the present, and a number of different forms of negotiation work to seal a final commitment to pay a price. This is what we will term the *preparatory imperative* – that once a commitment to sale has been made, a range of preparatory activities emerge over time, with the completion of each activity providing a step towards a sale being achieved. Preparation, then, is part requirement (legal demands, matching this sale with the standards set by a previous sale) and part discovery (as new requirements emerge that are demanded by various parties for a sale to go ahead). The imperative here is not a clear, single demand, but captures the range of emergent activities participants feel compelled to perform. The preparatory imperative in selling student loans is taken on and exemplified by government departments, not by universities. Given the uncertain consequences of selling tranches of student

---

[1] For an STS analysis of selling and prices, see the work of Cochoy (1998, 2009, 2010).

loans, universities in the UK are preparing for a future that is yet to be forecast.

This is not unique in the history of UK market-based interventions. We can find a significant background history of the selling of what were once (and might nominally remain), public goods in other state sectors beyond education. Harvey (2005) suggests that the Thatcher government of the 1980s "set out to privatize all those sectors of the economy that were in public ownership. The sales would boost the public treasury and rid the government of burdensome future obligations" (60). In a similar manner to the preparatory imperative that we set out above, Harvey suggests:

> These state-run enterprises had to be adequately prepared for privatization, and this meant paring down their debt and improving their efficiency and cost structures, often through shedding labour. Their valuation was also structured to offer considerable incentives to private capital – a process that was likened by opponents to "giving away the family silver". In several cases subsidies were hidden in the mode of valuation ... [organisations] held high value land in prime locations that was excluded from the valuation of the enterprise as an ongoing concern. Privatization and speculative gains on the property released went hand in hand. But the aim here was also to change the political culture by extending the field of personal and corporate responsibility and encouraging greater efficiency. (2005: 60)

From Harvey's work we can note that selling is not just a matter of achieving a price, but a complex weaving of the preparatory imperative with a political programme of action designed to shift responsibilities or costs. Yet this tying together of a political programme and a specific intervention requires the imposition of a coherent logic to a series of actions that, when explored in detail, evade this singular coherence. The history of privatisation – for example, in UK trains (CRESC, 2013) or in the US Federal Communication Commission's 1994 auctioning of communications spectrum licenses (Guala, 2001; Mirowski and Nik-Khah, 2008) – provides one useful way to consider some of the complexities of selling public entities that go beyond the coherence of a single programme of action. Selling often involves a successive almost opportunistic logic whereby a first action later enables a subsequent action, but it is not always the case that the later action was planned at the time of the first action. What form of sale might derive best price and what would count as best price for whom are preparatory matters that require resolution (and as we will show, then often create problems that also need to be resolved; see Chapter 8 for more on the recursion of problems and solutions).

This points us toward the broad complexity of the preparatory imperative – that when considering the efforts involved in selling student loans, we must be attentive to the range of work involved. Heeding the warning of Guala (2008), we must be attentive to the practices of selling developed for this specific sale of this specific entity. Building on this point, in order to understand the selling of student loans, we need to know more about the specificity of these loans. We need to know how they are being sold to what potential buyers, in what particular timeframe, under what regulatory conditions, for what specific purposes, using what means of valuation, building on what successive conditions?

Student Loans

A History of Expanding State Engagement

Student loans have been in existence in the UK since the early 1990s and were first designed to help university students in the UK with the cost of living. These loans have continually been a matter of controversy, as the loan book has increased in size and value and the loans themselves have changed. What were once more or less straightforward repayment loans are now – as we shall see – subject to a range of different repayment rules and what were once designed to cover costs of living are now a tool for transforming the funding and some might say the nature of UK higher education. These changes have generated questions including the value for money of higher education,[2] the appropriate interest rate at which loans should be paid, whether or not and how much of university tuition costs should be covered by loans, when and how quickly repayments should be made, and when (if ever) loans should be cancelled.

Public debate, student protests and changes in support for major political parties[3] (Lewis, Vasagar, Williams and Taylor., 2010; Phipps, 2014; Gil, 2015) have all been attributed to student loans in the UK. With the financial crisis of 2008 onwards and the UK government's search for a means to reduce public spending, cut the deficit between spending and tax revenue, and concomitantly further reduce levels of public spending through cutting debt and its associated interest costs, increasing attention has been paid to a search for things to sell. With

---

[2] Although publicly funded universities have generally been praised for providing economic and social benefits (OECD, 2015; Mountford-Zimdars, Jones, Sullivan and Heath, 2013; AAAS, 2016), the extent to which they provide value for money depends on how value is calculated (and what benefits are included, at what price) and what costs are included, at what rate.

[3] The Liberal Democrats were said to have lost support after breaking their pledge to abolish university tuition fees and had in fact overseen a substantial increase in fees once in Coalition government (BBC News 2012, 2016).

student loans contributing to such public outcry, selling the loans might seem to provide a chance to sell off responsibility for this public problem, along with creating a positive contribution to public accounts. Except that the continuing nature of student loan controversies has dogged the sales themselves: questions now abound of the value for money of selling the loans, what these sales will mean for students, whether or not the sales actually contribute to a reduction in public spending (or are a mere accounting artifice) and so on. Selling these loans has not equated to selling off and shifting responsibility for the problem. To make sense of these challenges, we need to start with some history.

In their medieval form, Oxford and Cambridge Universities were the only English higher education institutions and they dominated higher education in England until the nineteenth century (Anderson, 2016). These institutions drew on their own assets (often land) as a basis for generating income. Government involvement in higher education only began in the nineteenth century as an attempt to expand university education (and the London universities were established during this period, with Manchester seeing its first university in 1851) and to encourage these existing universities to provide a more nationally oriented form of education (Vernon, 2004). Legislation between 1850 and 1880 was central to shaping the early financing by the state of university provision, with teaching staff becoming professionalised, curriculums modernised and a new examination system established (Anderson, 2016). These changes led to an initial expansion in student numbers to incorporate for the first time wealthy upper-middle-class students, including female students from the 1870s onwards.

This expansion in the number of universities and the student population accelerated in the early years of the twentieth century. This coincided with the establishment of the University

Grants Committee (UGC) in 1919 that enabled government to centrally manage financial support of higher education institutions through block grants. The growth in UK universities went hand-in-hand with a growth in state oversight. Oversight of the UGC itself was managed by the Treasury until 1963 and then moved under the jurisdiction of the Department of Education and Science.[4] However, the kinds of costs managed by the UGC were still limited. Until 1946 the UGC's role was the allocation of "deficiency grants" designed to help financially when required (Shattock and Berdahl, 1984: 472). This changed in 1946 when the Committee's purpose was reassessed: "the time had come when the Government was bound to assure itself that somewhere in the University system provision is made for every field of scholarship or science which is necessary to the national interest" (Hetherington, 1954, cited in Owen, 1980: 264). This required a significant further expansion of provision that was enhanced by the Education Act of 1962, which ensured that higher education was free. Local authorities (but effectively the Treasury) would now have to pay university fees for students.[5] As a result, the government financing of higher education grew from 33.6% of all income received by universities (including endowments and fees) in 1921 to 76.4 percent in 1973 (Owen, 1985: 46–47). Growth in the number of universities and the population of students involved growth in state management of higher education, but also an emergent dependency; university income was now much more dependent on the state.

---

[4] Although the Treasury as well as the Board of Education had been providing some financial assistance to universities in the form of grants since 1907 (Owen, 1980).

[5] Although tuition fee payments by local authorities "were partially means-tested until the late 1970s" (Hillman, 2013: 251).

As higher education expanded in the closing years of the twentieth century, this dependency was brought into sharper focus. From steady expansion of the university sector post-World War II to the 1990s (Collini, 2012),[6] the 1988 Education Reform Act and the 1992 Further and Higher Education Act created a more drastic change in the landscape. Polytechnics were reclassified into universities and these institutions expanded significantly. Higher education participation rates in England rose from 15% in 1988 to 47% in 2014 (McGettigan, 2013; UK Government, 2015). New oversight bodies were also established. The University Grants Committee was replaced by the Universities Funding Council in 1989, and in 1992 the Higher Education Funding Council for England (HEFCE) was formed to oversee funding of English universities[7] (see Chapter 3 for more on the role of these funding councils in managing the REF). The growth in participation required a growth in oversight, but also led to a significant growth in cost. The affordability of higher education provision came under government scrutiny.

Growing provision of higher education had been a lurking problem in the background of higher education discussions since the late 1970s and early 1980s, as "the virtual zero growth of GNP [gross national product] has meant that increased education expenditure in real terms can only come at the expense of real reductions elsewhere" (Craven, Dick and Wood, 1983: 579). However, post-1992 expansion in the number of universities, number of students, costs of provision for government and growth of oversight requirements, fed into these

---

[6] From the 1960s until 1992 the only new higher education institution was the University College of Buckingham founded in 1976 as a private university (Shattock, 1994).

[7] The 1992 Further and Higher Education (Scotland) Act made separate higher education funding provisions for Scotland.

discussions and accelerated policy changes. Growing funding for universities came with growing exposure to the potential for government cuts or changes in policy (Anderson, 2016).

This long history of change eventually fed into the formation of the Student Loans Company[8] in 1990 and the issuance of the first loans. As we will see, student loans – in tandem with the UK higher education sector – have also grown significantly since their inception. It was also in the 1990s that first efforts were made to sell parts of the student loan book. The preparatory imperative – to organise the loans, their value, relationships with buyers, rules for a process for negotiating price, how sales would feature on government accounts – was clear from this early stage. However, different types of loans and different moments of sale involved preparatory imperatives that took different forms. Comparing two sales – the first student loan sale in 1998 and the most recent in 2017–18 – will show the distinct features of the preparatory imperative that moved from one particular political climate to another. Our suggestion will be that changing political times changed the basis for selling.

A Tale of Two Sales

The First Portfolio and its 1998 Sale

The Student Loans Company put part of the UK government's student loan portfolio up for sale in 1996. This initiated a two-year-long negotiation process through which a price and a sale were achieved. Through what means did this sale and settlement of price come about? It required the establishment of the Student Loans Company, the issuance of loans, calculating

---

[8] The Student Loans Company is a non-profit organisation owned by the UK government that administers student loans.

the present value of those loans, preparing these loans for sale by accounting for them using specific technical terms, finding and building relations with specific potential buyers (who were themselves especially established just for this purchase) and developing rules for how price would be negotiated. Selling student loans provided some very specific complexities. To understand these complexities, we need to continue our history of UK higher education.

The growth in number of UK universities and the size of the student population meant that the government's costs for funding "free" higher education were rapidly escalating in the 1990s. Kenneth Baker (1986, cited in Wilson, 1997: 12), the secretary of state for education, argued that:

> student numbers in higher education are at an all-time record level [and] we want still more to benefit. [...] But in doing so we must have regard to the claims on national resources. That is why I think that the time is ripe to investigate with an open mind all possible forms and sources of support.

The costs of higher education at a time of constrained government budgets provided a basis for supporting the introduction of loans as a way to reduce state spending. Loans were not initially conceived as a means to cover the costs of tuition fees (as we will see, this came much later). Instead, the loans were designed to cover students' costs of living, partially replacing maintenance grants, whose value had been frozen (Barr, 1989).[9] Through the Education (Student Loans) Act of 1990

---

[9] From 1989 other changes had also been set in place: the introduction of the Research Assessment Exercise meant the block grant for teaching and research were set apart (see Chapter 4; Shattock, 1994).

(UK Government, 1990), maintenance loans were introduced. These loans were straightforward, at least in comparison to the loans that came later. They were more or less conventional repayment loans. Once a student's income reached 85% of national average earnings, they would be required to make 60 equal monthly payments. A graduate's salary was calculated through tax returns. Only through low earnings could a graduate apply to defer their repayments. To do so, they would need to apply to the Student Loans Company every 12 months for as long as they could demonstrate that their earnings were below the threshold. Once this threshold was met, monthly repayments began regardless of any subsequent fluctuations in the graduate's salary. From their implementation in September 1990, the Student Loans Company has handled the administration of these and all subsequent loans (Hillman, 2013).

Putting the first tranche of student loans on sale in 1996 required some work by the Student Loans Company. At this time, the Company had 615,000 student borrowers and a portfolio of £3.7 billion.[10] Through this continual issuing of loans, they had become one of the larger personal lenders in the UK. They had achieved a certain scale and so had the resources and financial expertise to pursue the sale of parts of the loan book. But the Student Loans Company could not act alone. On the one hand, they were directly accountable to the Department for Education and so had to negotiate potential terms of sale directly with ministers. On the other hand they also had to figure out with potential buyers what these loans might be worth. Financial expertise was not enough, as these were not quite standard loans. The loans could be deferred according to earnings. Some 48% of graduates deferred their repayments

---

[10] See www.slc.co.uk/media/5531/slc_annualreport_1999.pdf

of these initial loans. The loans were offered to all students, so their capacity to repay was uncertain. Of these initial loans, 9.1% were in default (meaning students had missed two or more payments) and court proceedings had been initiated. However, a large number of defaulters were difficult to trace. The Student Loans Company used debt reclamation services to eventually track down 81% of defaulters.[11]

What collectively did this mean for the sale of student loans? For the Student Loans Company in its annual report, it meant selling the loans required "the preparation of a large quantity of historical information and close contact with the potential purchasers" (1998: 2). The historical information was required to attest to the viability of the loan book; that these were good debts, of value, that would be repaid. Close contact with potential purchasers was required to establish exactly how much they might be willing to pay for these slightly unusual debts. The rules around student loans would not change, even with their sale. Hence the sale came with its own certainties: that repayments would not change, methods of payment would not change, interest rate calculations would not change, and terms and conditions would not change. The potential purchasers were not just buying debt, but buying into a set of agreements. The Student Loans Company also had to continually reassure ministers that the sale would provide good value for money (see more on value for money in Chapter 6 and the AMC). The Company was set targets to reduce levels of default, with ministers insisting that a default rate below 8% would be important for improving the price received on the loans. The Student Loans Company also needed to look after its own interests: the sale of loans would potentially result in a reduction in

---

[11] See www.slc.co.uk/media/5531/slc_annualreport_1999.pdf

their own role, as having fewer loans to manage would mean less work. The contract for administering the loans post-sale was competitively tendered and won by the Student Loans Company, ensuring their own continued size and scope.

A price of £1.02 billion was eventually achieved for the first portfolio in 1998 as a result of negotiations that began in 1996. The buyer was formed just for this purchase – a firm called Finance for Higher Education. They were, in effect, formed by NatWest, a major banking group in the UK. The loans were purchased in order to become part of a pension fund portfolio, with long-term income streams accorded a steady value.

The sale demonstrated the importance of the preparatory imperative: the interests of ministers had to be taken into account to ensure that the UK taxpayer received value for money in return for loans that students had been given; the concerns of the newly formed purchasers for long-term and reliable income streams had to be reflected; the future role of the Student Loans Company and its ability to administer its portfolio needed to be secured; the default rate had to be squeezed as a means to emphasise the value of the loan book (that loans would be repaid); and the rules through which loans were issued that would continue on beyond their sale needed to be cast as something that would not constrain present value nor should be of concern to student borrowers (as these terms would not change). Managing the preparatory imperative managed the sale. However, this did not provide a preparatory basis through which to manage all future loan sales. The changing preparatory basis of loan sales is made visible by the ever-changing political backdrop that these sales had to negotiate.

In the time it took for negotiations to be resolved and a sale to take place, the UK had changed governments, from a post-Thatcherite administration led by John Major to a (New) Labour government led by Tony Blair and Gordon Brown. The sale of the first portfolio proved that these loans had a value and could be moved off the government's books – but only if the preparatory imperative was accomplished. As we will see, a move to income-contingent repayment loans and a more extensive loan system covering larger amounts of money led to a significant increase in the complexity of preparing loans for sale.

Income-Contingent Repayment Loans and their 2017–18 Sale

The initial issuance of loans was considered insufficient as a solution to the problem of rising costs for government that had resulted from the continued expansion of UK higher education. Further change came through yet another government report. Among various recommendations made by the Dearing Report (1997) was to introduce a fee to cover 25% of the cost of tuition. As a result, government costs would be altered. Instead of covering the full costs of tuition, the government would lend students 25% of their fees and cover the other 75% through direct payments to universities. The Report also recommended that these newly expanded loans be accounted for in new ways to deal with a "classification problem" (Barr and Crawford, 1998). Here the issue was how to classify the loans on government account books. The report advised, "do not treat the repayable part of loans in the same way as grants to students". Instead of being classified as public spending on government accounts, loans should be accounted for in a way that recognised that at least some of the loans would be repaid.

The Report is spot-on in saying that this [classification] problem needs to be fixed, and fixed fast. If not resolved, it is terminal. It is true that loans will bring in additional resources from around 2020 – but you cannot revive a corpse. Resolution, in contrast, will release a "pot of gold" of over £1 billion, *immediately* and *every year*. (Barr and Crawford, 1998: 75, emphasis in original)

At the time of the Dearing Report, UK government accounting reform was underway (and had been since 1993), so a change in accounting for loans could be accommodated within this broader effort. This accounting reform was moving away from the cash accounting rules that had been in place since 1866 and which involved calculating profits and losses on a cash basis and focusing on cash flows in "real time". Reform of government accounting practices shifted the focus from cash accounting to accruals accounting: "Accruals accounts record costs and revenues as they are respectively incurred and earned. By contrast, cash accounting records cash payments and receipts when they are made" (Likierman, 1995: 563). The move to adopt accruals accounting meant that a government's financial performance could be monitored during a financial year. It also meant more could be done with finance than simply recording cash flows. Student loans could now be classified as "financial transactions" instead of expenditure. This meant that loans issued from 2001–02 could be classified in an entirely differently way in comparison to the more or less straightforward accounting terms used for the first portfolio of loans sold in 1998. The value of loans could now be directly linked to these new means of recording their financial performance, with consequences for calculating their saleability. The preparatory imperative for these sales, would now clearly have new figures to work with on financial performance – but, as we will see – these figures went beyond government accounting reform as new loans also introduced new rules on repayment. The preparatory imperative had to incorporate both sets of reforms.

When new loans were introduced as part of the implementation of recommendations from the Dearing Report, the terms of borrowing were transformed into income-contingent repayment loans.[12] In a similar manner to the original repayment loans, students would begin to pay back the debt once their salary had reached a milestone, although this changed from 85% of national average earnings to a threshold of minimum earnings of £10,000 a year rising to £15,000 in 2003. Income contingency then meant that instead of 60 fixed monthly repayments from the moment a student reached the milestone, monthly repayments would be linked directly to a graduate's salary: 9% of total earnings would be taken from a graduate's salary to cover the cost of borrowing and now outstanding loans would be written off initially when a student reached the age of 65 (although this was then changed to 25 years after graduation in 2006, then changed again to 30 years after graduation in 2012). Whereas the previous sale of the first portfolio of loans had to contend with some uncertainties regarding the value of loans that derived from the rules that would continue beyond their sale, now these new loans would come with further contingencies – specifically income contingencies and future write-offs.

Further changes followed. Continuing expansion of the higher education sector in the UK, notably rapid increases in the student population, were said to have led to "deficiencies in the university estate [of] £11bn" (Dearing, 2004). This figure was utilised by government to introduce tuition fees of £3,000 a year in 2006.[13] The cost of these upfront tuition fees were now

---

[12] Although initially these still only covered cost of living support.

[13] The reform was controversial and the Higher Education Bill only passed its second reading by five votes (UK Parliament, 2004).

to be covered by income-contingent loans. For Nicholas Barr,[14] these were an effective strategic change:

> The introduction of small mortgage type loans in 1990 was a response to fiscal pressures from the growing system. The 1997 Dearing Report said, in effect: "Loans are the right way to go, but income-contingent loans, not mortgage loans." This was Iain Crawford's and my great victory. Dearing had a rational strategy of income-contingent loans, and fees of £1,000 covered by loans. That was a strategy – more cautious than I wanted, but a genuine stepping-stone. The government then subverted the strategy by introducing fees but without loans to cover them. The next round of reform was 2006, which was the one time that the government stuck to its strategy, because we had an education minister, Charles Clarke, who was bright enough to understand the idea of a strategy and sufficiently a political big beast to be able to protect it from cherry-picking.[15] So, the 2006 reforms included income-contingent loans to cover living costs, variable fees of up to £3,000 fully covered by income-contingent loans, and pro-access policies earlier in the system. That was a proper strategy. (Barr interview)

Income-contingent loans were pushed forward as a means to implement changes in the way higher education was funded as part of a New Labour strategy to manage government spending at the same time as adhering to left-of-centre principles to maintain wide access to higher education that was also fair. In theory students would still be able to *access* higher education

---

[14] With Iain Crawford, Barr is described as the architect of student loan reform: www.theguardian.com/education/2003/dec/02/highereducation.tuitionfees

[15] Further emphasising the importance of a political champion (see Chapters 5 and 6 and the importance of political support for a Social Impact Bond and pilot AMC).

as income-contingent repayments would protect them from
the problems caused by a low salary in any particular month.
Having the debt written off after a fixed time also meant that
the prospect of a debt-free future was still in theory achievable even for those with no or low income. However, to sell
these income-contingent loans would now mean preparing
potential buyers for the prospect of investing in an individual's earning prospects (something of a risk in comparison to
the contractual returns settled by the Social Impact Bond of
Chapter 5, for example). Although it can be argued either way
that these terms might or might not have maintained a principle of easy access to higher education, the precise framing of
the debt prospect on these terms meant that selling these loans
would be more difficult: these were not a form of debt in which
potential investors had experience.

At the same time, the terms of the income-contingent
loans were designed with a principle of *fairness*. This principle
was summarised by former Conservative minister for universities and science David Willetts (2015: 14):

Even though there are public benefits from a graduate going into a
very-well-paid job, it is not clear that on its own it justifies less afflu-
ent tax-payers subsidising it. Repayments by graduates who enjoy
earnings above the average as a result of their university education
appears fair – otherwise lower income non-graduate tax payers would
be meeting the cost of a university education.

Accomplishing a principle of fairness then depended upon
the notion that the population of graduates now saddled with
ever-increasing debts, would be in a position to earn more as
a result of their qualifications. The income-contingent loans
would make these debts fair, as the graduates would have
a strong chance of repaying the costs of their education and

these costs would not have to be covered by the general population of non-graduate taxpayers. This would also, in theory, aid the preparatory imperative of selling these loans. Granted these loans were bigger than their predecessors, were tied to new terms and conditions of income contingency and a fixed write-off, but the graduates themselves would be among the most able to repay. These were good debts to invest in as these were good debtors. At least in theory.

The move by government to start to sell tranches of the 2002–06 loan book have been mired in controversy. The first attempt to sell these loans in 2014 was scrapped by Vince Cable of the UK Coalition government as the price offered was not, in his view, good value for money for the taxpayer. Calculating what might constitute good value could be achieved by comparing the likely sale price to be achieved with the future income stream the government would receive from loan repayments (McGettigan, 2015). Reviving the prospects of this sale in 2016, once the Coalition government had been consigned to history by the outright election victory of the Conservative Party in 2015, caused its own problems. Preparatory work for the sale, once again undertaken by the Student Loans Company, had to cover a range of different activities.

Income contingency had to be taken into account. To sell and buy these debts required a value to be negotiated for the rate at which graduates with remaining debts were likely to meet the salary threshold and stay above that salary threshold. A value also had to be placed on what 9% of the salary of those graduates over the salary threshold was likely to be – and these were not the kinds of calculation upon which investors could draw on a great deal of experience. Those with most knowledge about these figures were the sellers – the Student Loans Company – who would once again look to administer the sale.

Along with income contingency, the write-off of unpaid debt also had to be taken into account. Loans issued in 2006 were being offered for sale in 2016. At ten years old, these remaining debts were ten years closer to being written off. And the age of these debts in general was a problem for their valuation. As these loans were now over ten years old, around half had been paid off. The idea that graduates would be good debtors had proven half right: 50% had earned sufficient salary to begin repayments immediately and 9% of their salary had been sufficient to clear their debts. Now that these debts had been paid, however, what was going on sale was the 50% held by graduates who had not earned as much, had not paid off as much, and had in some cases never earned enough to make any repayments. In the outstanding loans, 60% of graduates had not made a payment in the preceding financial year (Financial Times, 2017). The value of these loans and the amount that could be made from their sale looked doubtful.

Further issues mounted up for the UK government. Subsequent to the sale of the first portfolio of loans, other pre-1998 loans had been sold to a firm called Erudio. This firm had caused controversy and stood accused by the National Union of Students of trying to get students to repay loans even when their incomes had not reached the appropriate milestone (Weale, 2017). The Union suggested that government policy was now oriented by the prospects of future sales rather than by the needs of students. Principles of access and fairness seemed to be taking a backseat.

So why sell the loans at all? Although it might initially appear that selling off a public asset[16] also provides the means

---

[16] For more on public assets, see Milyaeva and Neyland (forthcoming).

to sell off a problem (or at least shift responsibility for that problem away from the public sector) the history of privatisation suggests this is not the case. The sale of UK trains, for example, has done little more than inspire ongoing, continuous and perhaps even increasing criticism of the government for failure to adequately regulate the sector. And much the same seems to happen with, for example, privatised energy firms and the amounts they charge customers or the use of Private Finance Initiatives for public buildings such as hospitals that are seen to incur huge future costs. The sale of student loans has not resulted in graduates' ire being redirected toward the investors who have purchased such debts, but remains firmly focused on the state. Selling the loans has not sold off the problem.

Selling tranches of loans seems to have been motivated by other issues. The accrual accounting terms used to classify the loans means that at the time of their sale in 2017–18 they were not listed as a public cost. They were not a debt that would be wiped off the books once money was received from their sale. Instead, under the terms of accrual accounting, any amount received from their sale would make a positive contribution to public finance. Selling the loans was thus a useful way to rebalance government books and address (at least an amount of) public debt. As a result, the sale of loans was attractive in 2017–18 as a means to bring in revenue. At the same time, the importance of value for money calculations receded as any price achieved could be promoted as a positive contribution to public debt. The amount of revenue achieved through the sale, however, depended on the preparatory imperative. With income-contingent loans, much depended on impaired value.

It had been clear from the sale of the first portfolio that student loans could not be sold at close to their face value; that is, the total amount of money lent. In line with other similar sales of debts, investors look to place a value in the present on the income stream they are likely to receive in the future. As Muniesa et al. (2017) suggest, things make sense from the perspective of an investor when they can derive the "present value from an estimate of the future" (108). The risk to be taken into account in coming up with a value is the likelihood that the face value will not be paid in full. Although this is a technique of valuation that began in private sector investments, Muniesa et al. (2017) continue that:

The state realizes the political potential of this way of looking at things and acquires accordingly the dispositions that are required in order to do so. This means indeed new types of people in command and new forms of economic technocracy. And this means also, perhaps more importantly, an entirely different way of deciding what should be done with money. (109)

Following from this, we might note that selling loans is then part of a broader move to develop these techniques for valuation in relations between the public and private sectors. At the same time, these acts of valuation seem to signal a change in the technocratic arrangements of government, including who is recruited, the skills required and who is in charge and responsible for making what kinds of decisions. In a similar manner to Chapter 2 wherein technocracy (albeit negotiated) dominated design decisions, implementation and further changes in the European Union Emissions Trading System, we could note that the 2017–18 sale of loans depended for the completion of its preparatory imperative on similar technocratic abundance.

But how could a value be placed on a tranche of student loans with their fixed terms of sale, income contingency, fixed write-off period; when the loans were ten years old, good debtors had paid off their loans and exited the scene, and what remained were loans where 60% had not made a payment in at least a year? The distinction between the sale price (what it would be reasonable to pay or what investors would be willing to pay) and face value of these loans seemed potentially huge. However, the UK government had acquired some experience in valuing these kinds of debts. In 2012 a change in government policy as a result of austerity measures that sought to cut public spending, led to an increase in student loans to £9,000 a year to cover the cost of tuition for full-time UK and EU students. This combined with a removal of the cap on how many students could enrol at a university saw a surge in loans from £6 billion in 2011–12 to £11.8 billion in 2015–16, with the total loan book being valued at £76.3 billion (compared with £39.6 billion in 2011–12; Cartwright, 2016). These were still income-contingent loans and so their value had to be calculated on specific terms. The government calculated that a student taking out a loan in 2012 would achieve their highest rate of earnings growth in 2027–29 (Shephard, 2013: 3). Hence the debt would not be paid very quickly. And some debts would never be paid in full. On top of these costs, the government was also subsidising the interest rate. These issues had to be reflected in the valuation the government would place on these loans in order to account for them on government books. The distinction between the face value of these loans (£76.3 billion) and their market value meant they had to be calculated as an impaired asset.

The impairment for these large post-2012 loans involved a calculation of net present value that had to take into account the specific complexity of terms and conditions, costs to government, and probable future income from these debts. The figure put on these debts in 2017–18 was that for every £1 lent, the return would be 55 pence (although there was volatility in the cost charges applied by government). In this way, valuation techniques used to put a monetary figure on the book value for post-2012 loans could be used to value the 2002–06 loans that were being put on sale. That is, their value had to be considered impaired. The tranche of loans that had a face value of £43 billion thus had an impaired value of £30 billion (taking into account further factors such as the age of the loans). Within this group of £43 billion loans, £3.7 billion of loans were being put on sale, although these had an impaired value of £2.5billion (Financial Times, 2017).

Could the impaired value of £2.5 billion be achieved as the sale price? The short answer is no. In a similar pattern to the sale of the first portfolio of loans, the Student Loans Company used valuation techniques as only part of its preparatory imperative. It also had to set up specific relationships with potential buyers and use these to negotiate how much of the impaired value they could achieve as a sale price. Once again a specific organisation was set up for the sale – this time titled Income Contingent Student Loans PLC. Once again the loans would be purchased in order to derive future income streams for pension funds. The prerogative for the buyer was to achieve a price at which the potential, but quite risky, future income stream would provide more value than its cost. As the value of the debts was risky, a selling technique was borrowed from the pre-crisis financial markets – debts were bundled up together and rated.[17] The 2002–06 loans were put into four bundles

---

[17] In the run-up to the financial crisis, banks secured against their future risks and the uncertainty that debt would not be repaid by bundling and selling debts. When these became the uncertainty (Davies, 2017), a state response was required in the form of a series of bail-outs. In a curious twist, it was now the state looking to reduce the level of public debt partly attributable to the financial crisis in order to bundle up its own risks and sell them.

that ranged from a single A-rating (not as high as AAA-rating, but considered upper-medium-grade debt with low risk) to unrated (meaning the debt was unlikely to be recovered). This meant that the four bundles could then achieve different prices, rather than all bundles being dragged down by the worst-looking risks. With the preparatory imperative complete, the loans could be sold. The final sale price achieved was £1.7 billion, which was £800 million less than the impaired value of the loans, or £2 billion less than their face value. The riskiest bundle of loans achieved a price of 8.9 pence for every pound of debt.[18]

The government aimed to continue these sales and raise around £12 billion from the sale of other 2002–06 loans in the following five years. As these loans did not count toward

---

[18] In a similar parallel to the financial crisis, the value of debt is low here. When US banks were in crisis, Mirowski (2013) suggests that buyers were encouraged by government to pay around $1.67 for every $100 of toxic assets with a guarantee that 93% of losses would be covered by the state. He suggests that: "This ramshackle contraption of the government backstopping corporate failure through disguised asset 'purchases' on a grand scale has morphed into a mutant form of capitalism, one that sports its origins in the neoliberal precept that the solution to supposed market failures is more markets" (347). Mirowski supports the CRESC observation that in the financial crisis, gains were privatised and losses were socialised. With the sale of student loans, accounting terms enabled that losses were kept off government books as these were positive sum sales, while potential future profits for investors were instead presentable as a necessary means to cut public debt.

public-sector net debt, it seemed that their sale could provide a positive reduction in public borrowing (which stood at £1.79 trillion at the time of the sale; Financial Times, 2017). Immediate cash made available by the sale could then be used by government straight away, instead of having to wait on future repayments, even if those payments might bring in more income in the future (McGettigan, 2015). However, this situation was not static: in 2019, these accounting terms used by government to place a positive value on the loans and their sale had to be changed following a ruling against the government by the Office for National Statistics in which the accounting terms were described as a "fiscal illusion".[19] The government was then forced to account for the proportion of loans that would not be repaid as public spending, changing the accounting terms for loans, making their sale less attractive to the state, as any income achieved would now need to be accounted for against this newly acquired cost. This may in turn lead to a change in government policy, with sales no longer appearing so attractive, the loans themselves appearing less attractive and the costs of higher education once again placed under scrutiny.[20]

Conclusion

In this chapter we have focused on the market sensibility of selling as a basis for managing a market-based intervention: the provision of loans to UK higher education students.

---

[19] See www.bbc.co.uk/news/education-46591500

[20] This time, by the Augar review; see: www.gov.uk/government/news/prime-minister-launches-major-review-of-post-18-education

Several features of the activities that we have considered in this chapter seem to stand out in comparison to previous chapters. The nature of the problem at stake, for example, seems to change. What was initially a concern for government costs at a time of rising student numbers, then became a concern for rebalancing public spending with attempts at selling the loans (see Chapter 8 for more on the changing relations of problems and solutions). Unlike the EU ETS (Chapter 2), for example, that has remained focused on CO_2 emissions throughout its phases or the Social Impact Bond (Chapter 5) that fixed in place a single solution, student loans have been subject to changes in government and transformations in national concern.

Furthermore, the loans and their sale that we have seen in operation in this chapter suggest a distinct temporality to the intervention. While we showed that the REF anticipates a future of greater university contributions to UK competitiveness, the EU ETS expects a cleaner atmosphere, the GDPR is oriented toward a new privacy-sensitive data future and the AMC anticipates future health impacts through incentives, the case of student loans allows us to see how an intervention builds on the past as much as it builds a distinct future. Successive changes in student loan policies, the amount borrowed, and the terms of borrowing each open up opportunities to then sell anew. The past (of government policies and borrowing by students, government accounts and historical loan tranches) is thus reworked as a sales opportunity. In place of a coherent and singular logic that pervades these policies, much seems to be done in the moment. Indeed, some of the actions involved in selling student loans appear quite short-term: immediate access to the money achieved from a sale and a quick contribution to the balancing of government books, seem more important than the long-term income that might be derived from the loans themselves or to what extent their sale achieves an adequate price.

Through the preparatory imperative we have tried to capture something of the complex practices, relations and devices through which this market-based intervention takes place. In terms of devices and practices we have seen that valuation and accounting techniques, discount rates and the impairment of assets are central to achieving a sale. But we have also seen that the expertise of the Student Loans Company in building close relationships with potential buyers and using those relationships to negotiate a price over time has been important. These devices for valuation bear some resemblance to the forms of anticipatory techniques we have seen in previous chapters, projecting forward a value (see, for example, the EU ETS and carbon leakage projections). And the historical features of valuation that we have noted in this chapter connect with some of those we have witnessed previously (with, for example, the business-as-usual counterfactual relying on historical data in Chapter 5). Selling, however, provides its own kinds of idiosyncratic features. For example, we can see the successive nature of the action here. Selling involves a preparatory imperative, but this builds on experiences of other sales of public entities, specific features of early student loans, the problems these sales created, and the conditions generated by the new terms of later student loan issues. As Nick Hillman, the former chief of staff and special adviser for the Department for Business, Innovation and Skills once put it, "the fact that higher fees could make higher education more like a regulated market, with students coming to resemble consumers, was a bonus, but it was not the primary purpose" (Hillman, 2016: 338–9).

We can now start to discern a gentle shift in attention across the chapters of this book. We began with a strong focus on regulation and allocation in setting constraints on business and distributing money through various forms of bureaucratic infrastructures (in the EU ETS, REF and GDPR). Now we are starting to see a clear emphasis on issues of financing in attracting investors to a Social Impact Bond, raising funds through the pilot AMC and selling student loans. Bureaucratic infrastructures are not necessarily absented from the action, but on occasion they become market actors engaging with and sometimes even assimilating private, for-profit entities. In Chapters 8 and 9 we will now begin to draw together the features of our argument from the preceding chapters. We will consider the ways in which market sensibilities give particular form to market-based interventions as a way to solve public problems (Chapter 8) and how participants in these interventions go about assessing success. This will allow us to explore the notions of progress that the market-based interventions examined throughout this book presuppose (Chapter 9).

References

American Academy of Arts and Sciences (AAAS) (2016) *Public Research Universities: Serving the Public Good*. Available at: www.amacad.org/multimedia/pdfs/publications/researchpapersmonographs/PublicResearchUniv_PublicGood.pdf (last accessed 3 April 2019).

Anderson, R. (2016) University fees in historical perspective. *History & Policy*. Policy Paper, 8 February. Available at: www.historyandpolicy.org/policy-papers/papers/university-fees-in-historical-perspective (last accessed 3 April 2019).

Barr, N. (1989) The White Paper on student loans. *Journal of Social Policy* 18(3): 409–17.

Barr, N. and Crawford, I. (1998) The Dearing Report and the government's response: A critique. *Political Quarterly* 69(1): 72–84.

BBC News (2012) Senior Lib Dems apologise over tuition fees pledge. Available at: www.bbc.co.uk/news/uk-politics-19646731 (last accessed 3 April 2019).

BBC News (2016) Lib Dems blame general election defeat on "perfect storm". Available at: www.bbc.co.uk/news/uk-politics-35615285 (last accessed 3 April 2019).

Callon, M., Meadel, C. and Rabehariosa, V. (2002) The economy of qualities. *Economy and Society* 31(2): 194–217.

Canaan, J. and Shumar, W. (eds.) (2008) *Structure and Agency in the Neoliberal University*. New York: Taylor & Francis.

Cartwright, D. (2016) *Student Loans in England: Financial Year 2015–2016. Statistical First Release*. Student Loans Company (SLC), 16 June. Available at: www.slc.co.uk/media/7594/slcsfr012016.pdf (last accessed 3 April 2019).

Cochoy, F. (1998) Another discipline for the market economy: Marketing as a performative knowledge and know-how for capitalism. In M. Callon (ed.), *The Laws of the Market*. Oxford: Blackwell, pp. 194–221.

Cochoy, F. (2009) Driving a shopping cart from STS to business, and the other way round: On the introduction of shopping carts in American grocery stores (1936—1959). *Organization* 16: 31–55.

Cochoy, F. (2010) Reconnecting marketing to "market-things". In L. Araujo, J. Finch and H. Kjellberg (eds.), *Reconnecting Marketing to Markets*. Oxford: Oxford University Press, pp. 29–49.

Collini, S. (2012) *What Are Universities For?* London: Penguin Books.

Craven, B., Dick, B. and Wood, B. (1983) Resource allocation in higher education in Britain. *Higher Education* 12(5): 579–89.

CRESC (2013) *The Great Train Robbery: Rail Privatization and After. A CRESC Public Interest Report*. Manchester: CRESC, University of Manchester.

Davies, W. (2017) *The Limits of Neoliberalism*. London: Sage.

Dearing, R. (1997) *Higher Education in the Learning Society*. London: Her Majesty's Stationery Office. Available at: www.educationengland. org.uk/documents/dearing1997/dearing1997.html (last accessed 3 April 2019).

Dearing, R. (2004) We will all benefit from tuition fees. *Guardian*, 8 January. Available at: www.theguardian.com/politics/2004/jan/08/ publicservices.studentpolitics (last accessed 3 April 2019).

Financial Times (2017) UK government to book £800m loss from student loan sale. Available at: www.ft.com/content/726e3158-d522-11e7-8c9a-d9c0a5c8d5c9 (last accessed 3 April 2019).

Fuller, S. (2016) Markets as educators, or have we always been neoliberal? *Social Epistemology Review and Reply Collective*, 18 January. Available at: https://social-epistemology.com/2016/01/18/markets-as-educators-or-have-we-always-been-neo-liberal-steve-fuller/ (last accessed 3 April 2019).

Gil, N. (2015) LSE takes legal action to evict occupying student protesters. *Guardian*, 30 April. Available at: www.theguardian.com/world/ 2015/apr/30/lse-takes-legal-action-to-evict-occupying-student-protesters (last accessed 3 April 2019).

Guala, F. (2001) Building economic machines: The FCC auctions. *Studies in History and Philosophy of Science* 32(3): 453–77.

Guala, F. (2008) How to do things with experimental economics. In D. MacKenzie, F. Muniesa and L. Siu (eds.), Do Economists Make Markets? On the Performativity of Economics. Oxford: Princeton University Press, pp. 128–62.

Harvey, D. (2005) *A Brief History of Neoliberalism*. Oxford: Oxford University Press.

Hillman, N. (2013) From grants for all to loans for all: Undergraduate finance from the implementation of the Anderson Report (1962) to the implementation of the Browne Report (2012). *Contemporary British History* 27(3): 249–70.

Hillman, N. (2016) The Coalition's higher education reforms in England. *Oxford Review of Education* 42(3): 330–45.

Holmwood, J. (2014) Beyond capital? The challenge for sociology in Britain. *British Journal of Sociology* 65(4): 607–18.

Lewis, P., Vasagar, J., Williams, R. and Taylor, M. (2010) Student protest over fees turns violent. *Guardian*, 10 November. Available at: www.theguardian.com/education/2010/nov/10/student-protest-fees-violent (last accessed 3 April 2019).

Likierman, A. (1995) Resource accounting and budgeting: rationale and background. *Public Administration* 73(4): 562–70.

McGettigan, A. (2013) *The Great University Gamble: Money, Markets and the Future of Higher Education*. London: Pluto Press.

McGettigan, A. (2015) Cash today. *London Review of Books* 37(5): 24–8. Available at: www.lrb.co.uk/v37/n05/andrew-mcgettigan/cash-today (last accessed 3 April 2019).

Milyaeva, S. and Neyland, D. (forthcoming) English higher education: From a public good to a public asset. In K. Birch and F. Muniesa (eds.), *Turning Things Into Assets*. Cambridge, MA: MIT Press.

Mirowski, P. (2013) *Never Let a Serious Crisis Go To Waste*. London: Verso.

Mirowski, P. and Nik-Khah, E. (2008) Markets made flesh: Performativity, and a problem in science studies, augmented with consideration of the FCC auctions. In D. MacKenzie, F. Muniesa and L. Siu (eds.), *Do Economists Make Markets? On the Performativity of Economics*. Oxford: Princeton University Press, pp. 190–224.

Molesworth, M., Scullion, R. and Nixon, E. (eds.) (2011) *The Marketisation of Higher Education and The Student as Consumer*. London: Routledge

Mountford-Zimdars, A., Jones, S., Sullivan, A. and Heath, A. (2013) Framing higher education: Questions and responses in the British Social Attitudes Survey, 1983–2010. *British Journal of Sociology of Education* 34(5-6): 792–811.

Muniesa, F., Doganova, L., Ortiz, H., Pina-Stranger, Á., Paterson, F., Bourgoin, A., Ehrenstein, V., Juven, P.-A., Pontille, D., Saraç-Lesavre, B.

and Yon, G. (2017) *Capitalization: A Cultural Guide*. Paris: Presses de Mines.

OECD (2015) *Education at a Glance 2015*. Available at: www.oecd-ilibrary.org/education/education-at-a-glance-2015_eag-2015-en (last accessed 3 April 2019).

Owen, T. (1980) The University Grants Committee. *Oxford Review of Education* 6(3): 255–78.

Owen, T. (1985) Financing university education in Britain. *Western European Education* 17(3): 45–60.

Phipps, C. (2014) Demonstrators in "scuffles" with police as students march against fees – as it happened. *Guardian*, 19 November. Available at: www.theguardian.com/education/live/2014/nov/19/students-march-tuition-fees-live (last accessed 3 April 2019).

Popp Berman, E. (2008) Why did universities start patenting? Institution-building and the road to the Bayh-Dole Act. *Social Studies of Science* 38(6): 835–71.

Shattock, M. (1994) *The UGC and the Management of British Universities*. London and Buckingham: SRHE & Open University Press.

Shattock, M. and Berdahl, R. (1984) The British University Grants Committee 1919–83: Changing relationships with government and the universities. *Higher Education* 13(5): 471–99.

Shephard, N. (2013) *The Actual Financing Costs of English Higher Education Student Loans*. Available at: www.nuffield.ox.ac.uk/economics/papers/2013/FundingCosts20130508.pdf (last accessed 3 April 2019).

Smith, C. (1990) *Auctions: The Social Construction of Value*. Los Angeles, CA: University of California Press.

Student Loans Company (1998) *Student Loans Company Limited Annual Report 1998*. Available at: www.slc.co.uk/media/5532/slc_annualreport_1998.pdf (last accessed 3 April 2019).

UK Government (1990) *Education (Student Loans) Act*. Available at: www.legislation.gov.uk/ukpga/1990/6/contents/enacted (last accessed 3 April 2019).

UK Government (2015) *Participation Rates in Higher Education: Academic Years 2006/2007-2014/2015*. Available at: www.gov.uk/government/uploads/system/uploads/attachment_data/file/552886/HEIPR_PUBLICATION_2014-15.pdf (last accessed 3 April 2019).

UK Parliament (2004) *House of Commons Votes and Proceedings Tuesday 27th January 2004*. Available at: www.publications.parliament.uk/pa/cm/cmvote/40127v01.htm (last accessed 3 April 2019).

Vernon, K. (2004) *Universities and the State in England, 1850-1939*. London: Routledge

Weale, S. (2017) Universities minister announces sale of student loan book. *Guardian*, 6 February. Available at: www.theguardian.com/money/2017/feb/06/universities-minister-announces-sale-of-student-loan-book (last accessed 3 April 2019).

Willetts, D. (2015) *Issues and Ideas on Higher Education: Who Benefits? Who Pays?* London: Policy Institute at King's College London.

Wilson, W. (1997) *Student Grants, Loans and Tuition Fees*. Research Paper No 97/119. House of Commons Library. Available at: http://researchbriefings.files.parliament.uk/documents/RP97-119/RP97-119.pdf (last accessed 3 April 2019).

8

Problems and Solutions

Opening

In this chapter we will draw together the empirical and analytic insights from previous chapters as we now move to address more directly the question: *can markets solve problems?* Our focus throughout the empirical examples has been to explore market sensibilities as ways of thinking about, orienting, directing and intervening upon specific public problems. We suggested in the Introduction to this book that we would pursue an emergent definition of public problems, allowing the empirical data to speak of the possibilities this term offers. As a result, in the chapters we have examined the public bases of these problems in a variety of ways. For example, the problems we have considered are public through being widely shared and they have a broad membership called upon to recognise their importance. They are also public in their geographic extension, often crossing national domains or held up as examples for others to learn from. Responsibility for these problems has also been taken up by what would once have been termed the public sector (state, government, local authorities or superstate infrastructure) which now takes an array of forms. The problems are public, then, in their visibility, membership and spatial dispersion.

But these are not just any problems: these are particularly intractable problems, often of longstanding concern and this is partly why they have been addressed through market sensibilities. The policy-makers who took part in our research often consider these sensibilities to be transformative for the public characteristics of a problem: changing its membership, spatial location and transforming who and what is responsible. The hope is that in place of intractability comes recognisable and significant change. Here, trade and exchange, for example, can be seen as an initial means to anticipate industrial solutions to climate change through the trading of emissions allowances in the EU ETS. Competition is pushed forward in the REF as a basis for organising and resolving the challenges of how to distribute limited government research funds to a growing UK university sector. Property and ownership provide a means to reconceive two distinct markets for privacy through regulation in the EU GDPR or through start-up firms in the US. In a Social Impact Bond for children at risk, investment and return offers one way to address the apparently intractable costs of social care. An Advance Market Commitment for vaccination corrals incentives as a means to propel market actors into supplying low-income countries with new vaccines. And selling provides the UK government with a basis for trying to address the growing costs of university education. Reorienting market-based interventions through these sensibilities anticipates significant change in the public as a collective affected by the problem and the public sector as responsible for its solution.

This seems coherent. Yet our preceding chapters illustrate a variety of complexities made manifest through these interventions. What counts as the public is at stake in various forms as interventions develop. Students, for example, go from being given grants to being given loans and in the process they are transformed from public beneficiaries to debtors. At the same time, the state changes somewhat from providing a benefit to becoming a money lender. And although we have used each example to illustrate a market sensibility, in order to provide in-depth analysis of how these sensibilities are accomplished in practice, the examples do not remain narrowly focused. For example, aspects of competition also enter into the EU ETS through competitive pressures that industries suggest they are under. Or the REF contains aspects of property and ownership in discussions of intellectual property rights allocated to research outputs; the AMC also involves selling; the Social Impact Bond involves incentives; and so on. Complexity emerges around what counts as the public, the problem and the principal sensibility in each intervention. Our argumentative strategy has been to focus on the sensibility that seems most central to those managing each intervention as a means to interrogate its practical accomplishment. In this way, market sensibilities and public problems have been presented in detail, but also mediated through our own editorial decisions regarding what to prioritise.

Yet when we move between the specific detail of particular interventions and more general considerations of market sensibilities for intervening in public problems, further complexities arise with the very notion of problem and solution. It is not always the case, for example, that a problem straightforwardly precedes a solution (with children at risk being reconceptualised as an investment scheme in order to fit the demands of a Social Impact Bond) or that a solution retains a steady characteristic throughout an intervention (with the EU ETS being redefined through phases) or that a coupling of problem and solution proves consistent (with student loans being used to address distinct problems over 25 years).

In this chapter we will take on these issues and dedicate ourselves to the task of reconsidering our empirical examples with problems and solutions at the forefront of our analysis. This will provide a particular means to address the more general question of *can markets solve problems?* Hence instead of providing a narrow, single answer to the question *can markets solve problems?* – which would in itself be too limited given the range of problems addressed through markets and the need to consider the array of solutions brought to bear on problems – we will argue in this chapter that considering problems and solutions in detail has some key analytic advantages. First, by considering public problems in detail we can denaturalise the problems at the centre of each of our empirical case studies. This is important insofar as the specific nature of what a public problem is, we suggest, requires study as part of the effort required to make sense of why and how a particular solution has been articulated. The composition of problems requires study. Second, the relationship between problem and solution in each of our cases is not stable or necessarily enduring. These relationships also, then, need to be placed under scrutiny to make sense of how they came about. Solutions and their relationships to public problems require study. Third, the practices of making sense of a public problem in a specific way and putting together a specific solution appears deeply entangled with the kinds of consequences that emerge through particular couplings of problems and solutions. It is somewhat limiting, we suggest, to only explain these differences via the analytic pursuit of a single political programme of action (coherent or otherwise) such as neoliberalism and its derivatives. As a prior step to understanding how these couplings of problem and solution come to share common features (and hence might make sense as part of a shared programme) their distinctive characteristics and histories need to be understood in order to trace out how these play a part in giving effect to specific consequences.

The chapter thus opens up a detailed consideration of problems, solutions and market sensibilities. To achieve this, we will turn back to our empirical examples and consider different ways in which problems, solutions and market sensibilities can be illustrated. In a similar analytic strategy to our preceding chapters, we will use our empirical examples to illustrate the specific shape given to problems and solutions while also being aware that the examples could be reoriented in various ways to achieve distinct analytic effects. Our editorial strategy has been to utilise our examples in ways that we think respect the views of research participants at the same time as providing a means to interrogate different aspects of problems and solutions. The chapter will end with a consideration of what it means to treat these groupings of problems and solutions as in some way coherent or as having aggregate characteristics. We will explore the suggestion that finding (more or less) coherent, aggregate programmes of political action is the upshot of a search for the general at the expense of the particular. By starting with the particular, we will assess the possibility of building out toward different kinds of generals.

Problems, Solutions and Market Sensibilities

Throughout our chapters we have seen problems and solutions entangled in a variety of ways. For the regulators we have met in our chapters this is not always a straightforward matter of solutionism whereby "monumental, and narrow-minded solutions" are constituted in an attempt to solve problems that instead turn out to be "extremely complex, fluid, and contentious" (Morozov, 2013: 6). There are attempts, for example, to modify the terms of some interventions over time (such as the EU ETS) to better reflect the complexity of a problem and there are efforts made to intervene on a scale that is not national or international (such as the Social Impact Bond). Our interventions, then, are not all monumental in scale or rigidity. It would also be a little unfair to characterise most of the interventions we have looked at as instances of techno-fundamentalism, characterised by a "belief that we can, should, and will invent a machine that will fix the problems the last machine caused" (Vaidhyanathan, 2006: 556). Although, for example, the REF could be noted as a solution that tried to overcome some problems noted with its predecessor (the Research Assessment Exercise), it is not entirely machinic. As we saw in Chapter 3, human judgement continues to occupy a central role. Instead of solutionism and techno-fundamentalism, we need to carefully explore the terms on which problems and solutions are made. Our examples of market-based interventions that give effect to specific market sensibilities can prove central to this exploration.

1. Problem and Solution as an International Standard

In Chapter 4 we presented the EU General Data Protection Regulation (GDPR). Here we find a piece of legislation designed by regulators to act as a new standard for data protection and privacy regulation that others ought to follow. This normative agenda was partly designed to oppose or deflect critical voices from across the Atlantic that argued that any grand regulatory intervention into the data market would undermine economic growth. At a time of little or no growth in most industries, the booming trade in data was the thing that ought to be protected according to US politicians (echoing the voice of the data industry lobbyists). Normativities underscored both sides of the argument: for European regulators, users' data needed to be protected and here was a new standard that other

administrations ought to follow; for US critics, the data industry was a rare beacon of economic growth and itself ought to be
protected, undermining the free flow of data would only damage economic growth prospects.

Each side of the debate makes sense of the problem and the
solution in different ways. For European Union regulators, the
problem of users' data is clear and apparent (while critics seem
to counter that the extent of this problem is unproven) and the
solution, as a set of rights to be invoked by data subjects and
conditions under which the data industry should work, would
prove a way forward (while for critics, this solution is the potential problem). This European coupling of problem and solution
went further. It was not just that this way of making sense of
the problem could be resolved through this form of solution.
The intervention could set a bold international standard. For
Viviane Reding, vice-president of the European Commission
and EU Justice Commissioner, in a keynote speech[1] at the time
of the drafting of the legislation, the GDPR was to "become an
international standard-setter in terms of modern data protection rules" (Reding, 2012).

The coupling of problem and solution that takes place in
the development of the GDPR – and in particular the effort
made to produce a standard setting intervention – is perhaps best illustrated as a form of Kuhnian exemplar. Kuhn's
(1962) work on natural scientists draws a distinction between
a puzzle-type problem and other types of problem – a distinction that rests on the degree to which there is the assured
existence of a solution. A puzzle presupposes that a solution
can, and maybe even will, be found.[2] For Kuhn this generates

---

[1] At the Innovation Conference, "Digital, Life, Design".
[2] Other types of problem leave the possibility of a solution
more open – rather than a puzzle with an assured guarantee

particular couplings of problem and solution. That is, a solution can become paired with a problem, and one can be continually noted as an adequate means to deal with the other. This pairing can accomplish such a strong relationship that the adequacy, extent or need to interrogate the problem–solution relationship can become overlooked. The pairing become the solution that they seem to be.

Accomplishing this kind of certainty of status, for Kuhn, means that the pair of problem and solution can become a paradigm-exemplar. These kinds of paradigm, according to Kuhn, can become accepted as the basis on which a problem can and ought to be resolved. The GDPR as international standard-bearer for data protection would thus act on the global stage as the solution that it appears to be, provide evidence that data subjects' concerns can be taken into account, and that this does not destroy the data industry. In this way a paradigm generates the assumption that a solution exists – it renders the problem puzzle-like, with the assured possibility that it can be solved. It is moved from the category of more complex problems wherein any pairing of problem and solution might be considered more fragile. As an exemplar it also intimates a preferred order to the problem–solution relationship. That is, the problem is now considered as a more or less naturally occurring entity that pre-exists this particular solution and can be eliminated through successfully carrying out the steps that this solution sets out. In this sense, to act as an

---

of a solution, there might be particularly complex issues that require a response, an attempt to alleviate some features of the problem, provide an initial step towards a possible future in which a more comprehensive solution might be found, and so on.

international standard for data protection, the GDPR must prove that it has formulated the problem correctly as much as it has formulated an adequate solution.

These efforts to build what would become a more or less settled coupling of problem and solution that might work as a new regulatory exemplar, seemed to be required to gain sufficient initial support and momentum for the GDPR from businesses, from national regulators and European politicians. Support could then help further set in place the precise coupling of problem and solution that the regulatory text could accomplish. It did not mean, however, that the exemplar as a regulatory text was straightforward to compose. As we saw in Chapter 4, 3,999 amendments to the draft Regulation were submitted, national data protection authorities rallied against aspects of the proposed legislation, data industry lobbyists sought ways to raise concerns and negotiating the final text took years. And the coupling of problem and solution proposed in the draft text meant that the regulators had to carefully manage the relationship between the Regulation and the market. The GDPR was unlike other market-based interventions where industry might be set a target to achieve, and regulators assumed that target would be achieved by industry through a cost-sensitive search for the most efficient and effective means (like in the EU ETS). Instead, through the GDPR, the data industry was expected to take on certain concerns (for example, around consent) but it would be data subjects who would now be equipped with rights to set demands for the data industry (for example, around data portability and the right to be forgotten). The Regulation would be market-enabling by ensuring the same distribution of obligations for the data industry across Europe, but this would also enable market participants in the sense of giving data subjects rights that went beyond standard consumer rights. The consequences that would follow on from implementation of the GDPR would then depend on how these rights were interpreted by data subjects, how often and to what extent they enforced them, how industry responded and to what extent, and in what manner industry was punished for not meeting data subjects' demands.

The exemplar coupling of problem–solution did not, then, simply involve producing a single text (the policy document) that other nations might follow. It was about producing a market situation in which the data industry would have new obligations and have to meet new demands and data subjects would be newly equipped to set demands. The work of people like Reding (and numerous civil servants, politicians, and law-makers at the European Commission and the European Parliament) was not a reflection of an easy-to-compose exemplar, but instead emphasised the hard work required to specify the nature of the problem as being amenable to solution by this Regulation and the compelling need for this coupling of only this articulation of the problem and solution. As we also noted in Chapter 4, re-specifying the nature of the problem of privacy in terms of control via the articulation of modified forms of property rights over data were each significant accomplishments. As to whether or not, or to what extent, the GDPR will indeed turn out to be future-proof and fulfil its aims to operate as a regulatory exemplar, it is currently too early to tell. For our purposes in this chapter, we can note that the GDPR provides one initial basis for articulating a relationship between problem and solution. In place of the constraints imposed by trying to answer the question *can markets solve problems?* in a narrow sense, we have one initial step toward moving from particular intervention to more general description: market-based interventions can anticipate paradigm-exemplar-like couplings of problem and solution. In the next section we will turn our attention to a different basis for making sense of problem–solution relationships, more focused on dialogic democracy. We can find here some illustrative material from the GDPR, but also more comprehensively via the EU ETS, the REF and the AMC.

2. *Problem, Solution and Participation*

Although the paradigm-exemplar provides us with one way of exploring the coupling of problem and solution in market-based interventions, we can also interrogate the ways in which such interventions promote a sense of ongoing, participatory negotiation. Rather than focus on the setting of a singular standard, turning attention to these forms of negotiation can open up a space for analysing the ways in which change is articulated through market-based interventions. These more or less rigorous forms of participatory action involve what Callon, Lascoumes and Barthe refer to as "dialogic democracy" (2009: 188). Herein a set of procedures "are designed to promote the organisation of a debate that is respectful of scientific and political uncertainties so that it is better able to take responsibility for them and manage them," (2009: 188). In this sense, dialogue provides a means for specific form to be given to problem and solution, for these to be discussed and even for implementation to be monitored and further changes negotiated. Hence uncertainties regarding climate change and how it ought to be managed, or privacy in a new data saturated world, or government funding for university research at a time of limited budgets, might each be engaged by drawing relevant participants together. This "drawing together" would act as a kind of problematisation, a focal point for engaging a range of participants, their differences and uncertainties, around a concern that might then be transformed into a course of future action. In this way, rather than establish an expectation that a market sensibility would solve a problem, the sensibility might provide the focal point for orienting dialogue around the nature of how a problem and a solution could be articulated.

According to Callon: "problematization possesses certain dynamic properties: it indicates the movements and detours that must be accepted as well as the alliances that must be forged" for a proposed course of action to succeed in creating an effect (1986: 203). But the ongoing, participatory aspect of this approach to problems and solutions should not be overlooked – this is crucial to keeping open the possibility of change in making sense of the problem and the solution. Dialogue is thus not reducible to procedures alone. Instead, engaging with problems and solutions is about drawing up a map of externalities (things currently not taken into account), concerned groups, positions and relations. As Callon et al. suggest: "No debate is possible without this cartography" (2009: 189).

What would a cartography of market-based interventions look like? It seems that problematisation and forms of dialogic democracy are not directed toward fixing in place a single or rigid problem–solution relationship in the manner of a paradigm-exemplar. In contrast to the search for an established means of coupling problem and solution for others to follow, the problematisation is closer to a local matter of potential projection: a "hypothesis" (Callon, 1986: 221) of sorts that would enable a way forward if sufficient numbers commit to the actions it presupposes and if those actions turn out to have the effects anticipated. These courses of action can contain a specific market referent. But here markets enter into the action as both problem and solution. First, markets appear to offer an efficient and effective way to resolve a public problem by stripping away externalities:

Markets, when calculating interest, profits and returns on investment draw a strict dividing line between that which is taken into account and that which is not. This is where their strength lies, since they can be deaf to the protests of residents, spokespersons of future generations, or orphan patients. (Callon et al., 2009: 236)

Efficiency comes through casting out externalities. Left to itself, the market "tends to produce injustice" (Callon et al., 2009: 236) as expensive and overlooked externalities tend to include the voices of those most subjected to the consequences of market-based action. Second, dialogic democracy can then provide a basis for equipping the excluded with the means to participate. The market is always "on the lookout for new needs it can express, but it has every interest in waiting for these identities to become consolidated and credit worthy" (Callon et al., 2009: 237). Processes of dialogic democracy can engage in identifying externalities and giving them measure and even attributing a cost to this measure. What were externalities become equipped to participate in dialogue and the market-based intervention is provided with a means to take former externalities into account.

Certain features of the GDPR, such as consultations with concerned parties, could be open to this kind of treatment – although the 3,999 requested amendments suggests that the form of dialogue is not without its own problems. And the primary focus of the GDPR seemed to be standard-setting – the production of what we have termed an exemplar. This required extensive negotiation up to the point where a regulatory text was agreed, rather than ongoing discussion that might continue post implementation. By way of contrast, the EU ETS as another large-scale European regulatory framework, established a regulatory space within which different views have been drawn together and given voice in a continuing process of dialogue. Here in the EU ETS, the notion of externalities is particularly appropriate given its centrality in environmental economics and the theoretical rationale of cap and trade systems to address a problem of pollution. As we have seen in Chapter 2, the EU ETS allows "a lot of learning by doing" (interview, DG CLIMA 1). With the EU ETS we chose to focus on its present incarnation, and no doubt a historical study of its development would have opened up various points of interest and concerns with participatory processes (see, for example, MacKenzie, 2009). But even in its current form, efforts to establish the future phases of the EU ETS can illustrate features of participatory forms of problem–solution relationships. The EU ETS provides a means for the problem of climate change to be grasped in the form of emissions allowances, a price for allowances, their passionately negotiated rules of allocation and their trade and exchange. What might otherwise be the primary illustrative example of an externality – pollution – is drawn in to the heart of a market-based intervention. But as we also suggested in Chapter 2, problems with this intervention continue to arise. For example, despite a broad array of relevant participants, coming up with and settling what the cap ought to be for the next phase has not been straightforward.

In this way the EU ETS has to deal with a range of emerging concerns: the effects of behind-the-scenes lobbying of MEPs as concerned industries looked to get their views incorporated into discussions; the ability of environmental activists to counter the forecasting ability of industries with their economics-inflected reports; the level and depth of expertise contained in these reports that did not seem to be matched in parliamentary debates; and parliamentary decisions that seemed to incorporate some concerns (climate change, European competitiveness and carbon leakage) and not others (changes wrought by the financial crisis). Participatory forms of problem–solution relationships can then become characterised by an uneven distribution of concern for the issues that might be taken into account. What comes to count as an adequate rendition of the problem from which a solution might follow is a difficult accomplishment. For some, the participatory form can start to seem like the problem.[3] For example, as environmental activists found that their proposals for a more rigorous cap were not adopted, they grew weary with the EU ETS (BBC News, 2010). They had to choose between continued participation in a disappointing intervention or withdraw in order to maintain credibility but also risk damaging the EU ETS.

Considerations around participation in the EU ETS seems to go hand-in-hand with problems raised about participation: to participate is to prolong a particular approach to the problem–solution relationship that (at least according to activists who took part in our research) may no longer be helpful. The participatory form is not guaranteed to bring about a harmonious solution and the solution itself can become identified as central to the problem.

But we should not assume that participatory forms or their problems are exclusive to European legislation like the EU ETS or GDPR. At the level of national interventions in the UK, the REF (Chapter 3) has used ongoing consultations and reviews (such as the Stern review) as a means to give voice to concerns about its regulatory framework and effects (see Chapter 9). Once again, whose voice is heard and whose voice has consequences are not always clear, along with questions stubbornly persisting on the origins, content and format of these

---

[3] This runs in some contrast to the somewhat optimistic conclusions of Callon et al. (2009), who look to participation through hybrid forums as a means to, for example, democratise democracy.

consultations.[4] Participatory, dialogic democracy is not a guaranteed or straightforward way to resolve couplings of problems and solutions, but for our purposes does enable the equipping of market participants to be drawn to analytic attention.

One means to extend these ideas on problematisation and dialogue has been proposed by Marres (2011, 2012, and with Lezaun, 2011), whose work is focused on the various entanglements surfaced in moments of issue formation. We can explore the development of the Advance Market Commitment for pneumococcal vaccines (see Chapter 6) and its particular coupling of problem and solution through these terms. In place of any strong emphasis on democratic fora, the range of possible ways to understand vaccination, health problems and poverty that the AMC would take on, instead emerged through a series of socio-material entanglements. Initial work by economists and the Center for Global Development produced a report establishing a means to consider the problem of low-income country populations and their lack of access to vaccines. A problem of sorts was articulated, but only made to make sense through its entanglement with infected bodies, epidemiological evidence, economic reasoning, budgets, G8 diplomacy, particular ways of understanding and making sense of government interventions. And this was not a deterministic entanglement; initial reports exploring and then advocating an Advance Purchase Commitment, and then Advance Market Commitment, changed over time. Initially the aim was to focus on the apparent problem of absent incentives for pharmaceutical firms to invest in research into new vaccines for diseases prevalent in

---

[4] See, for example, https://wonkhe.com/blogs/hefce-launches-consultation-on-ref2021/ and www.fasttrackimpact.com/single-post/2016/12/13/HEFCE-consultation-impact-REF2021

low-income countries (for example, malaria). With the involvement of a new global health partnership (GAVI) to take up and explore the possibilities this new policy mechanism might offer, the focus shifted to incentivising pharmaceutical firms to scale-up manufacture of near-to-market vaccines (for pneumococcal diseases). This change emerged through the continuing work to build a socio-material basis for intervention: drawing in governments as donors and recipients of funds, philanthropists as funders, epidemiological and advocacy work around the importance and urgent need to intervene in pneumococcus, practical work to ensure that an intervention could logistically operate, pharmaceutical firms who would do the manufacturing, more work from economists on pricing, and consultants' efforts to make sense of the pharmaceutical industry, what level of price might constitute an incentive, and whether the AMC did have an incentivising effect.

In place of a democratic participatory forum came ongoing efforts to carefully plait relations between these entities that could become binding over time, but also through which issues could be raised and to some extent addressed. As we noted in Chapter 6, the binding nature of the intervention was deemed particularly important as time inconsistency (changes in donor government's priorities, or changes in government over time) was considered a disincentive for pharmaceutical firms to commit to new manufacturing investments. Issue formation here required a range of different participants and recognition of the actions that each participant was required to perform in order for a solution to take place. The production of this preferred outcome – vaccination and the possibility of saving lives – required a range of different actions for entities to become entangled into the form of solution to which they would respond. Governments required legally binding contracts and payment terms attuned to their specific demands. Pharmaceutical firms required a level of subsidy to encourage them to invest in expanding their manufacturing capacity. Populations of potential disease sufferers required a vaccine of certain efficacy. The Advance Market Commitment did not become an exemplar from which others could learn and did not promote a specific participatory fora through which problem and solution could be coupled. Instead, issue formation seems to provide a means to capture the action here: the successive entangling of entities that helps specify and re-specify the nature of the problem and build commitments to accomplish what seems to be the emerging requirements for a solution.

3. *Problem, Solution and Contractual Obligations*

Treating problem and solution relationships as exemplars from which others might learn or as a process of dialogic democracy or issue formation each suggests a degree of flexibility in intervention. However, we also encountered interventions that seemed to rigidly set in place problem and solution. In Chapter 6, for example, we analysed the significant efforts to set in place a contract for the AMC in order to overcome the apparent threat of donors' time inconsistency. In Chapter 5, we investigated a form of contracting given even greater significance in a market-based intervention. Here we analysed the Social Impact Bond for children at risk of going into residential care run by Essex County Council on the east coast of England. We showed that Social Impact Bonds have been presented by national government (in the form of the Centre for Social Impact Bonds), as a form of intervention that provides a structure for bringing private investment into public problems. Bonds are pushed forward as enabling new investment to be drawn in to interventions, along with apparently new and dynamic, effective and efficient private sector approaches to problems delivered by investors. A problem is marked for attention – in our case children at risk of going into care – and investors are invited to use their funds to cover the costs of a solution – in this case Multi-Systemic Therapy designed to keep children out of care.

Given the number of Social Impact Bonds in operation across the UK (more than 30 at the time of writing), this could be utilised to further illustrate the kind of paradigmatic-exemplar that we saw in the GDPR. However, unlike a conventional exemplar through which a coupling of problem and solution demonstrate their capacity to succeed (and hence become a positive paradigm for others to follow), Social Impact Bonds seem to be shrouded in negativity. Lessons to be learnt seem to stem more from their failure than their success (see Chapter 9). In Essex, a significant concern was the contractual structure of the intervention.

As we saw in Chapter 5, extensive efforts were made in Essex to specify the precise nature of the problem and the solution, the amounts to be invested, returns to be paid, costs to be saved, evidential basis for assessing the intervention, form of therapy that should be used, timing of the contract and oversight for the intervention. A series of calculations thus underpinned this market-based intervention: how much money would be saved by a child not going into care was calculated on the basis of days of care averted; the amount this would save the county council as commissioner in relation to how many children were kept out of care was calculated; the number of children that would go through the chosen therapeutic intervention over five years was counted; the cost of Multi-Systemic Therapy and evidence of its success was compiled; and an assessment was made of how much the investors might receive in total, with the aim of achieving something in the region of a 10–12% annual return on investment, if the intervention met its evidentiary benchmarks. Articulating the problem of children at risk as a problem solvable by investment involved a rigid form of contracting that fixed these calculations in place and around which problem and solution were organised. The contract guaranteed investors would receive returns when evidentiary benchmarks were met. For example, investors received a frontloaded return each time a child was recorded as not going into care and the intervention was measured against historical evidentiary benchmarks that Essex county council had already surpassed. Although in theory Bonds are set up in such a way that if the benchmarks are not achieved, the investors do not receive their return and may even lose their capital investment, this was not the case in Essex. Although in theory the market sensibility of investment and return is delivered in an apparently ruthless manner with the investors' money wholly at stake, this was also not the case in Essex.

In place of a conventional bond that provides an investment vehicle came a series of contractual bonds that eliminated many conventional investment risks. The contract specified the problem and solution relationship in great detail. But for frontline workers in children at risk in Essex, the solution became the problem that now needed to be solved. Frontline workers developed a detailed critique of the intervention. They suggested the historical data collected as a basis for evaluating the intervention was out of date and the local authority had already changed its children's services to such an extent that the intervention might not have even been necessary (see Chapter 9). Furthermore, the form of therapy contractually fixed in place a single solution to the problem of children at risk, despite apparent concerns among frontline workers that its suitability was limited:

we're much more constrained than we initially thought ... I think if we did go forward we might not tie it to a rigidly evidence-based intervention – we might truly hold to the principles of innovation in SIBs and we might say we're only interested in the outcomes and we're going to work with a provider ... who will get us there somehow as long as it's legal and we've got defensible decision-making – but actually the outcomes and sustaining the outcomes are the really key thing. (Interviewee 1, local authority)

Although the contract seems to be the means through which problem and solution are given a practical, interventionist purpose by structuring investment–return relations, it is also the contractual obligations that are identified as a part of the problem. The contract seems both key to transforming a public problem into a problem amenable to a solution envisaged on the terms of the market sensibility of investment and return, and the contract is key to continuing discussions of issues that arise from the intervention.

Yet dialogic democracy seems to be a notable absence here. This absence seems to have been a strategic feature of the Social Impact Bond for children at risk. As the frontline worker in Essex noted, she and her colleagues were excluded from contract negotiations by their managers as it was assumed they might try and "scupper" the intervention before it got started. As a result, frontline workers "were effectively handed a project that was already three-quarters of the way through [set-up] but actually relied heavily on us to be operationalised" (interviewee 1, local authority).

Contract negotiation might have provided a means to draw together various parties to the problem in the articulation of a solution. Entities might have been drawn to the fore, calculative agency distributed and future problems pacified. However, in practice, the contract negotiations were lengthy and mostly technical matters that seemed to play into the hands of the investors (who appeared to have more experience in contract negotiations) and excluded key parties (the frontline workers in children's services). The process and outcome of the contract negotiation was thus more of an imposition than a dialogic form of participatory democracy.

In Essex, what seemed most apparent in the Social Impact Bond was the continual critique of the intervention as a viable means to solve the problem of children at risk. Although we have focused on frontline workers in this illustration, these were not the only concerned parties. It was not clear for many of the participants in Chapter 5 (aside perhaps from the investors), that the Social Impact Bond for children at risk of going into care coupled problem and solution in a way that worked. The intervention cost more than was anticipated, saved less than was anticipated and utilised a form of therapy that was only suitable for a proportion of the population of children at risk (see Chapter 9 for more on success and failure).

What we can note here is that a solution did not straightforwardly follow from a problem as, in this case, the solution was deemed to be a problem and this problem was deemed to require new solutions. At the same time, the problem of children at risk was not straightforwardly defined by the choice to intervene through a Social Impact Bond. The Bond took years to set up and its precise contractual form required extensive articulation of the terms of problem and solution. This ongoing movement back and forth between problem and solution – what Garfinkel (1967) termed the recursive relationship of problem and solution – is not unusual. The EU ETS, for example, seems to be formed around a participatory mode of dialogic democracy that itself becomes the problem. The GDPR is noted along the way as pushing forward a solution that might create future problems for the data industry. The REF is continually critiqued for putting in place a solution that problematically reshapes UK higher education research (see Chapter 3). What seems distinct about the Social Impact Bond is the contractual rigidity of problem and solution that bars entry to forms of change once the terms are set. One way to push this analysis along, that we will investigate in the next section, is to explore further the nature of composition in problem and solution relationships and how acts of re-specification (re)establish the nature of things to be intervened upon.

4. The Composition and Re-specification of Problem and Solution

Thus far in our analysis of problems and solutions we have noted that accomplishing an exemplar-like status for couplings of problem and solution is rare. This is not because the market-based interventions we study are themselves rare or consigned to an obscure background of politics. These interventions frequently tackle public problems that are significant in their membership and geographical scope. Often, then, our interventions are oriented toward achieving an exemplar-like status – a public demonstration of the ability of different market sensibilities to bring about anticipated change. But in practice something more complex and uncertain takes place. Ongoing problematisation proves more effective at drawing together various participants and, along with issue formation, seems to enable regulators to respond to ongoing changes in the nature of problems and solutions. At times, however, the participatory process itself is called into question and what we see is something closer to recursion with a solution becoming a problem that then requires a solution that then might become a problem. Or in the case of Social Impact Bonds, the terms of intervention – the solution – prove problematic, but contracts rigidly hold the intervention in place all the same. What we can also see in our analysis thus far is that the particular field of problems is important. The public aspect of these problems seem central in moves to accomplish an exemplar-like status, to be able to publically declaim that a major concern is being tackled by a solution from which others could learn. The market sensibilities involved are both implicated in the possibility of bringing about change to heretofore intractable situations, but often form the basis for critique and counter-critique leading to recursion.

Taken together, this suggests straightforward assumptions that, for example, we know what a public problem is, how a market sensibility can be used to solve it or even what the appropriate relationship between a problem and a solution ought to be are all somewhat oversimplified or overly optimistic. At the same time we need to move beyond the conventions of the social problem literature (see, for example, Gusfield, 1980), which merely suggests that experts' construction of a problem are in some way problematic. As Woolgar and Pawluch (1985) suggest, this kind of analysis depends on an uneven distribution of ontological interrogation whereby:

one category of claims [by the expert] is laid open to ontological uncertainty and then made the target for explanation in terms of the social circumstances which generated them; at the same time, the reader is asked to accept another category of claim [that of the social scientist] on faith. (1985: 218; also see Woolgar and Lezaun, 2013)

What is required is a more thoroughgoing interrogation of the nature (ontology) of the composition (Latour, 2010) of the problem at stake and its solution.

One means to develop such an approach is provided by a return to the situation we met in Chapter 7. Here student loans were identified as a problem in various ways over a 25-year period and developed in line with changing political priorities regarding the relative importance of budgets, public spending, balancing government books and public account reforms. In that chapter we looked at UK higher education student loans as, initially, a solution to the problem of widening access to higher education. As more people started to attend university in the UK from the early 1990s onwards and as the university sector itself expanded (with polytechnics becoming universities from 1992), the associated costs for government similarly grew. With an increase in costs defined as the central problem, the UK government sought to introduce loans as a cost-sharing solution. In place of student grants to cover the cost of living (where such costs all fell to the government) student loans would need to be repaid by students with fixed monthly payments required as soon as a student met the salary threshold for repayments. But this problem (of increased costs) and solution (of cost sharing) changed over time. This was not only a kind of flip-flopping recursion caused by public critique where a solution becomes noted as a problem. The same field of intervention was ontologically re-specified as a different form of problem for which new solutions could (and needed to be) composed. As student numbers continued to rise, the cost of higher education courses (rather than grants to support students) along with principles of fair access to higher education became defined as the problem. New loans were introduced to cover new fees that students were now expected to pay. The problem (rising costs) and solution (shared costs through loans to be repaid) remained nominally the same.[5] At the same time, the type of costs to be covered by the loans changed (from cost of living to course fees) and the forms of repayments also

---

[5] Although critics (Molesworth, Scullion and Nixon, 2011; Canaan and Shumar, 2008; Holmwood, 2014; McGettigan, 2013) have argued loans have provided a further problematic transformation of UK higher education towards a market orientation (also see Chapter 3 on the REF).

changed: instead of a mortgage-style loan with fixed monthly payments, these new loans would be income-contingent in an attempt to ensure fair access. This meant students would only pay loans on those months when their salaries met the repayment threshold. The nature of the problem and solution appear to be re-specified here. Drawing on Woolgar and Pawluch (1985), we might ask: how and through what means does this re-specification come to satisfactorily pass as an adequate means to compose the nature of problem and solution?

However, before we can deploy such an analysis, this situation has already changed once again. Following the financial crisis of 2008 and a squeeze on public spending following the election of a Coalition government in 2010 with an explicit agenda to cut public spending and rebalance public accounts, costs once again became a problem.[6] Partly this renewed concern for reducing costs was a consequence of the UK government's increased borrowing that stemmed from efforts to bail out financial institutions. Financial institutions had run into trouble from trading in securitised debt bundles that (turned out to) contain sub-prime debts and debtors. With student numbers still rising, the problem remained more or less the same (cost to government and fair access) but instead of a cost-sharing solution with loans covering a percentage of course fees, loans would now be used to cover full fees in most subjects. Although now much more substantial in value, the structure of loans persisted: students would make repayments in months when they met the repayment threshold.

We could try and describe this situation as recursive, with the solution becoming a problem requiring a solution.

---

[6] Exacerbated by a removal on the cap of how many students could enter higher education.

But there is more going on here. First, the subtleties of these changing loans are important for understanding the nature of the problem–solution at stake. The early loans introduced a relatively blunt solution that meant all students had to repay loans in the same way and more or less at the same speed. Later loans with income-contingent repayments slightly shifted the nature of the problem at stake: from an outright focus on costs to government in early loans, came a focus in later loans on costs to government combined with a sense of what might be fair to students (and non-students whose tax payments would otherwise cover the cost of universities) and what might promote wide access to university education. Costs, fairness and access as a problem–solution relationship were embodied by income-contingent repayment loans. Costs, balancing public spending and (a nominal notion of) fairness and access were then embodied by later and larger income-contingent repayment loans that covered higher fees for students and tended to leave students with a much higher debt. Hence the problem and solution did not remain entirely the same, either for government (with changes in the distribution of costs and motivation for redistributing costs) or for students (who were presented as needing fair access policies and income-contingent repayments and who, in practice, faced much higher debts, but also a much higher repayment threshold). For this composition of problem and solution, a broad array of new and different forms of expertise were required and this did not all arrive in one moment. Over time different UK governments acquired expertise in different forms of lending and repayment; students started to develop skills in assessing likely future debt and required earnings and repayment thresholds; universities started to develop means to market their student offers, taking loans and fees into account. From this we can say that making sense of the very specific nature of problem and solution and its consequences is crucial here. It is in these subtle changes in the formulation of the nature of problem and solution, the technical practices upon which they depend along with the policy-making speeches through which they are promoted, that the world changes for students and universities and to some extent for government.

Second, these formulations of the problem–solution of loans did not operate in isolation. Alongside this reshuffling of the levels of loans and how they would be repaid, the loans themselves presented an opportunity. They formed an asset (of sorts; Milyaeva and Neyland, forthcoming) that could be sold. Here composing the nature of the problem–solution depended upon the history of the intervention itself: having loan books meant the government could start to discuss the loans as part of a problem: an imbalance in public spending, with more money being spent than tax income received. Selling the loans could then be presented as a solution. However, from the early loans of the 1990s to the later loans of the twenty-first century, selling these assets itself became a problem. As we noted in Chapter 7, a preparatory imperative required navigation for the loans to fulfil a set of conditions that meant they could be sold. This often took years, with the first tranche of loans from the early 1990s selling in 1998 and loans issued in the early part of the twenty-first century selling in 2017 and 2018. The preparatory imperative required a re-specification of the problem–solution relationship: access and fairness were not important here and were relegated to the background; income contingency that was the financial mechanism designed to accomplish access and fairness came to centre-stage; the viability of the loans as having a value depended on what could be made of this contingency – just what repayments would be made, by who and when. The problem was now how to place a value on loans, the best of which had been repaid and the worst of which (in some cases) remained.

In a somewhat surprising mirroring of the activities that led to the financial crisis, the need for public bail-outs, an increase in public debt and the need to sell off the student loans, the solution to this new composition of the problem of student loans was securitisation. Securitising these loans in bundles and affixing different values to each bundle according to the likelihood of future repayment provided one kind of solution for how they could be valued by potential buyers. The nature of the problem was set through calculative means (bundling and valuation). But this method also presented problems. On the one hand, selling assets below their value on government books meant the loans contributed less than they might to the rebalancing of public spending. On the other hand, and thanks to government accounting reform, these were not listed on cash accounting terms and so any sale, at any price, provided a positive contribution to government accounts. Selling loans did not result in selling off a problem (the terms of loans would remain the same and government would still remain responsible for overseeing these terms), but it did result in re-specifying the nature of the problem. Loans went from small, mortgage-style repayment schemes to income-contingent debts. They went from a shared cost to a cost for students, and then they went from a cost listed on public accounts, to an (impaired) asset, to a positive contribution to public spending. The nature of the problem and the solution changed as opportunities were identified for re-specification. The search for these kinds of opportunities seemed to arise in the case of student loans not because there was a deep concern that the loans were not working but through a broader search for ways to balance government books. What was once a solution to one thing (cost and then fair access) could now become a solution to something else (problems with public spending).

In comparison to our other interventions, there seems little concern for dialogic democracy in the development and redevelopment of student loans. Although we might find work by, for example, the Student Loans Company to draw together an array of entities in preparing loans to be sold, there is little focus in this work on the development of a participatory fora through which all concerned voices might be heard (Callon et al., 2009) and little concern for issue formation (Marres, 2011). Few efforts are made to take student/debtors' views into account. Furthermore, preceding sales of UK government assets, for example, through privatisation, only provided a steer toward the possibility of selling the loans. They did not provide a steadfast coupling of problem and solution as paradigmatic-exemplar (Kuhn, 1962) that could be used to direct the sale of loans. The peculiar features of loans and specific difficulties in establishing relations with potential buyers meant that few previous sales of government property could provide a template for solving the problems encountered in these sales.

Also, in contrast to any rapid sense of recursion, here the problem of student loans took some time to take on a specific and recognisable form, and over time various solutions were composed in response to opportunities that seemed to arise. Even if some constituent elements of student loans, problems and solutions stayed the same over 25 years, much also changed. Rather than being dynamic, the pace of change was sporadic, and the sale of tranches of loans took years of pre-paratory work and were much delayed. What could happen to loans and how the nature of the problem–solution relationship could be composed – the opportunity that loans presented to government – were the result of successive changes. Early policies on loans did not envisage the sales achieved in 2018 in their initial inception in the 1990s. The loans did not give shape to the problem–solution relationship in a similar manner to the fixed contractual structure of the Social Impact Bond or in the form of an exemplar-like standard that others might adopt as proposed through the GDPR. The loans seem characterised by a more accidental trajectory of development.

Conclusion

In this chapter we have engaged with our empirical data to consider anew our moves between particular and general. This has enabled us to explore the diverse features of *public* made at stake in these interventions. To return to the question that opened this chapter, what can we now say about the public nature of the problems we have considered? What does it mean to say that a problem is public? What we can see across our examples, is varied activities to compose the membership of specific couplings of problem and solution. Couplings of problem–solution need to be articulated in such a way that they can be populated with the people and things for whom it should be a concern and that might be able to bring about change. Those doing the composition work – for example, the European Union, national or local government – approach member-shipping as a matter of articulating with clarity the public nature of the problem–solution at stake. Problem-solutions must be composed in such a way that their breadth and depth as concerns can be made clear and in order that accountability and responsibility for their resolution can be taken on by the emerging membership.

The precise form of this articulation work involves recognising and reproducing the constraints imposed by the public aspects of accountability and responsibility – paying heed to the publicly visible nature of being a member of a problem–solution coupling. At the same time, articulation work has to pay attention to the difficulties of putting in place and holding in place a membership that might adequately bring about change, with various devices such as incentives, contractual stability and returns on investment used to compel engagement. Ongoing recursion in couplings of problem-solutions can lead to future challenges with member-shipping, as public visibility, accountability and responsibility can lead to scrutiny when interventions are seen to fail and lead to members exiting the scene. Recourse to imposing interventions by excluding potential dissenting members from participation (as in the Social Impact Bond) or drawing up relations that limit the extent to which members can publicly voice concerns (the REF) recognise these potential future problems. Exclusions and limiting voice attempt to reduce future publicly articulated concerns about a problem–solution, although in practice this often seems to only defer these critiques. As a result, the public nature of problems is not composed in a single manner. We have seen active (dialogic, issue-forming) and marginalised publics (with little consultation or voice) as a form of membership. We can also discern forms of membershipping in which publics are actively created for consultation or strategically excluded from negotiation. We have noted distinct public spaces that interventions hold as their domain (from local to national to international). And we can elucidate various emerging and fading formats for what might once have been the public sector. This has opened up some different ways for our analysis to navigate between particular and general.

In eschewing an analysis of the extent to which these interventions fulfil a more or less coherent political programme of action, we have opened up a space for promoting the importance of considering market-based interventions, their challenges and consequences. In this chapter we have sought to accomplish this analysis by considering the coupling of problems and solutions. This provides another means to move from particular to general. If we accept that intractable problems are unlikely to be solved in any single moment and that solutions are likely to endure, then we need to be equipped with some general analytic tools for making sense of the continuing features of problem–solution relationships. Here we have considered four distinct means to couple problem and solution in market-based interventions into public problems. We have focused on the exemplar as a means to analyse the efforts made to not just create a policy, but to compose an intervention that might generate a standard, a means to combine problem and solution from which others might learn. We have considered participation and issue formation as means for opening up the possibility of problems and solutions to initial or ongoing consideration, building a kind of anticipated flexibility into interventions while also broadening the voice given to participants. In contrast, we have also noted rigid forms of market-based intervention wherein the coupling of problem and solution becomes contractually bound and change is not permitted. And we have considered the forms of re-specification and composition through which the same field can become reworked to address new problems through new solutions. These couplings have provided a basis for drawing together on the same page the aims and anticipated outcomes of interventions, what happens in practice, their consequence, critique and (in some cases) ongoing change.

The couplings of problem and solution provide a distinct means to move between general and particular in considering our interventions. They provide a basis for interrogating up-close the detail of specific market-based interventions, comparing distinct ways of formulating problems and solutions, without becoming enslaved by the search for a single programme of political action. But in addressing the question *can markets solve problems?* these couplings also leave us with a concern: just what kind of success or progress can be attributed to these market-based interventions and through what means? This is the concern to which we will now turn in Chapter 9.

References

BBC News (2010) EU can afford to increase its climate ambition. Available at: http://news.bbc.co.uk/1/hi/sci/tech/8629529.stm (last accessed 3 April 2019).

Callon, M. (1986) Some elements of a sociology of translation. In J. Law (ed.), *Power, Action and Belief: A New Sociology of Knowledge?* London: Routledge, pp. 196–223.

Callon, M., Lascoumes, P. and Barthe, Y. (2009) *Acting in an Uncertain World: An Essay on Technical Democracy*. Boston: MIT Press.

Canaan, J. and Shumar, W. (eds.) (2008) *Structure and Agency in the Neoliberal University*. New York: Taylor & Francis.

Garfinkel, H. (1967) *Studies in Ethnomethodology*. New York: Prentice Hall.

Gusfield, J. (1980) *The Culture of Public Problems*. London: University of Chicago Press.

Holmwood, J. (2014) Beyond capital? The challenge for sociology in Britain. *British Journal of Sociology* 65(4): 607–18.

Kuhn, T. (1962) *The Structure of Scientific Revolutions*. Chicago: University of Chicago Press.

Latour, B. (2010) An attempt at a compositionist manifesto. *New Literary History* 41: 471–90.

MacKenzie, D. (2009) Making things the same: Gases, emission rights and the politics of carbon markets. *Accounting, Organisations and Society* 34: 440–55.

Marres, N. (2011) The costs of public involvement: Everyday devices of carbon accounting and the materialization of participation. *Economy and Society* 40(4): 510–33.

Marres, N. (2012) *Material Participation*. London: Palgrave Macmillan.

Marres, N. and Lezaun, J. (2011) Materials and devices of the public. *Economy and Society* 40(4): 489–509.

McGettigan, A. (2013) *The Great University Gamble: Money, Markets and the Future of Higher Education*. London: Pluto Press

Milyaeva, S. and Neyland, D. (forthcoming) English higher education: From a public good to a public asset. In F. Muniesa and K. Birch (eds.), *Turning Things into Assets*. London: MIT Press.

Molesworth, M., Scullion, R. and Nixon, E. (eds.) (2011) *The Marketisation of Higher Education and the Student as Consumer*. London: Routledge

Morozov, E. (2013) *To Save Everything, Click Here: Technology, Solutionism and the Urge to Fix Problems That Don't Exist*. London: Penguin.

Reding, V. (2012) *The EU Data Protection Reform 2012: Making Europe the Standard Setter for Modern Data Protection Rules in the Digital Age*. Speech Innovation Conference Digital, Life, Design – 22 January, Munich, Germany. Available at: http://europa.eu/rapid/press-release_SPEECH-12-26_en.htm (last accessed 3 April 2019).

Vaidhyanathan, S. (2006) Rewiring the "nation": The place of technology in American studies. *American Quarterly* 58(3): 555–67.

Woolgar, S. and Lezaun, J. (2013) The wrong bin bag: A turn to ontology in science and technology studies? *Social Studies of Science* 43(3): 321–40.

Woolgar, S. and Pawluch, D. (1985) Ontological gerrymandering: The anatomy of social problems explanations. *Social Problems* 32(3): 214–27.

9

Progress

Opening

In the preceding chapters we have been witness to a variety of fields from healthcare to the environment, from education to social care, that have been composed as problems that might be solved by specific market-based interventions. As we noted in Chapter 8, these actions do not deliver solutions in any straightforward manner. The intractability identified among many of these fields of public problems appears to endure, even in the face of policy optimism at the launch of interventions. The REF is launched at least partly as a means to overcome criticism of its predecessor, the Research Assessment Exercise (RAE); the EU ETS heralds a new environmental future; Social Impact Bonds bring new, dynamic private investors and their funds into cash-strapped areas of government activity; the GDPR will establish a new international standard for privacy; and so on. And this optimism is bound up with clear expectations that the interventions will bring about fundamental change: saving children at risk, saving lives among low-income country populations previously too poor to afford vaccinations, or enabling UK academia to fulfil its potential to contribute to the nation's competitiveness. Such optimism seems to fade over time as, for example, negotiated technocracy rather than dynamic market exchanges dominate proceedings (EU ETS), or lengthy negotiations produce a contractually bound interaction that limits its own success (Social Impact Bonds), or the intervention itself starts to unhelpfully steer the field it sets out to measure (REF). Nevertheless, change does take place and this perhaps partly accounts for why there are so many market-based interventions in operation: they take part in the accomplishment of emerging consequences.

In this final chapter we will take a look at how these consequences become incorporated into the assessment of success and progress in market-based interventions. Most of our examples come with their own evidentiary practices, relations and devices that help set in place specific claims to progress. However, as we shall explore, this progress is by no means straightforward, nor does it follow paths that were anticipated at the beginning of each intervention. We will start with a brief consideration of progress and its evidentiary practices before engaging with our market-based interventions. We will end the chapter with a final note on equipping researchers with the means to engage market-based interventions.

Progress and its Evidence

According to Callon and Muniesa (2005), to be calculated, things must be made calculable. This requires detaching entities from their conventional associations and reordering those items into a single space. This reordering will then enable new associations to be formed, manipulations to be made and a result to be extracted. It does not matter, for example, that in writing an academic journal article we had a particular purpose in mind (to further some arcane and obscure aspect of Science and Technology Studies or ethnomethodology, for example, that we anticipated might lead to conversations at future conferences or in writing if anyone ever read the article). The article is shorn from these associations and entered into the calculative arrangements of the REF. It is scored from 0 to 4 and then its result is compiled with the scores gained by other members of our sociology department and contrasted with other sociology departments in order to form a new result: the value of our department in a ranking and how much government research funding it ought to receive. And we can witness other such calculative practices going on elsewhere: in Essex, children at risk are made calculable through costs; in the ETS, emissions allowances are given a price; or in Geneva, vaccines are assessed according to their cost effectiveness.

This initial rubric of detachment, ordering into a single space for association and manipulation in order that a result can be extracted seems quite useful. But what does this tell us about progress? Latour (1993, 2013, 2016) suggests that modernity demands a form of temporal linearity through which the past can become depicted as the negative from which progress is being made to an improved future, a progress from ancient to modern. In a similar manner to Callon and Muniesa, this depiction relies on separation and reassociation. To make progress clear, matters need to be clearly demarcated – for example, into nature/society, fact/value, human/non-human, science/politics – both for the resolution of the inadequate past and for progress toward a more effective future to be made apparent. But for our examples, this sets something of a challenge: the scoring system of the REF, for example, does not alone stand testament to the intervention's success, its ability to progress from a negative past to a more positive future. Our first aim in this chapter will thus be to explore how the forms of assessment we have already seen can become embedded within explicit rubrics of progress that might require their own evidential calculus.

A second aim follows from Latour's critique of the modern. For Latour, modernism's failure is to be continually overwhelmed by hybrids that prevent the purity of demarcations
(between nature and society, for example) from being maintained. What we need to also explore, then, is the ways in which
our examples of market-based interventions might limit otherwise overwhelming hybridity and impurity through their evidentiary set-up: benchmarks, ongoing monitoring and other
evidential practices might enable a linear movement from
negative past to more positive future. They might accomplish
a form of modernism. Making sense of this calculative, evidentiary move is important, as Lazzarato (2009) suggests attuning problems to interventions designed through, for example,
competition requires effort to calculatively hold the world
in place: "the world and the relations inscribed in it are the
result of specific compositions of apparatuses ... put into place
as a result of calculations aiming to constitute the world in a
determinate way" (110). In the next section we will return to
our examples and explore the ways in which progress involves
(and requires) specific evidentiary practices attuned to progress which at the same time are continually under threat from
messy forms of hybridity.

Market-Based Interventions and Progress

The EU General Data Protection Regulation (GDPR; see
Chapter 4) has only recently been enacted and so its progress is
somewhat difficult to discern. As we noted in Chapter 4, a general sense of progress has been used to articulate its very reason
for being: that data practices have changed significantly, that
legislation needs to maintain pace with the digitally saturated
world and that the new legislation might provide an international standard from which others could learn. But as far as its

impact on changing the data landscape is concerned, this will have to wait for the future. Others among our market-based interventions do provide more evidence of their calculative pursuits. The REF (see Chapter 3), for example, is designed in a similar manner to the GDPR as a successor to its predecessor (the RAE), but also comes with an array of means to assess its contribution as an intervention. These are not straightforward in the sense that the scoring system of the REF (and the RAE) only provides a calculative means of evidencing the success of the intervention itself if the results are separated out and re-associated, manipulated in new ways and with new results extracted. For example, it is possible to trace out the results of distinct departments over time and to say that one has made progress (or not) on the terms the REF establishes by taking data out from each set of previous RAE and REF results and creating a temporal narrative. And it is also possible to produce evidence that more high scores have been achieved over time. For example, the Funding Councils that ran the 2014 REF suggested: "The [2014] results show that the quality of submitted research outputs has improved significantly since the 2008 RAE," with the number of 4-rated outputs up from 14% in 2008 to 22% in 2014 and the number of 3-rated outputs up from 37% to 50%.[1] This means that 72% of UK research outputs assessed were either world leading (4-rated) or internationally excellent (3-rated). One upshot of these evidentiary benchmarks is that internationally excellent research now starts to look second-class.

Ignoring rampant grade inflation for a moment, we can see once again that the production of evidence requires much calculative work. Matters (such as output scores) are separated

---

[1] See www.ref.ac.uk/2014/media/ref/content/pub/REF%2001 %202014%20-%20introduction.pdf

from their previous associations (such as their link to a department or position in a league table), entered into new associations (for example, in comparison with preceding RAEs), manipulations made (such that REF and RAE become comparable) and results extracted (some sense of progress over time is attested). If we ended the story here then we might be tempted to say we have in a sense accomplished the kind of modernism of which Latour was sceptical: progress is discernible through the careful building of containers through which past and present can be separated and a linear form of progress from past to future narrated. Except that ending the story at this point would require ignoring the overwhelming evidentiary concerns that this method of scoring inspired. The comparison between RAE and REF was apparently flawed because, for example, looking only at the figures ignores the possibility that departments have become increasingly competent in game-playing. Indeed, promoting the notion that the amount of world-leading research produced by the UK has increased 8% in six years is almost an admission of the REF's performative effects: a consistent scoring system that encourages production of further research that meets the terms of the scoring system. This was not the only concern. Suggestions were also made that staff were submitted on a strategic basis, that large and successful institutions dominated the scoring, and that the low scores were predominantly achieved by newer universities (meaning that little changed in the hierarchy of UK research).[2]

---

[2] See, for example, http://blogs.lse.ac.uk/impactofsocialsciences/2018/02/13/the-raeref-have-engendered-evaluation-selectivity-and-strategic-behaviour-reinforced-scientific-norms-and-further-stratified-uk-higher-education/

Progress and its neatly purified linear narrative is redirected by calls to take the missing messes into account.

Yet progress and its calculation does not end here. The success of the intervention can also be assessed according to its cost. Universities are here called upon to provide a figure for the amount of time they have devoted to their REF submission (translated into a cost via, for example, calculating the amount of time different members of staff contributed to the composition and assessment of a submission, with some staff costing more than others) and these are aggregated and added to the costs faced by the Funding Councils themselves. But this is not success in itself; the bald cost of £246 million[3] tells us nothing of what was achieved. Cost must thus be combined with benefit or assessed through a value-for-money calculation. Through this, we are told that the total cost of the REF represents only 1% of the total amount of government research funding distributed to universities or 2.4% of the amount directly distributed as a result of the REF. This is deemed good value in Funding Council assessments. Although the REF cost more than the RAE, we are told the REF's demand for impact cases "quite reasonably increased" costs from £66 million for the preceding RAE that did not contain impact (Technopolis, 2015). A near fourfold increase in cost is apparently good value and not a sign that the UK research assessment system has costs that are spiralling out of control.

This is still deemed insufficient evidence of progress. The achievement of higher scores is critiqued as soon as it is

_____
[3] See the cost assessment of the REF carried out by Technopolis on behalf of the Funding Councils: www.hefce.ac.uk/media/ HEFCE,2014/Content/Pubs/Independentresearch/2015/ REF,Accountability,Review,Costs,benefits,and,burden/2015_ refreviewcosts.pdf

evidenced. The cost of the REF is critiqued for being too high.[4] And with the REF's ever emerging focus on UK academia's contribution to national competitiveness, the calculations, their careful separations, re-associations and manipulations are not producing the right kind of results. These calculations don't speak to impact or to contributions to competitiveness. Maybe these specific numbers are the problem – perhaps there could be a way to link the REF to something like GDP? With such a calculation still absent, it is numbers more generally that are the issue. The final refuge for progress is something more qualitative that pays recognition to the inevitability of complexity and mess in trying to figure out such notions as success and the difficulties involved in trying to impose purified and neatly contained calculative certainty upon progress. In the absence of evidence of numeric success, a review is presented as the way forward. For this to stand testament to the importance of the REF and to withstand the rigours of anticipated future debates about progress, the review needs to be able to stand its political ground. Lord Stern, an established expert in reviewing after his work on climate change, is called in to chair the review and the academic community is called upon to participate. This leads to 300 responses to a call for consultation, 40 qualitative interviews with academics and other relevant stakeholders and a small number of stakeholder workshops. The result is that progress is now made

---

[4] See, for example, www.theguardian.com/higher-education-network/2014/dec/15/research-excellence-framework-five-reasons-not-fit-for-purpose and http://blogs.lse.ac.uk/impactofsocialsciences/2015/08/03/why-did-the-2014-ref-cost-three-times-as-much-as-the-2008-rae-hint-its-not-just-because-of-impact/

discernible – no less a figure than Lord Stern can put his name to the report that claims:

Over thirty years the RAE / REF has supported a sustained improvement in the quality and productivity of the UK research base. It is used by universities to attract students, staff and external funding. Over that period, development of the process has delivered an exercise that is credible and transparent. (2016: 10)

Although it is now discernible, progress seems to have defied calculation and instead depends on the ability of more qualitative methods to engage with the messiness of progress.

We can see a similar pattern in attempts to assess the progress made by the Social Impact Bond we considered in Chapter 5. Various forms of calculation led to strongly worded critique and a more qualitative review of the intervention was carried out by the Office for Public Management. The central structure of the Bond, the contract[5] – unlike the central component of the REF – did carry its own calculative means of assessing progress. For example, historical data was used to establish a business-as-usual counterfactual. A trajectory taken from this data was used to project into the future what would happen to children at risk if no intervention was carried out. This trajectory then provided a means from which to assess the impact of the intervention: how many children would not go into care in comparison to the counterfactual. However, the historical data was critiqued by children's services in Essex for being out of date as it failed to take into account significant changes they had made to their service in the years it took to set up the Bond. The business-as-usual counterfactual was based on a business that was no longer usual. The results of

---

[5] Itself subject to critique, as we noted in Chapter 5.

the therapeutic intervention (MST) on children at risk could be presented on their own – that 70% of the children of families that entered into MST did not go into care – but without the comparative historical data, no linear trajectory could be cast from negative past to positive future.

This was not the only calculative means to construe progress. The intervention could also be assessed according to its costs. This data also turned out to be somewhat troublesome. Initially Essex County Council projected an anticipated saving of £17 million from the Social Impact Bond that would be divided between the local authority (£10 million) and repayments to investors (£7 million). As costs rose (for example, for staff training) and savings did not materialise (as MST was only suitable for certain children and so no residential care homes could be closed or staffing levels reduced), the County Council found itself facing a double-spend problem: covering the continuing costs of children at risk and the costs of repayments to investors. Progress in the form of more effective interventions achieved over time, utilising a decreasing local authority budget could not be demonstrated through calculations. The Office for Public Management report designed to review the intervention instead drew on qualitative testimonies, through interviews and stakeholder engagement workshops, as its basis for assessment.[6] Much like the REF, progress seemed to defy calculation and qualitative accounts were required. But on this occasion, even engaging qualitatively with progress seemed to generate some hesitancy in the presentation of results. In place of any definitive account of progress comes a warning: "we are unable to draw any conclusions on the extent to which the

---

[6] See https://traverse.ltd/application/files/9515/2285/2105/ Interim-report-Essex-MST-SIB-Evaluation.pdf

delivery of MST through the SIB adds further significant value in terms of outcomes or performance" (OPM, 2015: 5). This is followed by a more modest claim: "What the [qualitative] data does give us is descriptive evidence of where the SIB structure has added value to the process of MST delivery, which may in turn lead to improved outcomes" (OPM, 2015: 10). The focus is subsequently placed on learning outcomes for other future Social Impact Bonds: progress might be discernible between this Bond and other Bonds that are yet to take place rather than within this single Bond, and there is discussion of "confounding factors" (OPM, 2015: 30) that prevent success being attributed directly to this MST-led intervention.

Can it be said, then, that progress evades the grasp of calculation? That the modernist ideal of purity and neat containment that enables the casting of a linear temporal narrative of success is out of reach?

As we saw in Chapter 2, the EU ETS incorporated a phased structure meant to foster learning by doing. The intervention had integrated from the start the idea that it would not be successful at once. This sequential organisation and the ongoing evaluation conducted by the European Commission (through its reports and impact assessments) opened up the possibility of renegotiating the design of the trading system. The move from national caps and ad hoc distribution of emissions allowances to a single emission limit and harmonised publicly available allocation formulas, indicators and thresholds was a major change. But we also saw that the flexibility supposedly permitted by the phased approach was limited, especially in light of sudden events. The EU ETS has been constrained by temporal delays created by the decision-making procedures of the European Union. The accumulation of a surplus of allowances after the economic recession is a telling example. The emission cap had been established by heads of states and governments and renegotiation of its overly generous limits had to follow the rhythm of this high-level politics, thus introducing some rigidity. The cap might have appeared ambitious enough (achieving it would be considered progress) when it was tested against economic forecasts run by the European Commission, but it ended up being far too lax, hence the surplus. Meeting the environmental objective did not require any effort and thus could not be claimed as any kind of proof of success.

Although the political bodies of the EU and the negotiated technocracy dedicated to the (re)design of the trading system eventually tried to address the surplus problem, the solution put forward, the Market Stability Reserve, looks particularly convoluted. The Reserve would take out of the market excess allowances. However, this would not change the overall cap given that these allowances would not be destroyed, but reintroduced in the system once the surplus has run out. The adjustment ought to artificially create scarcity in order to increase, in the short term, the price at which allowances are exchanged. Price here worked as a proxy for success. Indeed, increasing the allowance price was desirable because the whole point of the EU ETS is to turn emissions into a cost. This cost would be factored in by industries (internalised) when deciding on low-carbon investments, as these could save on the cost of buying expensive allowances to cover the pollution of old production processes. But as the Reserve was being legally agreed as a new feature of the EU ETS, some economists already warned that it might not have any price effect at all, because companies would anticipate that the allowances temporarily removed from the trading system would be brought back later.

This might suggest that the policy mechanism required significant change to achieve success. But the extent to which policy-makers could change the EU ETS to make progress in targeting carbon emissions from industrial activities was limited.

As we noted, changes had to navigate the rhythm of EU politics. Manoeuvrability in making changes was also constrained by claims regarding the impact of policy transformations on competitiveness (again). The elusiveness of evidencing effects such as carbon leakage made definitive statements on progress more difficult. And more qualitative reports, for example on the cement sector and its behaviour toward the EU ETS, have become a feature of discussions in Brussels. Narratives of linear progress, in this case from a dirty past to a cleaner future, are once again undermined. In the EU ETS this is partly attributable to calculative difficulties in demonstrating progress, but this situation is also tied to changes in the intervention itself, the lobbying practices of industry and constant examination of the possible range of issues to be taken into account. As we noted in Chapter 2, the surplus emerges as a problem, then carbon leakage, only to be replaced by investment leakage.

The importance of making sense of the specificity of these concerns with progress can also be seen in the Advance Market Commitment (AMC) we encountered in Chapter 6. Incentivising the production of pneumococcal vaccines for low-income countries involved a series of evidential practices. We mentioned the modelling of investment decisions under different vaccine prices and subsidy levels and the calculation of the cost-effectiveness of funding the purchase of pneumococcal vaccines. These calculations helped to prepare the intervention, provide some insights into the possible reaction of the pharmaceutical industry, respond to donors' concerns with value for money and help set the legal and commercial terms and conditions of the conditional purchase agreement. Calculations in the AMC were thus crucial to creating the conditions through which its success could be witnessable. The conditions for witnessing success had to be secured in order to be able to confidently forecast the number of lives to be saved.

We also noted that the AMC moved away from the problem of incentivising research on radical innovation to target diseases (such as malaria) for which no vaccine existed, to incentivising production capacity for a close-to-licensure vaccine because the pilot needed to work. The calculations, the switch in focus to a more modest aim and the forecast of lives to be saved, could further secure the grounds for success when two pharmaceutical firms (GSK and Pfizer) committed to the intervention by signing the first supply agreements.

As a pilot scheme, the consequences of the AMC were not left unattended. The grounds for witnessing success that were established in the set-up phase of the AMC fed into a range of reports by GAVI (Cernuschi et al., 2011), an initial independent evaluation (Dalberg, 2013) and a more extensive assessment by the Boston Consulting Group (BCG, 2015). Yet in place of a straightforward narrative of success, the BCG report is full of cautionary messages, the difficulty of the task in hand and refuses to clearly assign specific consequences to the AMC alone. Instead the success of the AMC is presented as intertwined with the consolidation of GAVI as a professional organisation, market participant and the main financier of child immunisation in poor regions of the world. As a result, an AMC would probably be superfluous now that GAVI has become such a solid organisation deploying tuned market-shaping efforts in a much more flexible and ad hoc manner compared to the legally heavy and politically charged pilot AMC. The economic conceptualisation of the AMC and its momentum within G7/8 finance summits took place at a time when the financing of immunisation and access to new vaccines in low-income countries needed to be improved, a time when a new partnership, GAVI, had just been created to address the very same problem. The pilot AMC, then, contributed to the creation of a situation in which it found itself obsolete.

If the AMC was characterised by careful preparation of the grounds for witnessing success, even if that led to its own obsolescence, the student loans we encountered in Chapter 7 were characterised by a stronger sense of haphazard opportunism. As we noted in the chapter, unlike the EU ETS, for example, where carbon emissions have remained the problem in focus, student loans have been used to address the costs of higher education, the need to make access to higher education fair and the challenge of reducing public spending. Precisely what might count as progress, then, has not remained steady. As a result, what calculations might be required to discern progress, what matters might need to be neatly contained, or what kind of temporal narrative established across what timeframe, can each be subjected to question. If, for example, we hold our focus steady on access, then we could argue that progress is clear in increasing student numbers over time (see Chapter 7). If instead we focus on fairness, this requires some more complex calculations and a range of decisions regarding what fairness might mean and for whom. For instance, what counts as fairness might shift between accounts produced by different segments of the student population or among non-graduates for whom the policy was apparently designed (in order that those who did not go to university would not have to cover the costs of those who did). Or we could focus on the Student Loans Company itself and suggest it has made a success of continuing its own existence by issuing and administering huge numbers of loans and by winning contracts to administer loans after their sale.[7]

Our focus in the chapter, however, was on selling. One means to calculate the success of selling tranches of student

---

[7] In contrast to the AMC that demonstrated its own obsolescence.

loans would be to look at price. The 1996 tranche of loans was sold for £1.08 billion and the 2002–06 tranche was sold in 2017–18 for £1.7 billion. A little like the cost of the REF, these figures alone might not be the most compelling evidence of progress. The numbers can be detached from their initial associations (all the work done to make a sale), but require ordering through new associations to extract a new result. One way in which this has been done is by assessing the value for money of the loan sales. But much in the same way as messiness pervaded the calculations of progress in the REF and Social Impact Bond, here political controversy has been apparent. Vince Cable, Liberal Democrat business secretary for the Coalition government refused to sanction the sales of student loans in 2014 because they did not represent good value for money.[8] And the loans sold in 2017–18 achieved a price below even their impaired value (see Chapter 7). However, for the sale of loans in 2017–18, these concerns for value were not so central. The problem to be addressed here was not value, but levels of public spending. At this time, government accounting rules enabled the loans to be sold as a positive contribution to government accounts (rather than as cancelling out a cost, as would be the case in traditional cash accounting). Loans were accounted for as an asset and the hope was that these could be sold on before they had to be written off (if students failed to repay them). At the point of write-off, if they were still on the government books, they would then count as a cost. Any price achieved was thus "good" in the sense that it contributed toward achieving (even in a small way) a reduction in the public spending deficit. Over time, these contributions might not be so small, with figures

---

[8] See www.theguardian.com/money/2014/jul/20/vince-cable-cabinet-tensions-scrap-student-loan-sell-off

projecting that the student loan book would be worth 20% of GDP by 2040.[9]

Had modernism finally triumphed through the purification of these numbers, with £1.7 billion achieved through the sale of loans in 2017–18 the ultimate sign of progress because accounting terms enabled these numbers to stand alone, free from the requirements of association and manipulation? Perhaps. But change is already lurking round the corner. The Office for Budget Responsibility has referred to these accounting terms as a "fiscal illusion", and the UK government has been told to change the way these loans are costed to more standard accounting terms.[10] Purity, modernity and progress might be no more than a temporary illusion.

Closing

Can markets solve problems? As we noted in Chapter 8, we need to maintain an even-handed scepticism regarding the nature of the relationship between problems and solutions, the ever-emerging forms that public problems comprise and the challenges of moving from studying particular interventions to making more general statements. In this chapter we have also reformulated our question slightly to explore the extent to which market-based interventions into public problems can manage to demonstrate progress. Here we have presented a different way to move from our particular interventions to more general declamations on market-based

---

[9] See http://cdn.obr.uk/WorkingPaperNo12.pdf

[10] See http://cdn.obr.uk/WorkingPaperNo12.pdf and https://wonkhe.com/blogs/begone-fiscal-illusions-understanding-student-loans-in-the-national-deficit/

interventions. We drew up an initial rubric for making sense of progress through calculative means of detachment, the ordering of entities into a single space for association and manipulation in order that a result can be extracted (Callon and Muniesa, 2005). And from Latour's work (1993, 2013, 2016) we suggested that progress can be treated as a matter of temporal linearity from a negative past to an improved future that is constantly at risk of being overwhelmed by the vicissitudes of monstrous hybridity.

Utilising these starting points, the demonstration of progress in our market-based interventions becomes discernible as a challenge. Quantitative evidencing of progress is replaced by a qualitative move to engage stakeholders and hold workshops on progress in the REF and Social Impact Bond. The extent to which changes to an intervention can be made are limited by concerns for the political process and with competitiveness in the EU ETS and by contractual agreements in the Social Impact Bond. Interventions prove their own obsolescence by demonstrating that their role can be taken by the international partnerships through which they have been formed in the case of the AMC and GAVI. Or alternatively, success can be discerned by cutting away messiness – at least for a time – and holding the focus steady on a single set of figures, such as price in the example of student loan sales. The switch from quantitative to qualitative evidencing, progress evading calculation's grasp, the limits of policy-making manoeuvrability, obsolescence and the accomplishment of narratives of linear progress through the shedding of mess, each seem like interesting points to further pursue.

Drawing together these insights on progress with our other general principles provides us with a position to say something about the requirements for equipping researchers interested in studying market-based interventions into public problems. Along with these theoretical pointers to pursue in further studies on progress in market-based interventions, researchers can find in each of our chapters a distinct analytic entry point that could be pursued. Negotiated technocracy, the inequitable fairness of competition, provident investments, time (in)consistency, financial diplomacy and the preparatory imperative have each had a place in our chapters. Combining these theoretical ideas with our methodological approach developed around an in-principle flat ontology and an attention to market assembly work and calculation, might equip researchers with useful starting points for their own research. Our deployment of this approach has involved resisting the temptation to buy into ready-made assumptions regarding the nature of markets and intervention. Instead, we have pursued market sensibilities as ways in which interventions are oriented. Exploring the means of composing trade and exchange, competition, property and ownership, investment and return, incentives and selling have each provided a basis for exploring, analysing, comparing and contrasting market-based interventions in action. Taken together, these general principles collectively can operate as a means to carry out further studies of particular market-based interventions into public problems.

References

Boston Consulting Group (BCG) (2015) *The Advance Market Commitment Pilot for Pneumococcal Vaccines: Outcomes and Impact Evaluation.* Available at: www.gavi.org/results/evaluations/pneumococcal-amc-outcomes-and-impact-evaluation/ (last accessed 3 April 2019).

Callon, M. and Muniesa, F. (2005) Economic markets as calculative collective devices. *Organization Studies* 26(8): 1229–50.

Cernuschi, T., Furrer, E., Schwalbe, N., Jones, A., Berndt, E.R. and McAdams, S. (2011) Advance market commitment for pneumococcal vaccines: Putting theory into practice. *Bulletin of the World Health Organization* 89(12): 913–18.

Dalberg Global Development Advisors (2013) *The Advance Market Commitment for Pneumococcal Vaccines: Process and Design Evaluation.* Available at: https://marketbookshelf.com/wp-content/uploads/2017/05/the-advance-market-commitment-for-pneumococcal-vaccines-process-and-design-evaluation.pdf (last accessed 3 April 2019).

Latour, B. (1993) *We Have Never Been Modern.* Cambridge, MA: Harvard University Press.

Latour, B. (2013) *An Inquiry into Modes of Existence.* Cambridge, MA: Harvard University Press.

Latour, B. (2016) *Reset Modernity!* Cambridge, MA: MIT Press.

Lazzarato, M. (2009) Neoliberalism in action: Inequality, insecurity and the reconstitution of the social. *Theory, Culture and Society* 26(6): 109–33.

OPM (2015) *Evaluation of the Essex Multi-Systemic Therapy Social Impact Bond.* Available at: https://traverse.ltd/application/files/9515/2285/2105/Interim-report-Essex-MST-SIB-Evaluation.pdf (last accessed 3 April 2019).

Stern, N. (2016) *Building on Success and Learning from Experience: An Independent Review of the Research Excellence Framework.* Available at: https://assets.publishing.service.gov.uk/government/uploads/system/uploads/attachment_data/file/541338/ind-16-9-ref-stern-review.pdf (last accessed 3 April 2019).

Technopolis (2015) *REF Accountability Review: Costs, Benefits and Burden.* Available at: http://www.technopolis-group.com/report/ref-accountability-review-costs-benefits-and-burden/ (last accessed 3 April 2019).

Index